I hope you'll
find good value
in these pages.

Laurana

Conscious Spending. Conscious Life.

an uncommon guide to navigating the consumer culture

Laurana Rayne

Author photo: Kalliopy Koika of Kalambaka, Greece
Cover and interior design: K-tizo Graphic Design, www.k-tizo.com

www.TheUncommonGuides.com

Care has been taken to trace ownership of copyright material contained and credited in this book. However, the author welcomes information that enables correction of any reference or credit in subsequent editions.

Because of the dynamic nature of the Internet, web addresses or links may have changed since publication and may no longer be valid. Additional bibliographical information has been provided along with the links to facilitate searching if they have changed.

We gratefully acknowledge the following for permission to use previously published material:

Tom Atlee for his poem, Story Fields; www.co-intelligence.org

Mind Tools Ltd. for their illustration of the Urgent/Important matrix; www. MindTools.com

New Road Map Foundation for their illustration of the fulfillment curve and their method for calculating real hourly wage. This work is licensed under Creative Commons Attribution Share-Alike 3.0 U.S. License. It is based on the Financial Integrity materials developed by the New Road Map Foundation, available for free at www.financialintegrity.org

ISBN: 1481140116
ISBN-13: 978-1481140119
Library of Congress Control Number: 2012923141
CreateSpace, North Charleston, SC
Printed in the United States of America

To my parents,
Lewis and Doris Homme,
who made sure I grew up with both
a good education and plenty of common sense

Contents

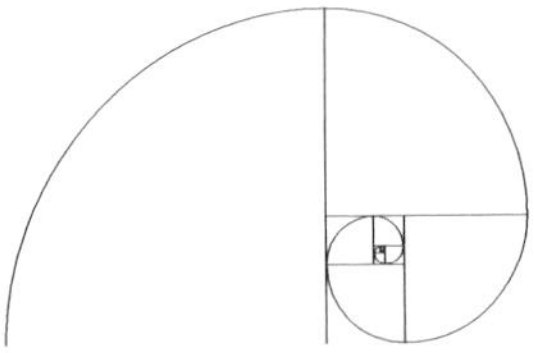

4 Health, Safety & Integrity of the Future

Notes from Laurana

It's tricky living in a consumer world. Subjected to so many pressures and ulterior motives, it's up to each of us to think for ourselves. There's a lot to know, and it's not necessarily just how to budget and invest. The purpose of this book is to enable you to make choices from an insightful position rather than reacting in knee-jerk fashion to cultural expectations. *Conscious Spending, Conscious Life* provides perspectives that can help you avoid being swept along with the tide, so that you don't end up living a life you didn't really want.

Why and how...

I wrote this book because I couldn't find one that adequately conveyed what I was discussing with my students. For many years, I taught a college course about issues in consumer economics. There are plenty of books and articles providing good money management information, and they were useful references for some aspects of my course. However, when it came to the philosophical issues, I had to rely on a ragtag assortment of articles, Internet readings, and book chapters. As my course evolved, this became cumbersome for my students...and for me.

Eventually, I realized my best option was to write a course-book to cover the issues we discussed and to clarify their interconnections. That summer, I travelled to a lovely retreat centre in Ireland and settled in for 12 weeks of writing. Following the course structure I'd developed over several years, I wrote a student supplement for my class. They found it helpful to have a focused presentation of the issues, and my teaching was more rewarding because we were able to get to deeper thinking and discussion.

As other people read that course-book, I kept hearing that it should be available to a wider audience, since the issues of consumerism affect us all. With that prompting, I began another round of writing to expand the content, so it could stand on its own without me there to elaborate on points and answer questions.

As it stands now, this book is a combination of the philosophical and practical. I've done my best to succinctly address the breadth of information and ideas that are essential to the subject of conscious spending. To get there, I updated my research, thought about what I've learned from my students, and drew on my own life experiences. Then I imagined I was speaking with you about these many issues and considerations.

There is so much to say about conscious spending, and I had to draw the line somewhere so the book could actually be printed. I decided to deal with extra information by developing a companion blogsite. That is where you'll find my blog—which allows me to continue exploring thoughts—and a resources section containing expanded information in certain areas such as mortgages and life insurance. These topics are best understood as an overview until you actually need to buy the house or some life insurance. Only then do you need more detail, so you know what to look for and the questions to ask.

My intentions...

The consumer world has become highly complex, and it's easy to become overwhelmed and lost in details. My intention is to provide context, so you can see how things fit together. Context is like the background in a painting: it is the aspect that gives meaning to the individual objects featured in that painting. Without background, they are floating and aimless. The consumer culture is the painting we live in. If we do not have any context for what has gone before, we are also floating and aimless. That makes it much more difficult to make constructive choices.

I have also intentionally handled this subject in ways that provide perspective. Perspective is the capacity to view things in their true relationships or relative importance. Perspective allows you to get to the essentials. This is crucial in the consumer world, which is confusingly complex.

Because I'm a generalist at heart, I've covered a wide variety of topics and introduced you to the work of many others. I want you to be able to follow up on topics that interest you, so I have included detailed endnotes and a bibliography. Many of my references are found on websites. To make connecting to them as convenient as possible, I've posted the endnotes, with hyperlinks, on my blogsite.

In the classroom, I taught with chalk in hand because a visual is often the best way to convey a concept. The illustrations in this book are tidier versions of my most useful blackboard drawings. I hope they have made things clearer.

I'm particularly interested in systems and how they work. I believe that when we understand a system, we are better able to navigate in it. I've shared my insights into aspects of the consumer world with the intention of empowering you to live well in it.

An uncommon guide...

This book is about questions more than answers. It is based on the premise that when we ask the right questions, we will be able to figure out what to do. This is one of the ways that it's an *uncommon* guide: it doesn't tell you what you *should* do. Instead, it provides insights and raises questions, which allow you to decide what you will choose to do for the life you want. This gives it a different tone from the many prescriptive self-help books. On my blogsite, I have posted a variety of questions that I've used with my students. You may find them a thought-provoking supplement to your reading.

Conscious Spending, Conscious Life is about financial sustainability rather than financial information or cleverness. Personal finance books usually speak in terms of managing your *money*. This book talks about managing *yourself*. Managing ourselves involves many things—monitoring our viewpoints and mindsets, cultivating resourcefulness, using time to maintain perspective, retaining our balance in changing circumstances, being aware of our ethics and holding ourselves to high standards, paying attention when we engage with the marketplace, and developing healthy skepticism and common sense. How we do these things has enormous impact on how we deal with money. That's why this book addresses much more than money.

At the back, I've included a section about learning the language of financial sustainability. It goes beyond the usual glossary: I've structured it for enrichment rather than simply repeating dictionary meanings. That's why it's subdivided into topic areas and has some additional comments with the definitions.

You'll also find a list of authors whose work has inspired me. Many are not in the bibliography, but all are found on my bookshelves. I thought they'd be useful for further exploration.

A highly noticeable, uncommon feature of this book is its wide margins. I insisted on this because I'm a fan of making notations in books. This is the kind of book that almost calls for it; you read something, it sparks a thought, and you don't want to lose the thread of the idea. It is so frustrating to be hampered by a narrow margin at those moments. I didn't want that to be your experience.

Finding your way...

Conscious Spending, Conscious Life encourages you to think about what works for you as you are making your life. In that spirit, I encourage you to engage with the content of this book in whatever ways work best for you.

Although we were all taught to read from front to back, you don't have to use that approach. You might want to start by reading the first section (Welcome to the Voyage) and the last (Living Consciously). They are like the bread that holds a sandwich together—the container for what is inside.

Or you may want to skip the bread and go directly to the meat of the matter. You could look at the Contents page and pick a chapter that seems relevant at the moment. You could pick one of the four main sections and read it entirely. You could look up a pertinent topic in the glossary.

Or you can go with your intuition, right brain, and serendipity. Open the book to a page and start reading there. It might be exactly what you need that day.

Starting conversations...

Consumer and money issues are relevant to all of us, yet they are rarely spoken about. Perhaps this is due to embarrassment over a lack of information or a feeling of not doing it well. In any case, it's time to change that.

This book can be a catalyst for starting conversations that will further our understanding of the issues and their implications. The "think-abouts" at the end of each chapter and the section near the end called "Strategies & Principles to Live By" are rich sources of things to talk about.

Because *Conscious Spending, Conscious Life* is about meeting the challenges of the consumer culture, these conversations pertain to our daily lives and can occur almost anywhere:

- Youth groups
- Continuing education classes
- Reading groups
- Post-secondary classrooms
- Post-secondary residences
- Premarital classes
- Dinner parties

The conversations do not need to occur in large or organized groups. They could be between

- couples who will soon begin living together,
- parents and their children who are on the verge of leaving home, or
- grandparents and their grandchildren who are graduating from school and entering adult life.

These discussions can be formal or informal. Often they will be prompted by something you read or hear in the news. It helps to consolidate your perspective by running it past someone else. In a group, more structure is needed to make good use of everyone's time. You will find a discussion guide in the resources section of the blogsite. My suggestions may not be exactly what you want to do in your group, but will be a good starting place.

We are all teachers...

As much as possible, I engaged my students in discussion during class. It wasn't difficult because the topics were relevant, or soon would be. I found they readily responded to the invitation to share their perspectives and explore new ideas. Students came out of this experience feeling more confident of their ability to navigate life in the consumer culture, as illustrated by these comments from their course evaluations:

> *This course was a surprise to me. I learned a lot of things I didn't know I'd be learning and that was pretty cool. Most of it can actually be applied to my life; I'm sort of young and naïve and I learned a lot of things where before I was like 'What?'*
>
> *Excellent. Makes you think and helps you make good life decisions.*
>
> *At first I thought this class was going to be a drag, but quickly found it to be EXTREMELY helpful.*

Very few post-secondary students have access to consumer economics courses. Parents and grandparents must, and can, provide this education for their children. Here's what I suggest:

- The basic step is to give them this book to read. I've often thought the perfect time is when a young person graduates from high school, heads off to college or university, or finds a job and moves away from home. They are at a teachable moment then—in transition and aware of the new responsibilities they are about to undertake.
- The next step is for the giver to read the book and start a conversation about a particular point from it—perhaps one they disagree with. Selecting

a point of disagreement is a good strategy because it gets away from sounding as if the parent is pushing predetermined viewpoints. Any of us who have raised teenagers know that this gets us nowhere.

- The third step is an idea from my friend and colleague, Patti. I think it's brilliant. She said that, before giving the book to her kids, she would read it and make notes in the margins. These comments would reflect her family's values and perspectives. Then she'd ask her husband to do the same, in a different colour ink. Individualizing the book this way will enrich it immensely, and I hope other people are inspired to also do that.

That brings me to the end of what I want to say about this book, except that I'm pleased to share it with you, and I trust you will find value in the time you spend with me on the subject of conscious spending. If you're inspired to share your thoughts and experiences with me, I'd be delighted to hear from you via my blogsite at www.TheUncommonGuides.com.

A Special Note of Thanks

This book is richer for the contributions of so many people. Heartfelt thanks to colleagues, friends, and family—so generous with encouragement and expertise.

Thank you to my army of advance readers—Susan Bitner, John Coxhead, Thomas Crutcher, Margaret Field, Gerald Gardner, Ian Gardner, Rosemary G, Jen Gareau, Sylvia Harnden, Patti Hawryluk, Ambrose Leung, Doug McClintock, Patricia McGowan, Megan McPherson, Sybille Melotte, Lorraine Pawluk, Brenda Purschke, AMR, CDR, Leigh Rees, Amy Ropchan, Rae Stephens, Dominique Vail, Teresa van Bryce, and Lois Wood. Without them, this book wouldn't have been as robust.

Three cheers for Frances Purslow of Purslow Communications, who copy edited my prose with skill and patience; Diane M. Cox, who applied her eagle eye to proofreading the manuscript multiple times; Kalliopy Koika, whose photo of me in a Greek mountain village turned out to be just right for this cover; Becky Thompson, who serendipitously arrived in the room next to me in Bali and brought long-awaited inspiration for the title; and Jeff Cummings of K-tizo Graphic Design, for his insightful visual interpretations and meticulous technical work.

Sincere thanks to Carol Koopmans and Nollind van Bryce for their assistance in bringing this book to its readers. Without them, you may not have found it.

I acknowledge with gratitude the work of other thinkers and writers whose ideas have inspired me. Without them, my mind would have operated in a much smaller playground.

Then there are two long-ago teachers—Mrs. Brox, the Grade 10 language teacher who drilled us in grammar, and Mrs. Higginson who did the same in Grade 8 math. Without their dedication to making sure we understood both the principles and processes, I wouldn't have had the confidence to undertake this work.

And finally, to all my students in ECON 1060, 1160, and 0260. They asked me questions, made me think, and gave me the opportunity to play with my ideas. Without them, this book wouldn't be.

Welcome to the Voyage

It is one of the illusions of these times that we can control our world and the people in it—an understandable desire, certainly, because it's comforting to think we can make everything go our way. For many people, being in control gives them a feeling of security. And truthfully, it is possible to live that way for a while. But eventually we encounter something beyond our control—an extreme weather event, a dramatic economic downturn, or a serious illness.

Control is not possible...

Sailors, who deal with the uncertainty of weather and the continual possibility of unseen hazards beneath the surface of the water, understand the principles of navigation—awareness of their surroundings, skill in utilizing the tools at hand, and mastery of themselves and their impulses. You will need to apply the same principles when navigating the consumer culture.

As in the natural world, human-made social structures such as our economic system are unpredictable and have numerous unseen pitfalls. When we live unconsciously, it is easy to stumble into these pitfalls. By becoming aware of them, we are able to choose different courses of action. We are able to respond consciously rather than react mindlessly.

Frequently, people run into difficulty because they don't have the tools to make good decisions. The tools for navigating the consumer culture are techniques, strategies, and information. There is more than enough information out there. In fact, the danger is information overload. This book focuses on those things that are fundamentally important, and equips you to look for further information when you need it. Until then, a lot of information simply becomes clutter in your life.

Sometimes, people run aground because they have no mastery over their impulses, reacting impetuously in ways that are temporarily satisfying but ultimately counterproductive to their overall well-being. The consumer culture fosters short-term thinking and impulsive behaviour, making it difficult to think and act mindfully. Yet it is possible, if we pause to see the big picture and apply common sense.

Common sense is the ability to exercise sound practical judgment. It is distinctly different from intelligence and high scores on IQ tests. You probably know intelligent people who do stupid things; they seem to lack common sense.

Psychologist Karl Albrecht, among others, uses the term *practical intelligence*, which he defines as the mental ability to cope with the challenges and opportunities of life. Practical intelligence is about making good judgments in real life situations and is called for in consumer decisions we make daily: what to eat, where to invest, how much of our income to spend. Applying practical intelligence or common sense in everyday life helps us avoid making irrational mistakes and poor decisions. Some people call it *street smarts.*

Practical intelligence depends on having an awareness of what's going on around you. This is crucial, because so much in the consumer culture conspires to keep you unconscious—reacting in knee-jerk fashion, rather than making deliberate choices. Undoubtedly, it's easier to default to the ready-made solutions, but that means we allow ourselves to be puppets of a system that disregards our well-being. The antidote is to be conscious, aware of ourselves and the forces impinging on us. When we are conscious in what we think and do, we focus our attention and intention, making better decisions as a result.

So, although control is not possible, mastery is. And that's what this book is about—mastering the art of living your life skillfully as you navigate the tricky waters of the consumer culture. Some people aspire to being financially clever. This book takes you beyond that to financial sustainability.

The way we see the world...

Much of this book was written in proximity to the Atlantic and Pacific Oceans. As I stood on various shores and looked across expanses of water that seem impossibly huge, I found myself thinking about the people who did the same thing, long ago. I wondered what would make a person willing to venture into such treacherous waters, particularly in the early days when no one knew what was on the other side.

Some of these adventurers might simply have been fearless or reckless, depending on "dumb luck" to see them through. Others would have prepared themselves by learning what was needed and marshaling their resources in an orderly way before setting out. They did this knowing they would encounter the unexpected, but reassured that they had prepared as best they could. All would have encountered adversity on their voyages, and the outcome would have been affected by their knowledge, their strength of character, and how they saw the world. The voyage through the consumer culture is not much different.

We don't all see the world the same way. Some see it as a safe and generally happy place, while others find it dark and dangerous. Most of us are somewhere in between.

We create our worldview from what we have experienced and what we've been taught by our families and culture. Our worldview becomes our definition of how the world works, and it shapes our interpretation of facts. In other words, facts are filtered through our worldview, which provides fixed grooves for our behaviour—automatic reflexes and unconscious responses. This gives us the comfort of not having to think through every new situation as it confronts us. However, acting on autopilot is not usually a constructive response. Reconsidering our perspectives and shifting them as necessary becomes part of the process of growing and maturing.

Immersion in the consumer culture gives us a ready-made worldview that suits those who profit from it. This book is designed to offer other worldviews for your consideration. This does not mean you have to immediately adopt those different viewpoints. But I would challenge you to consider the possibilities. As Laurence Boldt says in *Zen and the Art of Making a Living*, "If we are to change our experience, we must deliberately cultivate new beliefs..."[1] To do that, we must understand the issues and their implications. I hope this book will help you do that.

Deepak Chopra, a pioneer in the field of mind-body medicine, reminds us that we can't change the system, but we can change our point of view. And when we take a new viewpoint, our experience of life is different.

Seeing from a new viewpoint requires an open mind. When you have an open mind, you are able to stand apart from your beliefs and observe without judgment. This requires conscious effort. Here are some of Chopra's suggestions for cultivating an open mind:

- Know that you are going to identify with your worldview at every stage of personal growth.
- Accept that these identifications are temporary.
- Take a flexible attitude and be willing to change your worldview.
- Allow your ability to quietly observe without judgment to replace the ingrained ideas you reach for automatically.
- Use every opportunity to tell yourself that all viewpoints are valid.[2]

It is important for us to recognize that it's not easy to let go of old ideas…and equally important to be kind to ourselves when we cling to them because there is comfort in familiarity. Nevertheless, our lives are more satisfying when we open our minds to consider a wide range of possibilities. Here's something to try when you encounter a seemingly outrageous idea: instead of reacting by thinking, "No way!" ask yourself, "What if…?" You might be surprised where this approach takes you.

Conscious spending is your best ally…

There are two viewpoints about how to achieve a satisfying life. The predominant view in Western culture is that life is about the end result. That is, we have a satisfying life when we achieve our goals. The other viewpoint is that life is a process, and satisfaction comes from learning and growing as we meet the challenges that life presents. When we live in a consumer culture, we certainly have an opportunity to confront challenges and learn about ourselves. Everything about the culture propels us toward unconscious consumption.

The consumer culture comes under intense criticism on many fronts. Consumers are taken advantage of. Cheap goods are available because workers in very poor countries are paid less than a living wage. Corporate concern is usually for profits rather than the well-being of people. We are pressured to buy things we don't need in order to keep the wheels of commerce turning. People are pushed toward irresponsible use of credit by financial institutions profiting from the interest paid when we borrow their money. All of these things are true. Together they make it seem as if it's impossible to make our way through life unscathed.

That is one perspective. However, the consumer culture can also be seen as a great proving ground, an environment that continually challenges us. To live a satisfying life in such an environment, we need to keep our wits about us, think for ourselves rather than react in knee-jerk fashion to what marketers would like us to think, consider what is really important to us, and maintain a sense of the long term and the big picture.

In short, we must engage in conscious spending rather than unconscious consumption. Conscious spending is not just about what we do with our money. It's about how we use *all* of our resources—time, energy, health, intellect, and money—to create a life that is meaningful and worthwhile. There is great satisfaction in learning to skillfully meet the challenges of the consumer culture by living a conscious life.

The process view underpins my thinking. That's how I've experienced my own life, and it makes the most sense to me. This approach has led me to where I am today and made it possible for me to write this book. I will feel well satisfied if your life's process benefits from some of the information and perspectives offered here.

1

Economics, Illusions & The Consumer Culture

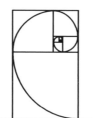

The Consumer Culture

Culture is a product of the arts, beliefs, customs, and institutions created by a society at a particular time. A culture is an expression of the values held by that society. Values are deeply held beliefs. They may be defined as principles, standards, or qualities considered inherently worthwhile or desirable.

To consume means to use up, destroy, expend, or squander; and a consumer is someone who consumes or buys things. A consumer culture instills a way of living that promotes buying and using things up. If a culture is an expression of the values held by the society, then a consumer culture might be said to be based on materialistic values.

Evidence of the consumer culture…

We can become aware of the values of the North American consumer culture by comparing it with others. Anyone who has lived in another country will be able to relate to this. Although it is true that more and more countries are adopting North American ways, there are still notable differences. In fact, some travellers experience culture shock upon returning home after being away for an extended time.

I had an "aha moment" when I returned from living in England for a year. While I was away, the coffee culture had swept into Canada. Arriving at the Calgary airport, I saw a coffee kiosk with samples of the three sizes of cups available. As I looked at them, I saw "big," "huge," and "gross." Having just come from a culture where the only available choice for coffee was a standard eight-ounce cup, it struck me how these three variations of big reflected the North American mindset that bigger is better.

If materialism is a hallmark of the consumer culture, then we only need to look around us to confirm that we live in a consumer culture. The number of shopping malls, the continual encroachment of advertising on our public spaces, and the growing market for counterfeit goods are evidence that we indeed live in a culture based on materialism.

Because we are immersed in it, we are largely unaware of the extent to which this culture influences and shapes us. Yet the first principle of navigation remains being aware of our surroundings. Understanding any system is crucial for successfully operating in it. Consider work environments, for example. When starting a job in a new workplace, most people find themselves in a state of heightened awareness as they observe and try to understand the dynamics of how it operates. They pay attention to the culture of the workplace (when to take breaks, the amount of leeway time allowed) and the power structure (who is in charge according to the organizational chart, and who has the real power). Understanding the dynamics—both overt and covert—gives us an advantage in successfully moving around in the workplace. The same is true of the consumer culture. The more you know about how it works, what the overt and covert motivations are, and who holds the power, the better equipped you'll be to navigate through it without making disastrous mistakes.

The Overspent (North) American...

Observations about how a system operates provide one means of gaining insight into the workings of the consumer culture. Research results also provide a useful perspective. Juliet Schor has studied the consumer culture for many years, originally investigating a trend that had been predicted for the 1970s—fewer work hours and more leisure time. Surprisingly, she found people were actually working more rather than less, and this became the subject of her book, *The Overworked American*. The obvious question was *why* Americans were not working less. This was addressed in her next book, *The Overspent American.* Essentially, she concluded that people were working longer hours to earn more money to acquire more goods; this she termed the *work-spend cycle.*

The work-spend cycle is like a treadmill that people can't seem to get off. You might logically ask why they don't just stop? According to Schor's research, at least two major factors fuel the work-spend cycle: upscale emulation and the aspirational gap.

Upscale emulation is the desire to imitate people who have more money than we do. The *aspirational gap* is the difference between the cost of what we want and the amount we can actually afford. In the past, this wasn't an issue. When people couldn't afford something, they simply didn't buy it, even if they really wanted to. The purchase was only possible when they had saved enough money. That attitude changed, and now it is quite possible to buy things when you don't actually have the money in hand.

The "buy now, pay later" mentality started with the American and British introduction of the all-purpose credit card in the 1960s. By the early 1970s, Canadian banks were issuing credit cards such as Chargex (the early form of Visa) and Master Charge (now MasterCard), and retailers accepted them as payment in increasing numbers. The impact of this is described in the historical section of the Royal Bank's website: "The introduction of charge cards to Canada marked a radical shift in the consumer habits of a country of savers. No other financial product changed Canadians' spending habits more than Chargex, by putting $300 of instant credit into millions of consumers' hands." [1]

Intensive advertising made the credit card a fixture of the culture in very short order. "Because there was no existing market for charge cards, Royal Bank used the powerful mediums of radio and television for the first time to intensively advertise Chargex... By 1980, 1.7 million Royal Bank customers had and were using charge cards."[2]

Appealing to our desire for security, the advertisements cautioned us, "Don't leave home without it" (American Express) and soothed our fears by reminding us that we could "Relax. You've got Master Charge." The latter was a 1973 television advertisement showing a young woman experiencing a car breakdown on a stormy night. She was frantic about not having the $45 for a tow, but the tow-truck driver reassured her that there was no problem because she had Master Charge.

The credit card companies also appealed to our desire for status and "the good life." A 1985 advertisement shows two beautiful people enjoying a luxurious beach vacation. The tag line says, "Visa. It's everywhere you want to be."

Despite the advertising, people used credit cards cautiously at first and mainly just as a convenience—paying the balance in full on the due date. However, rough economic times in the 1980s, coupled with the reassuring "you're worth it" advertising slogan, led people to spend more each month than what they could pay for. Over time, they lost sight of the principle of living within their means. As a result, today we see many people trapped in a work-spend cycle because of the debt load they carry.

Looking back...

Sometimes it's helpful to look back to see how we got to where we are today. It helps us gain perspective and reminds us that life has not always been the same as it is now. This exercise opens us up to the possibility of things changing again.

You've probably had enough exposure to museums and old movies to know that conditions a century ago were indeed very different from what they are today—not only in the objects people used in their daily lives, but also the systems and practices of society. In pioneer Canada, for example, people generally lived modestly, grew and preserved much of their food, and made many of the family's clothes. Garments were repaired, patched, and often remade into children's clothes. Then the scraps were made into quilts and rag rugs. People often constructed their own homes—usually modest structures built with the intention of adding more rooms as needed.

Back then, expectations and attitudes were considerably different. If you didn't have the money, you didn't buy it. If you wanted something, you saved until you could afford it. When more children were born, you moved extra cribs and cots into the existing bedrooms or put more children into each bed. It was a humiliating experience to ask a merchant for credit, although sometimes no alternative existed if the crop had been poor and the family had no food.

Shopping was much more a matter of necessity than a leisure activity. In rural Alberta, people purchased most of what they needed at the local general store or from mail-order catalogues. The Eaton's website describes the significance of "the catalogue" this way:

> In 1884, Timothy Eaton introduced his mail-order catalogue to Canada. This type of retailing was eminently suitable for the vast expanse that was Canada, which remained a largely rural country until later in the 20th century. The catalogue offered everything from clothing and furniture to farming equipment and even pre-fabricated houses. In the rural settlements, isolated communities and small towns that dotted the Canadian landscape, the arrival of the Eaton's catalogue was a major event and allowed people to avail themselves of the opportunity to purchase an array of products that were otherwise unattainable.[3]

Department stores, the forerunners of modern-day malls, were eventually built in all major settlements. The original Eaton's store, which opened in Toronto in 1869, was a very small establishment that prospered and later moved to a three-storey building featuring 35 departments and the first electric lights in any Canadian store. Eaton's expanded to Winnipeg in 1907. The Hudson's Bay Company had a presence in Western Canada much earlier, first with trading posts and then opening "saleshops" as early as 1857. Between 1911 and 1914, the Hudson's Bay Company opened downtown department stores in four major cities.[4]

The concept of "consumer goods" is a construct of the 20th century. Prior to that, the things people made, and occasionally bought, were basic items necessary to support their lives. By the early 1900s, Mr. Ford, Mr. Kellogg, Mr. Kraft, and Mr. Schneider all saw potential in manufacturing their products and selling them to a wider market. Since they sold beyond their local areas, they needed to let the public know what was available. This was the beginning of what we now call the marketing and advertising of consumer goods.

Early advertisements were fairly straightforward. Their intention was to introduce products to the public by describing the benefits and creating confidence in the trustworthiness of the manufacturer. After World War II, marketing efforts greatly intensified, as advertisers shifted their emphasis toward convincing us that our lives wouldn't be complete, or we wouldn't be worthwhile people, if we didn't use their products. As a result of this new approach, "things" shifted from their role of supporting our lives to being the focal point.

By the late 1970s, we were experiencing enormous pressure from manufacturers who put concerted effort into fueling our desire to buy. And we had a new means of buying (i.e., the credit card) even when we didn't actually have the money. Thus, the stage was set for one of the major challenges of navigating the consumer culture—avoiding unconstructive debt.

The Era of New Consumerism...

The late 1970s saw the beginning of what Juliet Schor calls the Era of New Consumerism. In *The Overspent American*, she describes in detail the characteristics and consequences of living in such a time. According to Dr. Schor's research findings, people in this era of new consumerism exhibit several common characteristics. Generally, from funding their aspirational gap, they incur high debt loads. They choose to ignore, or remain in denial about, where their money goes and their current level of debt. They live in a state of time poverty, and feel that their lives are out of balance. If you imagine living under such conditions, or perhaps already do, you can appreciate the degree of stress, alienation, and disillusionment that many people experience.

The consumer issues of our present time in history are challenging. However, the systems of thought and the rules that created these challenges are not written in stone. If we don't like how things are today, then we can individually and collectively make choices that will change them. In the end, this ability for making conscious choices is one of the advantages of being human.

Think-abouts

The fish is the last one to be aware of the water.

Why do you think there is such a prevalent desire to appear like the "rich and famous?"

Never spend your money before you have it.

~Thomas Jefferson

What are the costs of searching for identity and happiness through consumption? Think about financial as well as personal and social costs.

The Issues of Consumerism

Understanding the issues built into the system is crucial to successfully navigating through any culture. On that basis, let's look at some of the pitfalls and challenges of living in a consumer culture. These are largely avoidable, but you can only avoid them if you are aware of their existence. Otherwise, they will trip you up.

The issue of over-indebtedness...

Over-indebtedness has emerged as the primary issue of the consumer culture. Juliet Schor's research was conducted in the United States. However, issues of personal over-indebtedness are not limited to the U.S. An article in the *International Journal of Consumer Studies* tells us about the situation in Australia:

> Five years into the 21st century and consumer debt levels in Australia are still escalating. Simultaneously, there is concern that an increasing number of consumers may be unable to meet their future financial commitments, and also mounting alarm at the relative ease with which the majority of consumers can access additional credit facilities. At the same time, credit providers are avidly seeking greater profits by enticing consumers to borrow more and more.[1]

Ireland was hard-hit in the 2008 downturn, and the Combat Poverty Agency in Dublin is concerned that there is "no policy framework for dealing with over-indebtedness. This is a major deficiency, given the consequences of the current economic downturn and the associated increase in people experiencing debt problems."[2]

"Awash in a Sea of Debt," published in early 2010 by Canadian newsmagazine *Macleans*, tells us that Canadian mortgage and credit card debt is quite similar to the situation in the U.S.. According to author Jason Kirby, "Canadian families, already saddled with record levels of debt, have continued to pile on mortgage and consumer loans at a blistering pace. In the last 10 years the amount of consumer and mortgage debt hanging over our heads more than doubled to $1.4 trillion…"[3]

To put the extent of debt into perspective, he quotes debt-to-income ratios published by the Bank of Canada. The rate of indebtedness in the second quarter of 2009 was 142%. This is sometimes presented as the actual debt-to-income ratio, which in this case would be 142/100 (i.e., Canadians owed $142 for every $100 earned). Shocking? Yes. And the bigger question is: How do we think we can sustain this?

The concern is not just the magnitude of the ratio, but the rapid increase in the past 10 years. In 2000, the debt-to-income ratio was 98/100; in 2005 it was 116/100; and in its most recent report on the state of Canadian family finances, the Vanier Institute reported that the debt-to-income ratio of Canadian families had reached 153/100 by the third quarter of 2011.[4]

The practical problem is that such high levels of personal debt leave people unable to cope with emergencies or with an increase in interest rates because they have no money available for handling unexpected expenses. All their money is committed to basic expenses and paying interest on their debt.

One unexpected expense could be an increase in mortgage interest rates. While mortgage rates are currently at historical lows, this cannot continue in the long term. What happens when interest rates go up? The Bank of Canada, among others, is concerned about this. In assessing risk and vulnerability in its June 2010 report, it analyzed the rapid expansion of consumer and mortgage credit, and judged that "the overall level of risk to Canadian financial stability has increased."[5] News reports and government action since then confirm that this is a continuing concern.

Understanding debt…

One of the reasons for over-indebtedness is a lack of understanding about types of debt and how to use debt constructively. *Consumer debt* refers to borrowed money used to buy consumable goods. Nondurable goods are those that have a short lifespan. This category includes clothes, vacations, concert tickets, food, and gas for your car. Durable consumer goods are those with a life span of more than three years and include cars, furniture, and appliances.

Consumer goods are either quickly used up or their value depreciates as soon as you take ownership of them. When you use credit to buy consumer goods, you pay more than the listed price because interest is added to the cost. And, because consumer goods have short lifespans, you may not have fully paid off the first one by the time you buy its replacement.

Debt may also be incurred for a purpose other than buying consumer goods. There is an increasingly-common strategy that uses borrowed money to invest, referred to as *leveraging*. When you leverage an investment, you buy it with borrowed money, hoping that the investment will increase in value. The goal is to make enough money on the investment to pay back the loan plus interest and still make a profit. Leveraging can be useful in increasing your net worth but *only* when used skillfully.

There is risk in leveraging, and the degree of risk depends on where you invest the money. Putting borrowed money into stocks is a dicey proposition. By the very nature of the stock market, it is not a sure thing. If your stocks go down in value—as they could—you are still required to pay back the loan with interest. And if the amount you get from selling the investment doesn't cover the loan, you are responsible for the balance. That, in fact, was a major reason why investors hurled themselves out of windows when the Great Depression hit in 1929. They had borrowed up to 95% of the value of their stock purchases and had no way of paying back the borrowed money when the stock market crashed. They were financially ruined.

I did say, though, that leverage can be constructive when used skillfully. A common example is borrowing money to buy a house. Although people usually think of their house as a place to live, it is also the major asset in most people's net worth. They leverage their home purchase by taking out a mortgage, which is a long-term loan specifically for buying real estate. The property is the security for the loan and can be seized by the lender if the borrower defaults on the monthly payments—a process known as foreclosure.

A house has generally been considered a safe investment because real estate has historically increased in value over time. That rule of thumb no longer applies in the aftermath of the economic crisis of 2008, when we discovered that home ownership at all costs is not sensible. Just ask the people who took on high-interest sub-prime mortgages because they were unable to qualify for conventional loans. Or ask those who took on mortgages with very low initial rates that were scheduled to escalate to a more realistic value three years later. These people were forced to give up their homes when they could no longer make the payments.

Debt of any kind needs to be taken seriously. You can assess the wisdom of taking on a debt by considering it from the perspective of good (constructive) debt and bad (destructive) debt. There is a simple principle to differentiate between the two. *Constructive debt is used to buy something that can reasonably be expected to produce a return in the long run, such as a house or education. Destructive debt is anything that loses value over time; this category includes all consumer goods, both durable and nondurable.* By applying this principle, you can confidently navigate through the myriad credit "opportunities" that continually present themselves to you. Commit this principle to memory, or write it on a sticky-note and post it where you will see it regularly.

The issue of lack of resourcefulness...

A second issue of the consumer culture—not often recognized—is a lack of resourcefulness. This is particularly true of the generations born into the Era of

New Consumerism, when "money" (maybe not cash, but the means via credit) was immediately available to fulfill desires and solve problems.

This money-based approach to meeting needs leaves people crippled, without the incentive or imagination to figure out other ways of doing things beyond the ready-made solutions they can buy. Fix it, make it yourself, delay the purchase, do without—all of these are possibilities. But since the solutions are there for us to buy, why does it matter? There are two reasons—one practical and the other more subtle. First, the practical one. What would you do if the goods or the credit suddenly *weren't* available? Have you exercised your *resourcefulness muscle* enough to come up with alternate solutions in a situation where you had to be self-reliant? Many people haven't, or can't, or won't.

Then there is the far more subtle factor that generates a perpetual sense of unease by undermining personal independence. When people do not have a sense of self-reliance, they lose confidence in their ability to look after themselves. They become dependent on the system and on those who "call the shots." This is disempowering to the individual and is the real danger of our lack of resourcefulness.

Contrast our modern-day lack of resourcefulness with the self-reliance of a pioneering Canadian family. In the following passage from *Roughing it in the Bush,* Moodie is the author's husband, and John is a young Irishman who worked with them to earn shares of the farm. John's father had died when he was young and his mother's second husband had no interest in supporting the children, so John came to Canada to make a life for himself.

> On a wet day, when no work could be done abroad [outside], Moodie took up his flute, or read aloud to us, while John and I sat down to work. The young emigrant, cast early upon the world and his own resources, was an excellent hand at the needle. He would make or mend a shirt with the greatest precision and neatness, and cut out and manufacture his canvas trousers and loose summer-coats with as much adroitness as the most ex-

perienced tailor, darn his socks, and mend his boots and shoes, and often volunteered to assist me in knitting the coarse yarn of the county into socks for the children, while he made them moccasins from the dressed deer-skins that we obtained from the Indians.[6]

The issue of time poverty...

Poverty means "a lack of" and, although we more commonly think of poverty in terms of money, it is also applicable to time. Whether we're talking about time or money, poverty is the feeling that we don't have enough to meet our demands. Many of us have an aspirational gap when it comes to time as well as money—what we want to do requires more than we have. While a credit card can provide us with the means to spend more money, there is no credit card to use when we find ourselves short of time. We all get 24 hours per day and that is it, period. True, you can "borrow" time by spending less time sleeping in order to finish a project. However, you are just juggling your spending within your fixed allotment; you are not creating more time.

When we experience time poverty, we do what is expedient. This may meet the immediate need, but generally exacts a cost. Sometimes the cost is personal, such as the dwindling or loss of relationships because we don't have time to nurture them. Sometimes the cost is monetary, as in the following examples:

- When we don't have time to research and look for what suits our needs at a good price, we buy indiscriminately. This usually leads to one of two outcomes: We are dissatisfied with the purchase and end up not using the item, or perhaps discarding it and buying something else we hope will work better for us. Or, the item does meet our expectations, but we paid too much for it. In either case, the lack of time resulted in wasted money.
- When we don't have time to think about alternatives, we buy the first thing we think of. The consumer culture heavily promotes solutions that can be bought ready-made, and these will pop into your mind when confronted

with a problem to be solved or a need to be met. However, most situations can be resolved in more than one way. If you have time to think and time to implement the solution, you'll frequently find something that does the job equally well at a lower cost. But you need the time and mental space to make that happen.

- When we don't have time to manage what we have, we make duplicate purchases and unnecessary expenditures. Keeping tabs on our possessions takes time and energy. When pressed for time, we lose track of what we have and where it is. When we need something, we may know we have it but not where to find it. It's quicker and easier to buy another, even though financially it doesn't make sense.
- When we don't have time to look after the tasks of daily living, we pay others to do things we could do ourselves. The fast food industry thrives on people who think they haven't time to make their own meals. So does the packaged food industry, which caters to those wanting foods that take little time to prepare. Canned soup, frozen pizza, cake mix, pasta sauce, cookies—all cost more than making them from scratch.

Time poverty is a stressful condition. Usually it feels as if there are demands coming from many directions, often with great urgency attached. A paper is due tomorrow; the kids need to be driven to soccer practice and music lessons; it's 6 PM and everyone is hungry, including you. Under circumstances of external urgency, you have no time for yourself, no time to think about things that are important to you. Ironically, it is the time we spend thinking about these important things that helps us create lives worth living, yet in the very act of living our lives, many of us don't have the time to do that thinking.

My mother raised four children in a small house in a climate where winters were long and cold. We spent a lot of time indoors. I recall her saying many times, in exasperation, "Will you kids be quiet. I can't hear myself think!" As a child, I didn't appreciate her frustration, but now I understand. I realize that thinking time is when I'm in touch with myself, make plans for my life, and see ways to make them happen. I also know I can only think in that way when I'm not caught up in responding to the demands of others.

Understanding the interplay between urgency and importance is crucial to maintaining perspective and managing our time effectively. As Stephen Covey discusses in *First Things First*, it takes us the next step beyond day planners and to-do lists. It's not just about getting tasks done; it's about directing our lives. An excellent online article, "The Urgent/Important Matrix," explains:

> *Important* activities have an outcome that leads to the achievement of your goals. *Urgent* activities demand immediate attention, and are often associated with the achievement of someone else's goals. Urgent activities are often the ones we concentrate on. These are the "squeaky wheels that get the grease." They demand attention because the consequences of not dealing with them are immediate.[7]

All activities have an element of importance (high or low) and an element of urgency (high or low). Combining these dimensions in a matrix[8] gives us a way of seeing where our time is going and establishing priorities. This matrix appears on the next page. To apply it, ask yourself the following two questions about each of your activities:

1. Is this high or low urgency?
2. Is this high or low importance?

Using this matrix, your activities will fit into one of four categories.

High importance	+	low urgency	=	**important goals**
High importance	+	high urgency	=	**critical activities**
Low importance	+	low urgency	=	**distractions**
Low importance	+	high urgency	=	**interruptions**

Urgent/Important Matrix

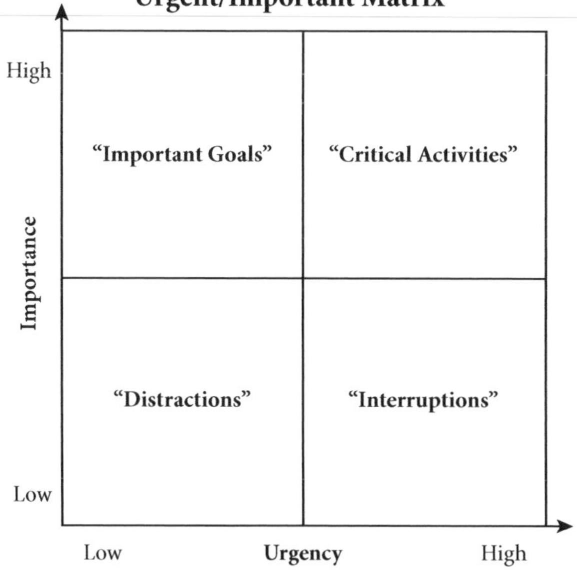

© Mind Tools Ltd. Reproduced with permission.

As you place your activities in the appropriate quadrants, you'll see a picture emerging that can help you understand time in the context of your life. If you spend most of your time dealing with low-importance activities, this could explain why you feel frustrated by never getting to the things you really want to do with your time.

If you spend a lot of time addressing critical activities that are both urgent and important, you may feel you are always "putting out fires." Either way, you're probably not getting adequate thinking time in the high importance, low urgency quadrant.

The challenge is to find a way to carve out some of this time for yourself. Using the urgent/important matrix can help.

The issue of a life out of balance…

My grandmother used to talk about *feeling off-kilter.* That was her way of saying her life was out of balance. These days, life coaches and the media speak of *work-life balance*—the idea of juggling the factors competing for our time and attention so they can exist in a harmonious whole.

Things go awry when one aspect is too dominant, creating a disharmony that we experience as stress, unhappiness, anxiety, or dissatisfaction. For example, a student who never stops studying to spend time with family is living a one-sided existence and will begin to feel that something isn't quite right. A student who spends a great deal of time socializing might experience stress because projects are neglected and the quality of work does not accurately reflect the student's ability. A mother of young children often feels she has no time for herself, whether she's a full-time parent or one with a full-time job outside the house. The desirable proportion of the various aspects of life will vary depending on a person's temperament, circumstances, and stage of life. The point is that they need to co-exist harmoniously for that person to feel in balance.

When we feel off-kilter, it's a sign to stop and re-assess. It may simply take a minor attitude adjustment, such as "I'll stop procrastinating." Sometimes a major realization is required: "It's unrealistic to think I can work 35 hours a week, take 5 classes, and get good grades." People caught in the work-spend cycle have to look deeper, as it could take some serious self-examination to find out what is keeping them there. It might be the need to pay interest on their huge debt load, it may be the cost of buying status goods to create a desired image of success, or they may be working extra-long hours to support a level of consumption based on the expectations of others.

The only way to regain balance in your life is to look closely at it, see what's off-kilter, and then take action. It's an on-going process, so be prepared to repeat as necessary.

Think-abouts

It is incumbent on every generation to pay its own debts as it goes. A principle which, if acted on, would save one-half the wars of the world.

~Thomas Jefferson

Time is free, but it's priceless. You can't own it, but you can use it. You can't keep it, but you can spend it. Once you've lost it, you can never get it back. ~Harvey MacKay

We are now surrounded with items that do things for us to an almost absurd degree—automatic cat food dispensers, electric can openers,... disposable toothbrushes that come with the toothpaste already loaded. People are so addicted to convenience that they become trapped in a vicious circle: The more labor-saving appliances they acquire, the harder they need to work; the harder they work, the more labor-saving devices they need to acquire. ~Bill Bryson

I'm A Stranger Here Myself

The Marketing of Culture

Because the system is based on generating profit, manufacturers are intent on convincing us to buy *their* products instead of someone else's. Thus, consumers are subjected to intense pressure to buy. If the pressure were exerted only on those who are secure in themselves, with extensive experience in the marketplace, it would be a fair game. However, that's not the way it is. One of the issues about marketing is that it takes advantage of the vulnerable—the poor, the insecure, the young, and the inexperienced.

Taking advantage of the vulnerable...

The poor are vulnerable because they have so many opportunities to see what others have, but they lack. Television, in particular, reinforces a distorted sense of what constitutes basic necessities. It creates a desire for "the good things in life." Since television is found in even the poorest households in North America, these images inevitably foster dissatisfaction.

This is also poignantly true in developing countries, where there are a surprising number of televisions. With the advent of the global economy, multinational companies have relentlessly promoted their products throughout the world. In "Cloning the Consumer Culture," the Center for Media Literacy discusses how advertisers create consumers and sell the Western lifestyle. A marketing professional describes advertising in Third World countries: "Once the TV set goes to work, the family is like a kid in the candy store. They're pounded by 450 commercials a week. They see all the beautiful things. And what they see, they want."[1]

Naomi Klein, author of *No Logo*, quotes Nike designer Aaron Cooper talking about taking shoes to low-income inner city neighbourhoods to gauge consumer reaction and to build up a buzz. "We go to the playground and we dump the shoes out. It's unbelievable. The kids go nuts. That's when you realize the importance of Nike. Having kids tell you Nike is the number one thing in their life—number two is their girlfriend."[2]

Advertisers have not stopped with the poor, though. The young have emerged as a prime target since the mid-1990s, when existing markets became saturated. In looking for new opportunities, marketers realized that preteens and teens were an untapped market with a huge disposable income. The 2001 book *Kidfluence*, written by Toronto-based marketing consultant Anne Sutherland, addresses the high degree of desirability of the youth market. The book jacket says:

> Welcome to *Kidfluence*—an era unlike any other. From what breakfast cereal they buy, to where they vacation, to what car would make a good family vehicle, today's kids are having a dramatic impact on their families' purchasing decisions and on Canadian commerce. And businesses are taking notice. Cereal advertising is geared to kids, cruise lines cater to their desires and car companies invite them into the boardroom.[3]

The market being described is a very young one. According to the YTV Tween Report released in February 2008, there were 3.3 million children in Canada between the ages of 7 and 14. Surprisingly, they spend $2.9 billion of their own money on food, entertainment, and clothing each year. They also influence $20 billion worth of spending by their families. This includes predictable categories, such as toys, movies, and fast food, but it also encompasses less-expected ones, such as personal care items, computer software, the family car, suntan lotion, and high speed Internet.[4]

Because of tween influence on spending, advertisers devote considerable effort to reaching this market. Schools provide a primary means for them to do so. With government funding cutbacks occurring at the same time schools are expected to provide more technology and enrichment opportunities, it is no wonder administrators are vulnerable to corporate overtures. Corporate logos emblazoned on team uniforms and in the gym generate money to fund the programs. Some schools grant exclusive rights for brand-name beverage dispensers in return for money to buy audio-visual equipment…or they allow Bus Radio, complete with advertising, to be played on school buses in return for installation of two-way radios and other safety features. In its fact sheet, "Marketing in Schools," the Campaign for a Commercial-Free Childhood highlights a number of concerns, including the use of corporate-sponsored teaching materials. Referring to a study by the Consumers Union, they tell us, "A review of seventy-seven corporate-sponsored classroom kits found nearly 80% to be biased or incomplete, 'promoting a viewpoint that favors consumption of the sponsor's product or service or a position that favors the company or its economic agenda.'"[5]

From a marketing point of view, a school is an ideal forum for gathering information about the target audience and promoting a corporate name. Until children are in their mid-teens, they must attend school for about 10 months of every year. In this environment, they are a captive audience. Besides that, schools are attractive to corporate researchers because of their implied aura of authenticity, order, and authority. For marketers, tapping into such credibility is to their advantage.

The digital world has added a whole new dimension in the corporate quest for access to our children. These days, many young kids routinely engage in unsupervised use of cell phones and computers. This is a marketer's dream. "Sophisticated technologies make it easy to collect information from young people for marketing research, and to target individual children with personalized advertising. By creating engaging, interactive environments based on products and brand names, companies can build brand loyalties from an early age."[6]

My issue with marketing to children is that it is not occurring on a level playing field. Psychologists have long known that until children reach the age of eight or nine, they are unable to distinguish between fact and fiction, and thus don't understand that what they see in advertising is not fact. Nor do they recognize that there are ulterior motives behind it. Even when they are old enough to begin making those distinctions, they don't have the experience to sort through the partial truths and emotional pitches being presented by adults with university education in psychology and marketing. It is not a fair game, and kids don't stand a chance. The consumer society has reached a difficult place with this. Although we understand that advertising to children is inadvisable, the wedge is in the door, and we may not be able to shut it again.

This puts a new stress on parents. "Young Canadians in a Wired World, Phase III" is a 2012 research report published by MediaSmarts, a Canadian centre for digital and media literacy. Children aged 11 to 17 were interviewed in three major cities. After talking with their parents, researchers reported the following:

> The parents we spoke to were beleaguered by fear of danger and exhausted from the burden of constant vigilance. Although the exact nature of that danger is poorly defined, many parents told us that surveillance is now equated with good parenting, and that the days of trusting their children and providing them with space to explore the world and make mistakes are long gone.[7]

This underlines the importance of active parenting. Besides monitoring online activities, parents need to build a child's sense of self and internal capacity to understand that advertisers have ulterior motives. Helping kids see through advertising claims and emotional appeals goes a long way to reducing their vulnerability. Other things parents can do: Challenge their children's definition of "cool." Encourage savvy consumer habits by talking to them about choices and the reasons for them. Discuss the effects of mass consumerism on the planet. Put shopping into perspective by being a good example. Although this sort of active engagement is a lot of work, it is also a great opportunity to help children grow into adults who will be able to function on their own terms in the consumer culture, rather than being puppets of it.

Branding and image…

Advertising was originally straightforward—here we are; this is a product we are offering you; here's why we think you'll want to buy it. Now there are many subtleties with added layers of complexity. You may look at an advertisement and see it only on a superficial level. However, you can be sure it has been carefully structured so the invisible layers have the desired impact, even though you aren't aware of them.

Creating a lifestyle image through product branding is one way they achieve this. Naomi Klein, in her video *No Logo*, shows how advertisers take social concepts such as family, democracy, and community, and apply them to products. The purpose of this strategy is to create an aura about the product that gives the person using it a sense of, or association with, that identity. Klein refers to groups of product-users as *brand tribes*. Once a person becomes a member of the "tribe," he or she is hooked into the lifestyle image and willingly pays for branded products to maintain that lifestyle image. Marketers refer to this as creating brand loyalty.

Creating brand tribes is a very powerful technique in a culture in which many people experience alienation from others, and even from themselves. Robert D. Putnam, professor of Public Policy at Harvard University, investigated the degree of this alienation. His research was published in *Bowling Alone: The Collapse and Revival of American Community*. The essence of this work is described on his website:

> … Putnam shows how we have become increasingly disconnected from family, friends, neighbors, and our democratic structures—and how we may reconnect.… Putnam draws on evidence including nearly 500,000 interviews over the last quarter century to show that we sign fewer petitions, belong to fewer organizations that meet, know our neighbors less, meet with friends less frequently, and even socialize with our families less often. We're even bowling alone. More Americans are bowling than ever before,

but they are not bowling in leagues. Putnam shows how changes in work, family structure, age, suburban life, television, computers, women's roles and other factors have contributed to this decline.[8]

The paradox of all this "aloneness" is that humans are innately social beings. We need to belong. Maslow's Hierarchy, which describes five areas of human need from the basic to the complex, places "belonging" right in the middle of these needs. We need to belong, yet North Americans have become increasingly disconnected from each other. It seems that marketers have found our Achilles heel. They are more than happy to provide a place for us to satisfy this deep and unmet need for belonging—as a member of their brand tribes.

A wolf in sheep's clothing...

Things are not always what they seem. Not all marketing strategies are identified as such, and these days much advertising goes undeclared. The industry refers to this as *guerilla marketing.* Product placement and street promoting are two examples.

Product placement, also known as brand integration, is attractive to producers of creative works because it helps fund their projects. For advertisers, it's a way to reach millions through television, movies, videos, video games, and books. Brand-name products are "integrated into the story lines...to provide a seamless synergy. It is not meant to stand out from the story. This kind of placement is attractive to the brand because it cannot be fast forwarded or Tivo'd out; it is integrated into the fabric of the story."[9] Other benefits for the advertiser are described on the website of a Canadian brand integration agency:

> When a well known brand is used by a star, an emotional connection is created with the consumer. It not only reinforces and validates a current purchase decision, it increases top-of-mind awareness and elicits positive brand associations. Once a brand has been integrated into a TV episode

> or film, it is there forever. It will be seen by millions of additional viewers every time the show or film is re-run, re-rented or re-watched. The Placement payoff never ends![10]

Another guerrilla marketing technique implements the hiring of "street promoters," people in the demographic of the target market. They get paid to create a buzz where none exists, without letting on that they receive money to do this. In *No Logo,* Naomi Klein describes the care taken by Pepe Jeans to ensure that its products are seen in the right places on the right people. She goes on to give other examples:

> By fall 1998 it had already started to happen with the Korean car manufacturer Daewoo hiring two thousand college students on two hundred campuses to talk up the cars to their friends. Similarly, Anheuser-Busch keeps troops of U.S. college frat boys and "Bud Girls" on its payroll to promote Budweiser beer at campus parties and bars.[11]

With the advent of digital social networks, guerrilla marketing became easier. Advertising has gone "viral." In this context, something appears to be word-of-mouth, but in actuality is staged by the advertiser. With the goal of exponential growth of the planted message, the advertiser creates an appealing message with a high likelihood of being passed along by network members.

Undeclared advertising such as this presents itself as something other than what it is—it is a wolf in sheep's clothing. Your best protection is to maintain a questioning mind when you read social media, so you can see these messages for what they are. And you might want to make it a policy to stop passing these messages along; then you won't be playing into the marketers' hands by freely promoting their products.

Telling the cultural story...

They say that the fish is the last one to be aware of the water. Those of us immersed in the consumer culture are often like the fish: we are unaware of the presence and impact of our surroundings. In the case of the consumer culture, the "water" is the overarching big-picture story that tells us how life ought to be. This is known as the *cultural meta-narrative.*

A culture encompasses the sum total of ways of living built by a group of people and transmitted from one generation to the next. A meta-narrative, as the name suggests, is the big story—a composite of all the messages, practices, and objects that make up the fabric of the culture. A meta-narrative may also be called a "story field," as in this poetic description by Tom Atlee, founder of the Co-intelligence Institute:

A story field is
a psycho-social field of influence
generated by the resonance and interactions
among a culture's many stories, events, roles, practices,
symbols, physical infrastructure, artifacts, cuisine, etc.

A story field shapes the awareness and behaviors
of the individuals and groups within its range.
It is the real-life field of influence associated with
a culture's Big Story, cultural Myth, or Metanarrative.

Our story field
frames what we think is real, acceptable, and possible,
and directly shapes our lives and our world,
often without our even being aware of it.
It shapes everything we see, think and do.

Change the story field of a culture
and we change what is real, acceptable, and possible...[12]

As this poem suggests, the cultural meta-narrative, which exists unseen and unidentified, exerts a surprisingly powerful influence on our lives.

In days long past, the story field of a culture was created by ordinary people. They were the storytellers who passed stories orally from one generation to the next. With the advent of mechanical printing, books became the means of telling the cultural story. Today, electronic media communicate what our society is meant to be about and how we should live in it.

This raises the question: If it's no longer people telling their children how to live in the society, then who actually *is* writing the story? As you look around, you'll see it's the companies who want us to buy—not just their product, but the image of a lifestyle that they have attached to that product through branding and advertising.

Sut Jhally, Professor of Communication at the University of Massachusetts at Amherst, is a leading scholar on the social role of advertising. In his film *Advertising & the End of the World*, he observes that when we talk about the effects of advertising, we usually ask the wrong question. Most often, people ask whether advertising is effective in convincing us to buy products. Instead, he says, the more pertinent question is: What impact does advertising have on the culture? According to Jhally:

> Culture is the place and space where a society tells stories about itself, where values are articulated and expressed, where notions of good and evil, of morality and value, are defined. Every society has a cultural field that talks about these things. In our culture, it is the stories of advertising that dominate the cultural field. Advertising, in fact, is the main storyteller of our society.... Because advertising seems to be about such trivial things, it is easy to dismiss as mundane or vulgar. But if it is now occupying the main parts of our culture, and is influencing how we think about ourselves and the world, then the stakes are simply too high for us not to engage with it.[13]

Being aware of the existence of the cultural meta-narrative is crucial for successfully navigating through it; otherwise, we simply react in knee-jerk fashion to the stories that corporations would like us to believe about what makes life worth living. When we are aware of the narrative, we can decide for ourselves if that's how we want to live the story of our own lives. This requires us to be willing to question, to have an open mind, to look for other ways, and to develop a sense of what is important to us. That's what this book is about.

Think-abouts

...use money in a way that *expresses* value rather than *determines* value.
~Lynne Twist
The Soul of Money

Can "brand tribes" satisfy our innate need for belonging? Have you been a member of a brand tribe?

Advertising is the main storyteller of our culture.
~Professor Sut Jhally

Change the story field of a culture, and we change what is real, acceptable, and possible... ~Tom Atlee
The Co-Intelligence Institute

What characteristics do you think would make a person vulnerable to the pressures of the consumer culture?

The Economics Underlying Consumerism

An economic system is the method used by society to organize the production and distribution of goods and services for its citizens. Western capitalism has its roots in the theories of Adam Smith, a Scottish professor of moral philosophy who published *The Wealth of Nations* in 1776. Smith proposed a *free enterprise* system, one in which the marketplace itself was left to determine the price of goods through the action of supply and demand, without interference from authorities. He also introduced the concept of the *invisible hand*, suggesting that individuals, all working in their own best interests, would collectively do what was best for society. Therefore, he believed, the market did not require regulation or interference.

These days you may hear Western economic systems described as capitalism, industrial capitalism, or market economies. All are variations of free enterprise that have developed over the years. There are things we cherish about these systems—most notably that we are all free to be entrepreneurial, to work in the kind of job we want (provided we take the required training), and to "move up in life" if that's what appeals to us.

On the other hand, we have also become acutely aware of some of the downsides of capitalism. Most notable is the extreme and rapid environmental destruction that is occurring as we remove resources from the earth, manufacture them into consumables, and discard the products when we're done with them. Capitalism is creating many environmental stresses, including toxic contamination of air and water, species extinction, climate change, depletion of the protective ozone layer, and waste disposal issues.

The attitude behind the environmental crisis...

Some of the increase in our consumption is simply due to population growth on the planet. However, an equally significant factor is the creation of artificial demand, which was described by retailing analyst Victor Lebow in the *Journal of Retailing* in 1955. This was after the end of World War II—the war that had generated enough economic activity to pull North America out of the Great Depression. With manufacturing for the war no longer needed, there was a sense of urgency to keep factories busy, and producing consumer goods was a way to do that. Thus, it became crucial to convince people of the importance of becoming active consumers so that the high levels of economic activity could be sustained:

> Our enormously productive economy demands that we make consumption our way of life, that we convert the buying and use of goods into rituals, that we seek our spiritual satisfactions, our ego satisfactions, in consumption. The measure of social status, of social acceptance, of prestige, is now to be found in our consumption patterns. ...commodities and services must be offered the consumer with a special urgency. ...We need things consumed, burned up, worn out, replaced, and discarded at an ever-increasing pace.[1]

Back then, we had no way of knowing the amount of environmental havoc this economic activity would eventually cause. Who would have thought that the weed spray developed in the 1950s to keep our lawns pretty would also kill birds and butterflies? Or that the propellant used in the hairspray to keep our 1960s bouffant hairdos in place would cause the ozone layer to thin and eventually split? We didn't know it then, but we do now.

The cycle of more...

It's a disturbing characteristic of the current economic system that enough is never enough. We are always being pursued to consume more. Deeply embedded in the cultural meta-narrative are the unspoken mottoes that "more is better" and "bigger is best." This serves manufacturers well in a system based on profit. Our perpetual state of dissatisfaction keeps us buying more, and ensures their continued income. It's not uncommon to hear someone jokingly justify a shopping trip by saying, "I'm just doing my part to keep the economy going." It isn't a joke; the system is set up that way.

This has put us in an awkward place. The economic system is designed to work on high levels of production and consumption, while Earth isn't. Opinions vary about the seriousness of the situation. At one extreme are those who say climate change is not occurring. At the other sits the Union of Concerned Scientists—an organization that includes half of the living Nobel Prize winners. In 1992, they issued a "Warning to Humanity," which said, in part:

> Human beings and the natural world are on a collision course. Human activities inflict harsh and often irreversible damage on the environment and on critical resources. If not checked, many of our current practices put at serious risk the future that we wish for human society and the plant and animal kingdoms, and may so alter the living world that it will be unable to sustain life in the manner that we know.[2]

The reason that we continue in these destructive behavioural patterns is explained by Sut Jhally, the communications professor who told us that advertising serves as the main storyteller of our society:

> The reason that consumer ways of looking at the world predominate right now is because there are billions of dollars being spent on it every single day. It's not simply erected and then held in place. It has to be held in place by the activities of the ad industry, more and more by the activities of the public relations industry. They have to try really hard to convince us about the value of the commercial vision.[3]

Doing things differently...

The commercial vision offers one, but only one, way of doing things. People all over the world have looked at the economy from their own perspectives and proposed changes in how things could function. What their proposals all have in common is a different philosophical base—one that values the well-being of people and the environment more than profit.

Historically, the environment has not been valued except for what can be taken from it. Profit trumps well-being. We see this when we look at how success is measured. The accepted indicator of economic success is the Gross Domestic Product (GDP), or Gross National Product (GNP). Some technical differences exist between GDP and GNP. However, in a broad sense, they both measure the amount of money that moves through an economy in a given year. If things slow down and there is less money movement, the indicator goes down. Conversely, when there is increased economic activity, it goes up. When the GDP or GNP is up, that says things are going well; when it goes down, the country has hit an economic rough patch. Half a year of decline in the GDP or GNP means we are in a recession. When a recession is severe or occurs over a period of several years, it is called a depression.

The irony of this viewpoint is demonstrated by its inability to take into account the source of the economic activity. GDP increases in times of war and in response to natural disasters such as Hurricane Katrina, the tsunami that hit Southeast Asia in 2004, and the devastating earthquakes in Haiti in 2010 and Japan in 2011. Disasters propel money though the system as a result of the economic activity generated by land reclamation, medical treatment, burial of bodies, and rebuilding of homes and businesses. Therefore, the GDP rises, and we say the economy is doing well. The system has no means of accounting for all the losses that have occurred, so it overlooks them.

Since GDP tracks the movement of money, it can only measure paid work. This means that a mother or father doing laundry, cleaning house, and cooking meals doesn't add to the productivity recorded in the system, even though hard work and a lot of time go into these activities. Conversely, a paid housekeeper doing those tasks *would* be counted as a contributor to the GDP and considered to be of economic value.

There are many forms of unpaid work done by dedicated people in our communities—serving as Scout and Guide leaders, visiting the elderly, packing hampers at the food bank, sewing blankets for hurricane survivors, canvassing for funds for medical research, and the list goes on. Traditionally, economics does not count these volunteer activities as contributing to productivity and well-being, dismissing them as *externalities* because there is no financial compensation. Unfortunately, this criterion excludes much of what contributes to the quality of our lives.

Because GDP is limited to measuring the movement of money, it reports only on standard of living, not quality of life. *Standard of living* measures whether people have enough money to buy basic food, shelter, and clothing. Governments often identify a *poverty line,* which is the minimum amount required for an adequate standard of living.

Money alone doesn't measure how well people and communities are doing. Levels of literacy, health, and happiness also indicate well-being. That is why there is a movement toward using a broader indicator—the Genuine Progress Indicator (GPI)—to measure economic growth and progress. The GPI includes the GDP, but also incorporates a variety of social and environmental factors. For example, crime is considered a negative, which therefore reduces the GPI. The same holds true for oil spills and natural disasters. These things actually *increase* the GDP because money is spent to deal with them; however, they *decrease* the GPI because they have a negative social and environmental impact.

Supporters of using the Genuine Progress Indicator as the yardstick for success point out that it provides a more balanced and realistic picture of a society's progress. Why? The Genuine Progress Indicator measures peoples' *quality of life* rather than just their standard of living, thereby presenting a more accurate picture of their overall well-being. Although switching to the GPI seems eminently sensible to many people, others find it difficult to accept.

The illusions…

When we do something a certain way for a long time, we may begin to think it's the best, or only, way. It's an illusion we hold onto because there's comfort in familiarity. It's not uncommon for us to keep doing it, even when it isn't working any more. Systems need to change, but we stick with the old ways out of habit and a desire for comfort.

My office at home is a good example. When I bought my condo, I decided where I'd like my desk, shelves, filing cabinet, and room divider, and that's exactly where they went. Initially, I had few projects and lots of time, so the arrangement worked reasonably well. As my workload increased and the type of projects changed, I began to feel as if the arrangement hampered my work instead of facilitating it. The location of my desk, computer, and filing cabinet was not efficient. The parts were all there, but the system had become a time waster. Given my new set of circumstances, my original setup no longer served its purpose. It took me months of frustration before I finally stopped to examine my feelings. Once the source of the problem became clear, I was able to rearrange things to serve me better. The key was recognizing the underlying problem and then making the necessary changes.

Could the same be true of other systems in which we live—even overarching ones such as the economic system? Do we need to rearrange and adjust things to better suit our current circumstances? Although making changes to an economic system implies much more complexity than rearranging a room, there are many visionary individuals saying, "Yes, we can make changes for the better. And here's how."

One such person is David Korten, a founder of the New Economy Working Group, created as a forum for freely exploring new ways of thinking about the economic system.[4] Early in his career, Korten went to Third World countries to tell them how to operate their businesses. As he did, he realized that what he said made no sense in the context of their experiences. That led him to wonder if it made sense anywhere. And so he began thinking differently. His latest book, *Agenda for a New Economy*, is the culmination of his work over the past 35 years, and is timely in view of the economic collapse of 2008. Whereas most of us see this collapse as a disaster, Korten sees it as an opportunity for creating a system that will work better. This is explained in "Why This Crisis May Be Our Best Chance to Build a New Economy," an article in *Yes! Magazine:*

> Wall Street is bankrupt. Instead of trying to save it, we can build a new economy that puts money and business in the service of people and the planet—not the other way around. Whether it was divine providence or just good luck, we should give thanks that financial collapse hit us before the worst of global warming and peak oil. As challenging as the economic meltdown may be, it buys time to build a new economy that serves life rather than money. It lays bare the fact that the existing financial system has brought our way of life and the natural systems on which we depend to the brink of collapse. This wake-up call is inspiring unprecedented numbers of people to take action to bring forth the culture and institutions of a new economy that can serve us and sustain our living planet for generations into the future. The world of financial stability, environmental sustainability, economic justice, and peace that most psychologically healthy people want is possible if we replace a defective operating system that values only money, seeks to monetize every relationship, and pits each person in a competition with every other for dominance.[5]

The current system, he says, is based on the illusion that money is wealth. He calls this "phantom wealth." What we should be generating instead is "real wealth." He explains it this way:

Real wealth has intrinsic value. Examples include fertile land, healthful food, knowledge, productive labor, pure water and clean air, labor, and physical infrastructure. The most important forms of real wealth are beyond price and are unavailable for market purchase. These include healthy, happy children, loving families, caring communities, a beautiful, healthy, natural environment. Money, a number on a piece of paper or created with an accounting entry, has no intrinsic value. Wall Street generates it in astonishing quantities through accounting tricks, financial bubbles, and debt pyramids. It appears from nowhere and can disappear in an instant, as a phantom in the night. Those engaged in creating phantom wealth collect handsome "performance" fees for their services and walk away with their gains. When the bubble bursts, borrowers default on debts they cannot pay and the bubbles and debt pyramid collapse in a cascade of bankruptcies. It is easy to confuse phantom financial assets with the real wealth for which they can be exchanged. Indeed, the illusions of phantom wealth are so convincing that most Wall Street players believe they are creating real wealth.[6]

Other economic visionaries...

Building genuine wealth is also the theme of *The Economics of Happiness* by Canadian ecological economist Mark Anielski. He observes that the old English meaning of wealth was literally "the conditions of well-being" and describes genuine wealth as "those conditions of well-being that align with our heartfelt values about what makes life worth living."[7] His model of genuine wealth redefines progress by measuring what really determines well-being, and prompts both governments and individuals to think about what is most important. According to Ray Anderson, "Mark Anielski has visualized an arresting and, importantly, a possible future, in which affluence will be measured in terms of more happiness and less stuff. That is a world to which all of us can aspire..."[8]

Ray Anderson was himself a visionary—a businessman who put his beliefs into action. He had an epiphany after reading Paul Hawken's book, *The Ecology of Commerce*, and committed himself to taking a path that, in his own words, was "right and smart." He explains:

> In 1994, at age sixty and in my company's twenty-second year, I steered Interface on a new course—one designed to reduce our environmental footprint while increasing our profits. I wanted Interface, a company so oil-intensive you could think of it as an extension of the petrochemical industry, to be the first enterprise in history to become truly sustainable—to shut down the smokestacks, close off its effluent pipes, to do no harm to the environment and take nothing not easily renewed by the earth. Believe me when I say the goal is one enormous challenge.[9]

Ray Anderson received numerous awards, including a posthumous presentation at The Guardian's Sustainable Business Awards 2012, in Britain. A brief video[10] tells us that he was courageous in doing things that were unusual and ahead of the times, and honest in publicly admitting when things went wrong so that others could learn from his company's mistakes. His integrity continues to inspire many, showing what is possible within a business environment.

Marilyn Waring, now a professor of public policy, began questioning basic premises of the economic system when she was a member of parliament in New Zealand during the 1970s. She challenged the conventional wisdom with penetrating questions and took strong stands for what she believed in. This period of Waring's life is the subject of *Who's Counting: Marilyn Waring on Sex, Lies and Global Economics*, a documentary produced by the National Film Board of Canada. She continues to write and speak about social and economic justice issues.

Korten, Anielski, Anderson, and Waring are by no means the only visionaries among us. Many others have described the problems and written about alternative ways of doing things. A sampling of some of these visionaries and their work appears on the next page.

Economic visionaries and their work…

- **E. F. Schumacher**
  - *Small Is Beautiful: Economics as if People Mattered*
- **Bill McKibben**
  - *Enough: Staying Human in an Engineered Age*
  - *Deep Economy: The Wealth of Communities and the Durable Future*
  - *Eaarth: Making a Life on a Tough New Planet*
- **Paul Hawken**
  - *The Ecology of Commerce: A Declaration of Sustainability*
  - *Natural Capitalism: Creating the Next Industrial Revolution*
  - *Blessed Unrest: How the Largest Movement in the World Came Into Being and Why No One Saw It Coming*
- **Lester Brown**
  - *Eco-Economy: Building an Economy for the Earth*
  - *Plan B 4.0: Mobilizing to Save Civilization*
  - *World on the Edge: How to Prevent Environmental and Economic Collapse*
- **Karl-Henrik Robert**
  - *The Natural Step: A Framework for Achieving Sustainability in Our Organizations*
- **Herman E. Daly**
  - *Beyond Growth: The Economics of Sustainable Development*
  - *Ecological Economics: Principles and Applications*

All of these visionaries have made thoughtful contributions to the debate about how the economic system could be better—more humane, more people-centred, more sustainable. They think in terms of increasing our quality of life rather than our economic standard of living. Their books are recommended reading for anyone wanting to gain a broader perspective about possibilities for the future of the economy.

Think-abouts

Discovery consists of looking at the same thing as everyone else, and thinking something different.
~Dr. A. Szent-Györgyi
Nobel Prize winner in medicine, 1937

The definition of insanity: Doing the same thing over and over again and expecting different results. ~Albert Einstein

Trees don't grow to the sky. Nor do you. Why would we think the economy could?

2

Fraud, Ethics & Justice in Our Transactions

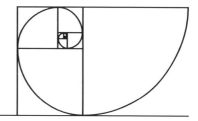

Some Thoughts about Ethics

When we think about ethics, it's often in terms of big moral issues such as war, poverty, and overpopulation. Since we can't do much about these things, we're able to pontificate while maintaining a distance. However, there is a much more immediate dimension to ethics—the everyday moral quandaries that we face. These are the challenges that require us to show who we are.

My favourite definition of ethics is "what you do when no one is watching." It expresses the fact that ethics come from the inside, not from external regulation. It is related to the concept of conscience—the inner voice that tells us what is right and wrong. It's about how we *ought* to act, not how we *do* act.

The principled choice between right and wrong is based on our values, and ensures that our actions achieve their goals without violating our values. When our actions are congruent with what we say we believe, then we are "walking our talk." When our actions are contrary to what we know is right, we usually justify to ourselves why it is okay to do it; that is, we rationalize our actions by giving ourselves reasons why they are acceptable.

Values are those things that we deem fundamentally important. Truth, honour, courage, humility, order, and compassion are generally considered to be universal values. One way of thinking about values is to ask yourself, "Where would I draw the line?" Consider the following questions. Would you…

- rob a bank?
- steal an old lady's purse?
- tell the server when you've been undercharged for a meal?
- tell your boss if you were overpaid by a *small* amount on your paycheque?
- tell your boss if you were overpaid by a *sizable* amount on your paycheque?
- take a credit card that a *friend* left on the table and use it to buy something?
- take a credit card that an *unknown person* left on the table at a party and use it to buy something?

Some answers will have been automatic; others may have been less clear-cut. Reflecting on your responses can be revealing, especially if your answer doesn't align with what you would say is the right behaviour if someone asked you.

> Most people would indeed like to live an ethical life and to make good ethical decisions, but there are several problems. One, we might call the everyday stumbling blocks to ethical behavior. Consider these: My small effort won't really make a difference. People may think badly of me. It's hard to know the right thing to do. My pride gets in the way. It may hurt my career. It just went by too quickly. There's a cost to doing the right thing.[1]

Much of everyday ethics is about the way we interact with each other. The guiding principles and standards have developed over time as people grapple with moral dilemmas and seek ways to act in alignment with their best standards.

The price of ethics...

There is often a personal cost for choosing to do the right thing. The cost may be monetary, as in the case of telling the server you were undercharged for your meal. In other instances, you may be inconvenienced or even ridiculed for taking an ethical stand.

In a consumer world, we all pay for theft and fraud in its many forms. Certainly the price of retail goods is increased because retailers add an amount to cover *shrink*, which refers to their losses due to theft by employees, customers, and organized crime. These losses cost the global retail industry $119 billion in the 12 months ending in June 2011.[2] In Canada, shrink averages about 3% of sales.[3] And even the most honest of us is now subject to much stricter return policies, as retailers attempt to prevent fraudulent product-return scams that have become all too common.

Retail is not the only area in which businesses encounter unethical customers. According to the Insurance Bureau of Canada, "Insurance crime continues to be a destructive and costly problem for all Canadians.… In 2007, auto theft cost Canadian insurers $542 million, a cost that is ultimately borne by consumers, averaging about $35 per automobile insurance policy."[4]

Consumer behaviour and choice…

One of the biggest challenges about ethics is that it is all up to us: it's *our* choice how we behave because ethics are not externally dictated. Doing the right thing is often the harder choice, but sometimes that is what we must do to express our highest standard.

How do you know if your choice is congruent with your values? Think about how you would feel if you had to tell your family about something you did. Would you be able to tell them without feeling a need to justify your action? Or think about how you would feel if everyone you knew read about your action in the newspaper. Would you be able to face the family and friends who read about what you did?

A choice changes us, moving us in the direction of the quality of that choice. You might think of it as going down the high road or the low road, depending on the quality of the choice. Your great-grandparents' generation thought of making the right choices in terms of building character. In *First Things First*, author Stephen Covey introduces his concept of a *personal integrity account.* He explains this idea as "a metaphor that describes the amount of trust we have in ourselves, in our ability to walk our talk."[5] When you do the right thing, it is a deposit in your personal integrity account. And when your actions are ethically questionable, that is a deduction from your integrity account. So all of your choices either contribute to your integrity and strength of character, or they subtract from it.

When we do something that we know we shouldn't, *we often justify what we've done, telling* ourselves why it is okay to do that. It's how we rationalize to ourselves that in this instance what we're doing is acceptable, so it isn't really a withdrawal from our personal integrity account. It takes courage to stop justifying and to make choices on the basis of doing the right thing. It is only possible if we are willing to act consciously, rather than acting for immediate gratification or taking the easier way.

Think-abouts

There may be times when we are powerless to prevent injustice, but there must never be a time when we fail to protest.

~Elie Wiesel
novelist and political activist

The time is always right to do what is right.

~Martin Luther King Jr.

Is it easier to be ethical when you have plenty of money?

Money can be a temptation, especially to those with very little and those with a lot. Why would that be so in each case?

Social Responsibility

These days, the challenge is to include social justice in our ethical framework. We cannot isolate ourselves from the conditions under which our consumer goods are produced. Social justice concerns us with the welfare of workers, and requires us to think about practices such as sweatshop production and unfair trade.

In this era of globalization, workers who produce our goods are generally located in the poorest countries and work under close-to-intolerable conditions in what have come to be called sweatshops. It costs very little to hire workers in these countries because they tolerate extremely long days, unsafe conditions, isolation, and very low wages. The truth is that for most of them there is little other choice for work, except prostitution.

If we think of social justice as focusing on what is humane and what is not, then sweatshops are clearly unjust. Why do they continue to exist? The simple answer is that it is the cheapest way to produce consumer goods. It is how you and I can have our inexpensive shoes and toasters, while corporations still make a profit.

Cheap at any cost...

There are ethical questions that arise when corporations and consumers participate in sweatshop production. Corporations frequently side-step the issue by structuring their businesses to avoid direct responsibility for workers' wages or their working conditions. Nike was the first to develop this arm's-length model of product production. Until that time, goods were typically produced in factories owned by the company selling a product. Nike's model reduced both cost and accountability by subcontracting production to a factory in a Third World country. Many companies now use this model, which has become known as the Nike Paradigm.

Since the objective is to keep costs down, it makes corporate sense to seek contracts in countries where labour costs are cheaper than in North America. Initially, that was Taiwan and Japan. As costs increased there, contracts were moved farther and farther south in Asia to poorer and still-poorer countries. Because the corporations can easily find new and cheaper factories, there is pressure on the owners of contracted factories to cut prices so they are competitive enough to keep their contracts. Since they can't do much about reducing the materials used to make the product, cost savings are achieved by reducing wages and neglecting the facilities. The quest of consumers and corporations for ever-cheaper goods thus results in a squeeze to the bottom, and it's the workers who suffer.

This raises the question: Is it ethical to buy goods made in sweatshops? Perhaps not, although we have to consider that the abused workers are at least earning some money to support their families in circumstances where few other options exist. The real ethical issue is the structure of the system itself. That is where change needs to occur. A corporation should not be absolved of responsibility for the welfare of workers simply by arranging for its products to be made at arm's length. It should be unacceptable for a corporation to hide from its social responsibility to be humane. Were there a willingness to be socially responsible, a company could set standards for its contractors to follow as a condition of the contract.

As for our responsibility as consumers, we need to look at our attitude that cheaper is better. If we were to return to valuing our possessions for their quality and longevity, and if we were willing to pay an appropriate price for such goods, we could make a contribution toward stopping this pressure on those at the bottom. We cannot place all the blame on corporations.

Fair trade…

Fair trade principles offer an alternative to "cheap at any cost." They are meant to ensure that production is sustainable and workers are fairly paid. Under a fair trade arrangement, the producer is paid a fair price, which is intended to provide a *living wage*. This is the amount it takes to pay for basic food, shelter, and clothing. In contrast, the free market system is based on supply and demand, and may result in the market price being considerably lower than a fair price based on a living wage.

Fair trade principles go beyond the price paid to the producer. There is a commitment to a safe and healthy work environment, and to not exploiting children as cheap labourers. Sustainability is encouraged through improved environmental practices and responsible methods of production. A subtle but important community benefit is the development of a producer's ability to remain independent. This is unlike the typical approach of global corporations, whose practices usually leave the local people either dependent on the company or forced out of business and off the land, as in the case of cash cropping.

Cash cropping is a practice that evolved out of a need in poor countries to meet their obligations for international balance of trade payments by growing crops for export. In order to grow sufficient food for export, large corporate farms take over the land. Usually, this is land that has been used for years for *subsistence farming*—small patches of land on which families grow the plants and animals they need to feed themselves. When their land is taken over for cash crops, these families are forced to move to city slums, where they struggle to find work so they can afford to buy food.

Encouraging corporate social responsibility...

We can all be proactive by supporting socially responsible companies. Corporate websites give you easy access to their mission statements, where you will find a company's stated intentions. The Body Shop, Ben & Jerry's, and Mountain Equipment Co-op are examples of companies that were founded on ethical philosophies. The Body Shop, started in England by Anita Roddick in 1976, states the following on its Australian website, in the section under Values & Campaigns:

> The Body Shop is committed to social and environmental justice on a local and global level. This goes way beyond "corporate social responsibility". For us, our success in contributing to the common good is just as important as making a buck. We're not perfect, but we strive to continually improve and live out our values every day. Being concerned with our sustainability and ethics is only the first step. We are proud retail activists and we feel a great responsibility to educate our customers on important issues and help them take action. We do this by creating close Values Partnerships with some of Australia's best non-government organisations.[1]

Ben & Jerry's divides its mission statement into three segments. One is a product mission and the second is an economic mission. Both are standard for any company wanting to stay in business: it needs to have a good product and make money from selling it. The remaining part of Ben & Jerry's mission, which addresses social responsibility, says that they intend "to operate the Company in a way that actively recognizes the central role that business plays in society by initiating innovative ways to improve the quality of life locally, nationally and internationally."[2] Other parts of the website describe programs that carry out their mission to improve quality of life at home and abroad.

Mountain Equipment Co-op (MEC) is a member-owned Canadian cooperative that has grown into a large business while maintaining its original business approach. MEC identifies a number of values and commits to them by specifically describing action they take in each area. Some of these values include:

- *Integrity:* We listen carefully to one another. We deal in good faith. We are honest, fair, and ethical.
- *Sustainability:* We work to make and market our products sustainably. We strive to build and operate our facilities with minimum ecological impact.
- *Stewardship:* We act to preserve and restore wild places. We do so actively, consistently, and generously.[3]

These three companies are used as examples to give you an idea about what to look for. Of course, there are many more. By seeking them out and consciously spending your money on products from ethical companies, you are voting to support them, in a sense.

Corporate accountability…

Of course, it's easy for a company to pay lip service to lofty concepts and not follow through with congruent action. This is when consumers, acting collectively, can take steps to hold the corporation accountable.

Consumer action may be in the form of publicity campaigns to expose questionable practices. Sometimes it's a call for consumers to boycott products of the company in question. When consumers boycott a company and stop buying its products, they show they are serious about the issue. As an individual, you can participate in a boycott and therefore become part of the voice requiring corporate accountability.

Boycotts aren't always the best way to address an issue. Moral and ethical dilemmas posed by sweatshops require action to change the structure of the system, not just practices of individual corporations. One proposed solution is a code-of-conduct clause in contracts between multinational companies and the factories making their products. This approach is favoured by the Fair Labor Association, headquartered in Washington, DC. In a brochure entitled "Protecting Workers' Rights Worldwide," it explains this philosophy:

> The Fair Labor Association joins forces with…companies that are committed to respecting their workers' rights. By joining together to maximize their impact on industry practices, Fair Labor Association members create the potential for lasting change at thousands of factories around the world. Every company that joins the Fair Labor Association agrees to transparency and accountability, an essential contribution to ending sweatshop labor.[4]

Lobbying government for new or revised legislation is a means of requiring businesses to improve their practices when they don't do so voluntarily. Lobbying is often used by organizations representing groups of individuals with particular interests. The Consumers' Association of Canada, for example, has lobbied government on issues such as telephone rates, auto insurance rates, bank mergers, and the future of health care in Canada. You can participate by donating to or becoming a member of organizations whose aims are in line with yours.

Personal accountability...

Holding corporations accountable is significant, but we can also make a difference by how we ourselves act. If we say we are in favour of small business, then we should purchase their goods and services. This might translate into shopping at a local pharmacy rather than a mega chain, or at your local farmer's market instead of a supermarket. The challenge is to remain true to your principles when local prices are higher than those of mass-production and mass-marketing.

If you are serious about walking your talk, you may want to help a small business in a developing country. Small amounts of money lent to people living in poverty can make a big difference, helping them start businesses and support themselves. You can do this by making a microloan through an organization such as Kiva or the Grameen Foundation.

The field of microfinance was pioneered by economist Muhammad Yunus. In 1976, he started the Grameen Bank in Bangladesh with just $27 and a vision. He believed that microloans could raise people out of poverty by giving them a chance when traditional lenders would not. He established a loan program and discovered that women in poverty rose to the challenge, using the profits of their businesses to improve quality of life for their children and repaying their loans with rarely a default. The Grameen Bank is fully owned by its clients and now serves more than 7 million poor families; it has become a model for microfinance around the world. In 2006, Professor Yunus and Grameen Bank jointly received the Nobel Peace Prize. The Grameen Foundation, its sister-organization, accepts donations from people wanting to make a contribution to breaking the cycle of poverty.

Kiva, another microlending organization, was founded in 2005 by Matt Flannery and Jessica Jackley of the U.S. Kiva is an online means for lending amounts as small as $25 to people in many of the world's poorest countries. According to the Kiva website, Jessica was "first inspired to start Kiva in the spring of 2004, working in East Africa with rural entrepreneurs. She became deeply moved by their stories of success, and wanted to provide a way for her friends and family to participate in the next chapter of those stories."[5] Matt was a computer programmer at TiVo Inc. and began developing Kiva as a side-project. Since Kiva was founded in 2005, 811,766 lenders have loaned $314 million at a repayment rate of 98.97%.[6]

There is also a need for microloans here at home. Jessica Jackley recently founded another online organization—ProFounder. ProFounder is aimed at helping U.S.-based entrepreneurs raise investment capital from their communities. It is one of several websites based on the idea of *crowdfunding*, which is a means of obtaining small amounts of capital from many people interested in supporting the development of a project or business.

Momentum is a not-for-profit organization established for the purpose of dealing with the issues of poverty in Calgary, Canada. Their website explains: "Central to Momentum's work in community economic development are the principles of the sustainable livelihoods model. Simply put, this model is based on the notion that in order for a person to increase their financial assets and stay resilient, they need to build strength in five different asset areas. Those areas are personal, physical, social, human and financial."[7] One of Momentum's many programs is micro business loans, which are based on the person's character and require participation in Momentum's business training program in order to qualify. Their website suggests several ways to contribute to their work: be a donor, volunteer your time, buy from the graduates, or hire the graduates. If you are interested in making a difference locally, these are powerful ways to contribute.

Contributing to microfinance to lessen poverty, holding corporations accountable for their actions as they go about their business, holding yourself to a high standard—these are opportunities for us to make things better for others. That is what social justice is about, whether out in the world or right where you live.

Think-abouts

It's not solely about the answers. It's about each person having a consciousness that the way we live affects the next person, and affects our community, and our country, and ultimately affects our planet.

~Sheryl Crow
musician and activist

We will have to repent in this generation not merely for the vitriolic words and actions of the bad people, but for the appalling silence of the good people.

~Martin Luther King Jr.

We can live a better life if all we do is care.

~John Paul DeJoria
businessman and philanthropist

Looking After Yourself in the Marketplace

It's challenging to function effectively in a money-based culture. Not only do you need to look at your own ethics and behaviour, you must also avoid being victimized by unethical people who will take your money through scams and questionable business practices.

Scams...

Scams are schemes to take your money without providing value in return, even though something is promised in order to persuade you to participate. Many scams have endured for years and are known under names such as the bank inspector scheme, Nigerian money letter, and Ponzi scheme. In the past, they were primarily conducted by telephone and mail; now e-mail provides cheap and easy access to potential targets. Some scams are highly sophisticated, whereas others are not. However, the results are the same: someone takes another person's money with the intention of providing nothing in return.

There is a long history of the elderly being targeted for scams because they have retirement savings and many are easy prey. A variety of circumstantial factors contribute to their vulnerability. Many of our elderly live alone and are isolated from the changing ways of the world. Some have lost confidence as they aged; some have lost their mental acuity. They were brought up in a different time, making them less skeptical and more willing to comply with a con artist's requests. If you have an elder in your family, watch for odd activities, such as frequent bank trips or large bank withdrawals. They could be doing these things in good faith but with disastrous financial consequences if it is at the bidding of a con artist.

Young people used to be of little interest to con artists because they didn't have much money. That has changed with their easy access to credit. Coupled with their high levels of Internet use and lack of life experience, this makes the young a primary target.

Surprisingly, the wealthy and the middle-aged are also susceptible to being defrauded—largely because of their wide-acceptance of the Internet for all kinds of legitimate business dealings. Online transactions are so commonplace these days, it's easy to forget that not everyone out there has honest intentions.

Why would someone fall prey to a con artist? Partly because we innately want to trust people. Sometimes there's an element of greed: we want something even though it sounds too good to be true. And sometimes we are just taken in by a person who seems believable. I recall a documentary in which a reformed con artist demonstrated techniques he had used. He was charming and charismatic, and his pitch was highly refined; it would have been difficult to refuse to buy whatever he was selling. The term "con artist" is shortened from the original—confidence artist. Con artists have personalities that engender confidence, and thus are able to get people to suspend critical thinking and do things they wouldn't do normally. Not all are charming, though. The same film also showed a con artist who had filmed himself outlining an elaborate scheme he'd devised to defraud investors. He came across as arrogant, ruthless, remorseless, devious, and highly intelligent—clearly, a formidable opponent.

Identity theft...

As the name implies, identity theft involves stealing pertinent personal information to use for fraudulent purposes. In pre-electronic days, thieves sifted through garbage bins behind stores and restaurants to gain information. They were looking for credit card numbers and corresponding signatures on carbon papers that had been discarded after the impression was made on the imprint machine. Now that we've moved to digital processing, they've developed other means of obtaining your information.

Phishing (pronounced fishing) is a primary means of fraudulently obtaining identity information. Much phishing is done by e-mail, and you probably have received some of these attempts in your inbox. Typically, it is a letter from a "bank" saying they need to clarify your details and urging you to "click here" to confirm the specifics of your account to keep it open and active. Don't. The link will take you to a *clone site*, set up by the scammer. As the term "clone" suggests, it looks like your bank's web pages, so you could easily believe it is legitimate and not give it a second thought. On the clone page you will be asked to type in details such as your card number, personal identification number (PIN), name, address, and secret identifying words. With that, a thief has everything he needs to undertake transactions in your name and withdraw money from your account.

Smishing is the variation used to reach you via texting. You will be asked to click on a link in a message to deal with some "urgent" situation or to claim a prize. This will either take you to a webpage where you are asked for information, or it will download malware onto your cell phone that allows the scammer to access your device and read details such as your banking information. Your best protection is to install an anti-malware program on your cell phone, and to make it a policy to never click links in a text message.

RFID theft of your credit card data is a growing concern. The RFID (radio frequency identification) chip enables your credit card to make payments wirelessly. Although it speeds transactions and seems very convenient, the chip leaves you wide open to others accessing your card information and using it.[1] Shielded wallets are being developed to prevent this, or you can wrap your credit card in aluminum foil to protect your personal information.

Identity theft is no joke. By the time you discover your identity has been stolen, there could be credit card purchases in your name, your social insurance number might have been used to apply for social benefits, and a collections agent could be demanding payments in arrears on the vehicle you purchased three months ago. The catch? You didn't do any of these things.

According to "Measuring Identity Theft in Canada: 2008 Consumer Survey," almost 1.7 million Canadian adults were victims of identity theft, about half of which involved credit card fraud. The cost of credit card fraud is generally borne by the card issuer, so is not too traumatic for the individual. However, identity thefts that did not involve credit cards cost Canadians more than $110 million of their own money and took 12 million hours to resolve.[2] When your identity is stolen, you have to prove it wasn't you that racked up the bills, and that can be surprisingly difficult.

The survey, undertaken by McMaster University, also investigated what consumers do to prevent or reduce identity theft. Preventive practices included doing less online shopping, reducing online banking, monitoring accounts frequently, checking their credit report each year, not giving credit cards to waiters and gas station attendants, and carrying fewer identity documents with them. In addition, many people reported the usual precautions, such as shredding documents before disposal, using a locked mailbox, and making sure no one can see the PIN number being entered at an ATM (automated teller machine) or POS (point-of-sale) machine.

Remember, as well, that e-mail should be used with caution. Never send personal information or credit card numbers via e-mail, which is not encrypted and can easily be read by hackers. Sending something by e-mail is like sending a postcard—what you write is out in the open for anyone to see.

Debit cards are also of great interest to scammers, who gather card numbers and their PINs in various ways. One method is to install a camera above the PIN pad to photograph your finger movement. That's why you should always shield your hand when entering your PIN. Card numbers and corresponding PINs can also be obtained by installing a false front on an ATM or pay-at-the-pump machine. This provides the thief with the information necessary to withdraw money from your bank account.

How would a false front get on a machine? A television documentary showed footage of a gang being followed across Canada by police. It was mind-boggling to see how quickly and seamlessly the false front was slapped in place at a pay-at-the-pump gas station. In just two hours, the gang obtained card details of 35 customers, and in a few days they had enough to steal nearly $650,000 from them.[3] Protect yourself by paying attention when you insert your card. If the front looks suspicious in any way, pull on it; a fake one will come off without much effort.

I could describe a long list of scams. But truthfully, as fast as the details are uncovered and exposed, other variations spring up or old scams are brought back with different twists. It is impossible—and perhaps not particularly useful—to attempt to remember the details of all of them.

A better strategy is to adopt an attitude of healthy skepticism. I'm not suggesting paranoia, by any means, but there are precautions you might consider. For example, you can reduce your risk of debit scam by using your card less and being more selective about where and when you choose to use it. A retailer told me he finds that Canadians use debit cards much more than people of other nationalities. He speculated that Canadians tend to be very trusting, and I think he's probably right. The downside of that trusting attitude is that we can be taken advantage of more easily.

Pay attention to your mindset…

If you believe that whatever someone tells you is true, you leave yourself open to being scammed. To protect yourself, always check things out thoroughly before getting involved. Ask people with more experience what they know about a deal or an offer. Check with the Better Business Bureau to see if there are complaints against the company. Check with the government to find out if this type of business is legitimate. Appropriate steps depend on the particular offer you are investigating. However, the important thing is that you do investigate.

The Canadian Anti-Fraud Centre is a reliable source of information, operated by the Royal Canadian Mounted Police (RCMP), the federal government, and the Ontario Provincial Police (OPP) since 1993. According to its 2011 annual statistical report, the Canadian Anti-Fraud Centre "plays a key role in educating the public about Mass Marketing Fraud (MMF) scams such as telemarketing fraud, West African fraud, Internet fraud, and identity theft."[4] If you don't know what some of these scams are, it's worth checking their website for solid information to support your sense of healthy skepticism.

Lacking a sense of boundaries can make you vulnerable. From a societal perspective, this started in the 1960s. In rebellion against the high degree of repression in earlier decades, the mantra became "let it all hang out." This mindset, coupled with recent widespread use of social networking sites, has created a situation that leaves people highly susceptible to giving out too much information.

Remember that personal boundaries are psychologically healthy, and it is neither required nor a good idea to casually give out personal information. When someone asks for such details, your first response should be to question why. For example, when a retail clerk asks for my address and telephone number, I simply say, "I don't give out that information. Why would you want it?" If a Facebook "friend" asks personal questions, you might stop to wonder if you actually know that person and if it's any of their business. If you get an e-mail from your bank asking you to confirm details, you should automatically think, "No way." So hold your boundaries, and you will avoid some potential problems.

If you believe in the *money fairy*, you are a con artist's dream come true. You may not call her the money fairy, but she's the one who whispers in your ear that lots of money can land in your lap with very little effort. The myth of the money fairy has been greatly strengthened by the legalization of lotteries in Canada. Of course, it's true that a few people do win very large sums of money. However, the sadder truth is that most of the money they win comes from the pockets of low-income people buying tickets they can ill afford in the hope of solving all their financial problems. Apart from that, the lottery system has contributed to the cultural meta-narrative—the part of the story that says it is possible for huge sums of money to come to people with little effort on their part. So when a con artist makes the same proposal, we no longer have our natural healthy skepticism working. Remember—when something sounds too good to be true, it probably is.

When things go awry…

Even if you have a healthy mindset and do your homework before jumping into something, things may not work out. It happens. The car repair shop charges a lot and your car still isn't working, you are talked into signing a gas contract for heating your apartment and discover it's costing you a lot more than your previous supplier charged, or your new computer isn't working properly and the dealer won't do anything about it. What to do?

As the following diagram shows, consumers, businesses, and government all interact in the marketplace. Understanding these players and their roles is useful when you have consumer problems to resolve. Ideally, consumers and businesses conduct themselves ethically in their mutual dealings, government legislates business activities when businesses don't self-regulate, and government provides education to help consumers learn about their rights and responsibilities in their relationship with business.

The Players in the Marketplace

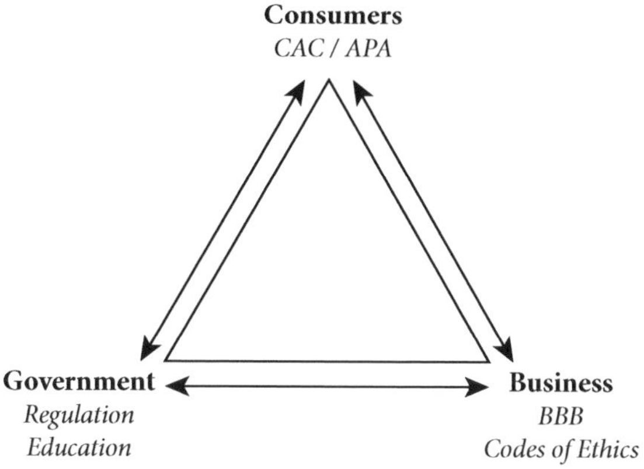

Consumer rights and responsibilities…

Consumer protection received minimal consideration during the first half of the 20th century. Manufacturers produced and promoted their products as they saw fit. Over time, it became evident that there was a need for legislation to ensure product safety and truth in advertising.

Then in 1962, U.S. President John F. Kennedy put forth a "Consumer Bill of Rights." The four rights identified at that time were the right to choose, the right to safety, the right to be informed, and the right to be heard. In 1985, the United Nations General Assembly adopted those rights and four more. In 2012, Consumers International—an organization providing a global voice for consumers—listed the eight rights as the right to the satisfaction of basic needs, to safety, to be informed, to choose, to be heard, to redress, to consumer education, and to a healthy environment.[5]

Rights are one side of the coin. Responsibilities are the other. Regrettably, some consumers embrace their rights but not their responsibilities. What are those responsibilities? As the marketplace became more complex, we moved past the simple responsibility of doing our research and getting a good buy. The following list from the website of the Consumer Rights Commission of Pakistan is a good summary of our major areas of consumer responsibility in the 21st century:

- **Critical Awareness:** The responsibility to be more alert and questioning about the price and quality of goods and services we consume.
- **Action:** The responsibility to assert ourselves by acting to ensure that we get a fair deal. As long as we remain passive consumers we will continue to be exploited and manipulated.
- **Social Concern:** The responsibility to consider the impacts of our consumption patterns and lifestyles on other citizens, especially the poor, disadvantaged, or powerless consumers whether they be in the local, national or international community.

- **Environmental Awareness:** The responsibility to realize the environmental costs and consequences of our consumption patterns and lifestyles. We should recognize our individual and collective social responsibility to conserve natural resources and to preserve earth for present and future generations.
- **Solidarity:** The responsibility to come together and organize consumers in order to enhance the strength and influence required to promote and protect our interests.[6]

Consumer organizations…

Refer again to the diagram showing the players in the marketplace. At the point of the consumer, I've named two organizations out of many that represent consumer interests. The Consumers' Association of Canada was started in Ottawa in 1947 as an independent not-for-profit organization. Its purposes are to inform and educate consumers, to speak out on consumer issues, and to work with government and industry to solve marketplace problems.

The need for such an organization became apparent during World War II when the Canadian government took steps to prevent price gouging by asking women's groups across the country to monitor prices. As these women did so, they became aware of other concerns, particularly the lack of standardization and safety regulations. When the war was over and their price-monitoring services were no longer required, these women still felt a need to look after consumers' interests. They arranged an initial meeting to discuss how this could be accomplished, and the Consumers' Association of Canada (CAC) was formed. As times changed, the issues under consideration changed as well. They have included—among others—standards for food labelling and electrical safety, gasoline pricing, international trade and standards, harmonization of provincial legislation, pensions insurance, privatization of utilities, and air transportation.

Another not-for-profit consumer organization is the Automobile Protection

Association (APA). As its name indicates, the APA's interest is motor vehicles. Based in Montreal, the APA was founded in 1968 by Phil Edmonston. Initially, he assisted car owners in launching class action lawsuits to make corporations accountable for manufacturing defects in their vehicles. Later, the APA introduced the yearly *Lemon Aid* guides to car buying. These books are based on reports from owners about problems they have encountered and provide a good way to see repair trends in particular brands and models. When researching the purchase of a used car, you'll find this an invaluable source of information. *Lemon Aid* guides are readily available in the reference section of public libraries, where you can access them at no charge.

The CAC and APA are examples of organizations of consumers speaking on behalf of Canadians. If you live elsewhere in the world, look for similar groups wherever you are. You can access their information when you need it and support their work by becoming a member if you are so inclined.

Protection from unethical businesses…

The Better Business Bureau (BBB) is a well-known business organization. It was established by businesses to create an ethical marketplace in which buyers and sellers can trust each other.

The Better Business Bureau is directly useful to you in several ways. When researching a product or service before making a purchase decision, you can check the BBB for information about the companies you are considering. This information, available online or by telephone, will advise you how long they've been in business, the number of complaints against them in the past three years, and whether there are any unresolved complaints. This provides useful information when making your final decision.

The Better Business Bureau can also help when you encounter difficulty in dealing with a company. The BBB's dispute resolution process assists in negotiations between consumers and member companies to resolve problems. Their complaint-filing system makes it possible to warn other consumers about unreliable companies. When seeking general information as part of your pre-purchase research, check their online resource library.

Professional practitioners such as doctors, lawyers, and realtors are typically set up as businesses but are not members of the Better Business Bureau. Instead, their respective professional associations require them to follow prescribed codes of ethics. A *code of ethics* is a statement that defines what is considered right and wrong in the practice of that profession. If you have dealings with a professional whose conduct is contrary to the code of ethics, you can lodge a complaint with the relevant professional association. If the ensuing investigation determines the conduct did contravene the code, then a variety of penalties may be imposed, depending on the severity of the infraction. This could range from a reprimand for mild transgressions to being banned from membership in the profession, if there was a serious ethical breach.

Legislation to protect consumers…

The government—the third player in the marketplace—is responsible for passing laws to ensure that the system works fairly for both businesses and consumers. Consumer legislation varies from country to country and within municipalities of a particular country, depending on its political structure.

For many years in Canada, there was little consumer legislation beyond the *Combines Investigation Act* (now the *Competition Act*) to ensure fairness in the marketplace, and the *Food and Drugs Act* to prevent the adulteration of these products. By the middle of the 20th century, there was a growing consumer movement in North America. The Consumers' Association of Canada lobbied the government to form a department of consumer affairs to address consumer issues. This came about in 1967, and within a few years several laws were passed, including the *Packaging and Labelling Act*, *Hazardous Products Act*, *Textile Labelling Act*, and *Care Labelling Act*.

Because Canada has a federal system, provincial governments assume some of the legislative responsibility. It was determined that the federal government would pass consumer laws that had to do with standards, while the provinces would address matters related to business dealings. The government of Alberta established its department of consumer affairs in 1972. Provincial consumer legislation includes the *Fair Trading Act,* with 20 regulations ranging from door-to-door sales to Internet sales contracts, and *The Residential Tenancies Act,* which addresses landlord and tenant concerns. Both deal with people engaged in business transactions.

It's important to note that provincial laws apply only in the province in which they are passed. Thus the details of the Alberta *Residential Tenancies Act* apply only in Alberta. If you live in another province or country and are renting accommodation there, you will probably find a law with similar intent. However, details such as notice periods and requirements for accommodation inspection reports may be different. Therefore, it's important to become familiar with specifics of the law that applies where you live.

By being aware of existing legislation, you can know when and where to complain if you encounter business practices that are contrary to the law. For example, to complain about an unsafe product, you would contact the federal government, since the issue has to do with product standards. If your landlord refused to pay the required interest when refunding your security deposit, you would contact the provincial government, since it deals with matters pertaining to business transactions.

Dealing with your consumer problems…

When you encounter a consumer problem, don't immediately report it to a government office. The first step in resolving a problem is to contact the retailer or service provider to bring the matter to their attention. Start with the person on duty; if that doesn't get the desired results, ask to speak to the manager. If you discover that person *is* the manager, then ask how you can reach the manager's supervisor. In other words, work up the chain of command until you find someone who can help you.

If that doesn't yield results, your next step will depend on the particular issue and may include contacting previously mentioned sources of assistance, such as the BBB, APA, or the government consumer services office. Failing that, you may decide to contact Legal Aid or Legal Guidance, small claims court, or perhaps the consumer affairs reporter at your newspaper or television station. Or you may choose to let other people know what has happened by spreading the word via social media. These are approaches of last resort, and should be taken only after you have exhausted the possibilities through the usual channels.

You can catch more flies with honey…

When solving problems, your attitude and demeanour make a considerable difference. Aim for an assertive, professional approach, although admittedly that isn't always easy when you are frustrated by unhelpful responses.

The best way to appear professional is to keep a log of your attempts at resolution. Include dates, person contacted, and details of discussion. Also keep copies of your receipts and all correspondence you send and receive by either post or e-mail. This permits you to be precise when you need to escalate the complaint and improves your credibility.

When it's necessary to send a letter, use a proper business letter format. If you don't know what an inside address is, find out. An Internet search of "business letter format" will produce all the information you need to make a professional presentation of your case.

Whenever you put something in writing, choice of language is crucial because it is permanent. If you choose poorly, your words can come back to haunt you. It's never a good idea to bluster and make threats. Instead, start from the viewpoint that the other person also wants to see the problem resolved, and the two of you are working out how that can happen. When you write from that perspective, your letter will have a very different tone—one that is much more likely to encourage cooperation.

As for the content of a complaint letter, give specific details about the product or service in question, the problem you encountered, what you've done so far, what needs to happen to resolve it to your satisfaction, and how and when you may be contacted. Make it complete but concise; you don't want to lose the point in a lot of excess words.

Be pleasantly *assertive*—stating what you want, firmly and without antagonism. This is in contrast to an aggressive approach, which is likely to involve shouts and threats. You can imagine how that approach affects the possibility of negotiating a satisfactory resolution. Remember, you'll be more successful if you are politely persistent rather than rudely aggressive and confrontational.

An ounce of prevention…

Avoiding consumer problems is much easier than having to solve them later. There is a way of approaching a purchase decision that increases your chance of achieving satisfying results. This strategy takes some time and is worth it when you're buying a relatively expensive item. What you consider expensive will depend on your budget. It might be a computer, a used car, new tires for your car, or a winter coat. Whatever the item, this process will prevent being swept away by appearances and deter you from buying on impulse at the first store.

Before going to any store, research the product and the sellers. Start by looking up product review articles in books, magazines, or online. Ask family and friends about brands they've purchased, who they dealt with, and what they like or don't like. The "don't like" question is significant because it gives you clues to problem areas and questions to ask in the next stage of research.

Once you've done this background evaluation, you're ready for in-store research. This is still a research phase, and you will not be making a buying decision on your first trip to the store. It helps to state this clearly to store staff, so they know they'd be wasting their time pressuring you to buy at this point. It also encourages them to be as helpful as possible, so you'll come back to them when you do decide to buy. Utilize their expertise. Ask them to tell you about the product. Ask about the potential problem areas that came to light during your research. Ask about service—where is it done and how long does it take? That's a crucial question if you're buying a computer because you probably don't want to be without it too long. Also ask whether the sales representative is on commission. If so, take a business card, so that person gets the sales credit if you do purchase from that store.

Conduct in-store research in at least three different stores. You'll find that after you talk to the first sales rep, you'll have other questions you want to ask the next one. Collect any literature they can give you, make notes in the store, and take this all home to digest.

Only then are you ready to make your decision. Consider the amount of money you are prepared to spend, looking closely at your financial figures and projections. Evaluate the features and repair records of various brands. Think carefully about exactly what your needs are, and separate these from the features that are glitzy and "nice to have." The latter can go on a B-list that you will revisit after meeting your primary needs for product function.

By taking time to digest all the information and process it on the basis of what you need in your life, you will stand the best chance of making a sound decision. It doesn't mean you'll never have problems because cheaply built goods and planned obsolescence[7] have become the norm. When your carefully selected product fails, you'll have to deal with it. Until then, you will have the satisfaction of knowing you spent your money consciously.

Think-abouts

People tend to forget their duties but remember their rights.
~Indira Gandhi

I'm not sure which upsets me more: that people are so unwilling to accept responsibility for their own actions, or that they are so eager to regulate everyone else's.
~Uri Blumenthal

Sometimes good things fall apart so better things can fall together.
~Marilyn Monroe

Our dilemma is that we hate change and love it at the same time—what we really want is for things to remain the same but get better. ~Sydney J. Harris

Self-knowledge is the most powerful form of self-protection.

3

Money, Power & Making a Life

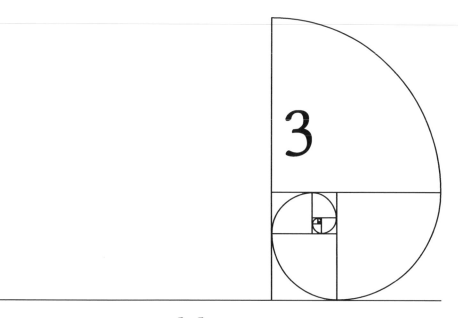

Making a Life

There is an advantage to making your own decisions rather than reacting in a knee-jerk manner to cultural expectations: you get to create your own life. Creating your own life is not as easy as living by default to cultural beliefs about what it should be. Nevertheless, the rewards of living a satisfying life make it worth the effort.

When you live by default, you let society dictate how you live. Bernice Wood, founder of Living the Balanced Life, describes it this way:

> When you install computer software, it comes with standard defaults, but you can make changes. You can add your preferences, your settings. If you leave things on default, the program will work as it was supposed to. It will get the job done. If, however, you choose the preferences, the software does things just how you want them to. It works more efficiently and effectively, based upon choices that you made. And it helps you do what you want to do better.... By choosing not to choose, you are choosing to leave your future in the hands of chance.[1]

Making decisions...

When I refer to making your own decisions, I'm not talking about deciding which sweater, pair of shoes, or new computer to buy. In the world of consumerism, that is what decision-making is usually about. But truthfully, those are decisions that don't matter all that much. What I'm thinking of here are the *life-forming decisions*—for example, not *which* new computer, but *should* I buy a new computer at all? Would my life be enriched by keeping the old computer and doing something else with my money?

One easy way to approach decisions is to ask, "What if...?" What if I don't buy a new computer? This allows you to play with possibilities without being committed to any particular course of action. If you don't spend money on a new computer, then you'll have a sizeable sum to put somewhere else. What if you put it into a special bank account to save for a trip to Greece that you'd like to take two years from now?

Generate multiple possibilities: What if I used it toward my living expenses next semester, so I can take a smaller student loan? What if I stopped buying things with my credit card and used the unspent computer money to pay off the balance of the card in full? What if I didn't buy the computer on credit and started saving money to buy it with cash when I have enough to cover the cost? What if I used it to build up my emergency fund, so I could have greater peace of mind?

The blessing and burden of choice...

When you're an adult, you can do pretty much what you choose, as long as you aren't breaking any laws. This sounds like a blessing, but choice can also be a burden: the burden is that you have to accept the responsibility for the choice. Some people avoid that burden through living by default; they let life happen *to* them without actively participating. In that way, they avoid taking responsibility for the outcome.

The blessing of choice is that you can create your own life. If you choose the route of active decision-making, then you'll need to call on all your resources. Logic is the obvious one, and this helps you assess the pros and cons after you've gathered information and generated a list of possibilities by "what-if" thinking. But logic on its own gives you a superficial answer because you are using only half of your resources.

Using *all* your resources...

The brain has two halves, left and right. The left side is the logical mind that sees things in detail and analyzes in a linear way. The right brain is entirely different.

It takes a holistic view, looking at the big picture rather than details. In the example of buying a new computer, it's the left brain that generates the list of other possibilities for using the money, but it's the right brain that questions the need for buying a new computer and asks, "What if." In doing this, the right brain is taking the holistic viewpoint—looking for the best course of action in terms of your whole life and what you want to do with it.

Practically speaking, how do you bring your right brain into the thinking process? The surprising answer is that you start with your body. Brain Gym is a set of 26 movements aimed at integrating the two halves of your brain. It was developed by Paul E. Dennison—an educator and reading specialist—and his wife, Gail E. Dennison to enhance learning through movement. The Dennisons report that people doing these movements experience improvement in a number of areas, including concentration and focus, memory, physical coordination, and organization skills.[2] Not everyone believes this; there are those who say these claims are based on poor science.[3] If Brain Gym seems intriguing, check it out for yourself.

Why would you care if your whole brain is working or not? According to Daniel H. Pink, author of *A Whole New Mind,* the ability to engage both sides of the brain will greatly contribute to success in life and career in the midst of the change we are experiencing:

> For nearly a century, Western society in general, and American society in particular, has been dominated by a form of thinking and an approach to life that is narrowly reductive and deeply analytical. Ours has been the age of the "knowledge worker," the well-educated manipulator of information and deployer of expertise. But that is changing. Thanks to an array of forces—material abundance that is deepening our non-material yearnings, globalization that is shipping white-collar work overseas, and powerful technologies that are eliminating certain kinds of work altogether—we are entering a new age. It is an age animated by a different form of thinking and

> a new approach to life... Today, the defining skills of the previous era—the "left brain" capabilities that powered the Information Age—are necessary but no longer sufficient. And the capabilities we once disdained or thought frivolous—the "right-brain" qualities of inventiveness, empathy, joyfulness, and meaning—increasingly will determine who flourishes and who flounders. For individuals and families, and organizations, professional success and personal fulfillment now require a whole new mind.[4]

Consciously engage your right brain, as well as the left, when making decisions. Also pay attention to your gut feelings or intuition, which is something that many successful business people do. Ways of reading our bodies can vary. Instead of gut feelings, you may "know it in your heart" or "feel it in your bones." Wherever it is for you, pay attention. It will help you make the life you want.

Writing your own story...

Making a life allows you to write your own story—that is, you get to engage with the consumer world on your own terms. The first step is to become aware of what you want your life story to be. The second is to question the cultural meta-narrative, and the third is to practice consciously making your own decisions.

Living in a consumer culture as we do, we are immersed in a story field that is created by corporations operating under the profit motive inherent in our Western economic system. The messages they send create the meta-narrative—the story most people unconsciously live by. It is a story that tells us we are not good enough as we are and promises that products will compensate for our deficiencies. This message relentlessly bombards us through a growing variety of media that have taken over our public spaces. It is a story that identifies participants as investors and consumers, rather than citizens. It gives you and me our value based on what and how much we buy.

This pattern of thinking, known as the consumption paradigm, has created the meta-narrative of the consumer culture. Beliefs and values underlying this meta-narrative include the following:

- Bigger is better.
- More is best.
- Resources are scarce.
- Human beings have insatiable wants.
- Material goods can satisfy these wants.
- Our role is to consume.

It is in the best interests of sellers for you to believe this. However, is it in *your* best interest to believe this? Remember that the consumption paradigm requires spending a lot of money. Credit cards have given us a means of spending without actually having money, but there are consequences for this. Sooner or later we pay the price, literally. In addition, high levels of consumption are creating enormous environmental stress that may make Earth an unsuitable habitat for humans. That, too, has obvious consequences for us.

Intentional simplicity...

If you are under 30, you may not be disillusioned yet by the seductive promises of the culture. However, by the time you hit middle age, you'll probably have discovered that many of the cultural promises are not true. Psychologist Tim Kasser, in *The High Price of Materialism,* describes scientific evidence relating to materialism and happiness. In a nutshell, he shows that a high level of materialism actually works against happiness.

Shifting to an intentional simplicity paradigm will change the meta-narrative. A paradigm is a theory or a group of ideas about how something should be done, made, or thought about. The *intentional simplicity paradigm* says that *we choose* how we see the world and how we engage with the systems that exist. For example, you can choose to see the world as based on scarce resources. Seeing things this way may allow you to stay within your comfort zone and maintain the status quo. Or you can choose to adopt another way of thinking, such as the viewpoint of plenty described by L. G. Boldt in *Zen and the Art of Making a Living.*

The chart that follows is based on his description; it contrasts the paradigms of scarcity and plenty.[5] To get the sense of each viewpoint, read it completely from top to bottom before going to the other. As you read through it, pay particular attention to the different quality of experience expressed by each column. (This will probably be a feeling you get, rather than thoughts that appear in your head.)

Contrasting Paradigms

	Viewpoint of Scarcity	**Viewpoint of Plenty**
based in...	fear	care, concern
fosters...	conflict struggle poverty oppression	thanksgiving cooperation abundance reverence for life
life is...	an account to be settled	a gift to be enjoyed
leads to...	competitiveness greed	attitude of praise thanksgiving
feelings of...	guilt obligation	mutual support responsibility
creates...	distrust feelings of never enough	trust experience of abundance

How much is enough?

If more is not necessarily better, then how much *is* enough? Under the scarcity paradigm, we will never have enough; it can't be otherwise. That's one of the inherent weaknesses of our current economic system: there is a built-in premise of scarcity.

Scarcity is one viewpoint. Another is offered by Lynne Twist—a global activist, fundraiser, speaker, consultant, and author. Over the past 30 years, Lynne has raised hundreds of millions of dollars to address world hunger and related issues. This has put her in contact with people from the richest to the poorest, and the experience has shaped her unique views about money. Among other things, she founded the Soul of Money Institute "to express her commitment to supporting and empowering people in finding peace and sufficiency in their relationship with money and the money culture."[6]

Lynne Twist is the author of *The Soul of Money*. In the chapter entitled "Sufficiency: The Surprising Truth" she makes the point that sufficiency, rather than scarcity, is a mindset we can choose. As she explains it, sufficiency is not a quantity of anything. "It isn't a measure of barely enough or more than enough. Sufficiency isn't an amount at all. It is an experience, a context we generate, a declaration, a knowing that there is enough, and that we are enough."[7] She further develops this idea by pointing out that this mindset moves us from one of fear to one of possibilities. "The struggle for sufficiency has nothing to do with the amount of money you have. It is all about the relationship you have with money."[8]

Enough is not a number...

How much is enough? Viewed from the intentional simplicity paradigm, "enough" is not a number—it is what is deeply satisfying. We indulge in excess when what we purchase is not fully satisfying. We try and try again, usually not realizing why we still want more. This applies in all areas of consumption—food, clothing, cars, entertainment, and our homes. Excess wastes a lot of resources, both financial and environmental, on things that are under-used or soon discarded.

The concept of satisfaction is illustrated in the following diagram of the fulfillment curve from *Financial Integrity: Transforming Your Relationship with Money* by The New Road Map Foundation.[9] They say, "Everything after the peak of the fulfillment curve is excess. We call it clutter."[10] As they explain, this is the point at which possessions become burdens.

The Fulfillment Curve

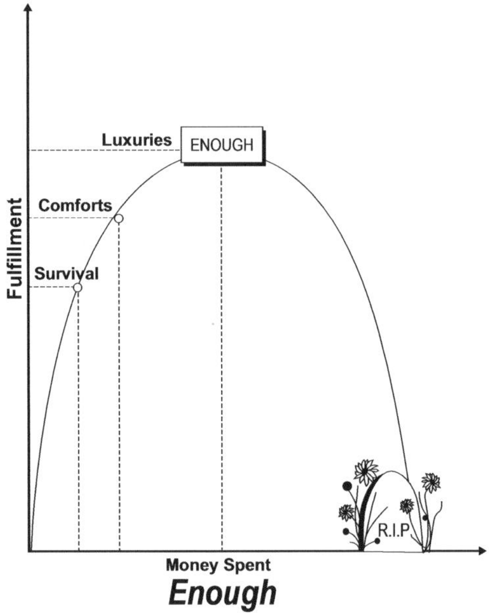

Reproduced with permission. This work is licensed under Creative Commons Attribution Share-Alike 3.0 US License. It is based on the Financial Integrity materials developed by the New Road Map Foundation, available for free at www.financialintegrity.org

Economists call this the *law of diminishing marginal utility*. Stated plainly, this means that after a certain point, each item is of less use than the previous one. As an example, think of a holiday meal with your family. Imagine you've been away at university for four months and had to do your own cooking. You're home for the holidays and your mom has made your all-time favourite dessert. You eat it with great gusto after polishing off a full meal. The first helping of dessert was so good that you have another, then another, then another. By the time you're on the third and fourth helpings, your enjoyment is much less than with the first. In other words, you've gone past the satisfaction peak and are encountering a diminishing degree of satisfaction with each additional helping. More helpings are actually *decreasing* your overall satisfaction.

The same principle translates to acquisition of material goods, yet few people understand this. Consequently, they don't know how to identify the point of enough, and keep consuming more in a search for satisfaction. *If you learn how to identify enough, you will find it much easier to navigate the consumer culture because more things will be non-issues.*

Enough is enough…

How do we know when we have enough? I really like this answer from the New Road Map Foundation:

> How do we know when we have ENOUGH? When we have everything we need, but nothing in excess. We have enough for our survival, for our comforts, and even for a few luxuries; we feel satisfied, and there's nothing in excess to burden us or complicate our lives. Enough is appreciating and enjoying what money has brought us but not buying anything that we don't really want or need; feeling pleasantly "full" of money without that constant yearning for more.[11]

The big question is, how do we get to a place of such peace with what we have and don't have? My students usually answered that question in terms of buying what we need instead of what we want. Although this is a common viewpoint, I've never found the needs-versus-wants approach to be helpful. Typically, it leads to mental gymnastics and justifications: we start inventing reasons why we "need" the things that we just want. It becomes an activity of the mind that is not grounded in the bigger picture of creating a satisfying life.

"Need" is defined as a lack of something that is required, desirable, or useful. Meeting a need compels us to fill the lack, sometimes to the point of desperation. In a mindset of neediness, we are not freely making our decisions; our actions are motivated by necessity, not by choice. And when we decide we can't have something, there is a sense of scarcity and inadequacy, so we feel deprived.

This is a disempowered state of mind. A more constructive alternative is to think in terms of essentials rather than needs. "Essential" means "of the essence"—the inward nature, true substance, or constitution of anything, including ourselves. When we consider the essential qualities of something and reflect on how it fits with our own character, we change the game completely; we are actively creating rather than reacting. When we choose on the basis of what suits us, we proactively create our lives.

A sensible approach to making a life...

- Focus on essentials rather than wants and needs.
- Ask yourself what you can't live without, rather than where you can cut back. This puts your focus on the essentials.
- Live in a house that is less expensive than you can afford.
- Filter decisions through this question: How does this fit for me?
- Reflect on your actions. Are you reacting to needs that demand to be met, or creating a life on the basis of what is essential?

Think-abouts

We make a living by what we get; we make a life by what we give.

~Sir Winston Churchill

Any intelligent fool can make things bigger, more complex, and more violent. It takes a touch of genius—and a lot of courage—to move in the opposite direction.

~Albert Einstein

Living simply is not a matter of living cheaply or feeling deprived. The idea is not to deny yourself the things you want, but to free yourself from the things you don't want.

~Elaine St. James
author

Choosing "enough" does not mean you should cut back expectations, or not strive to aspire.

~Lynne Twist
author and philanthropist

Power and Money

Money was originally developed to serve as a medium of exchange. This literally means you exchange money for goods and services, which makes transactions less cumbersome than bartering items you have for what you want. Money is a fact of life in a consumer culture. We use money to buy goods and services that fulfill our current needs, and we put some into savings and investments to be available when we require it later. This ensures our survival, provides financial security, and allows us to keep our options open.

However, people also utilize money for other purposes. Some use it for wielding power over others, often by withholding it and making the other person dependent on them. Some use money to buy their way out of difficulties, both physical and psychological, and thus avoid taking responsibility for their actions. Others use money for conspicuous consumption, buying expensive and flashy items in an attempt to bolster their self-image by portraying status.

Think for a moment about your relationship with money. Does money have power over you? Are you defined by the money you have (or don't have)? Do you feel that all your problems would be solved if you just had a bit more (or a lot more) money?

Learning about ourselves from ourselves…

It's an interesting phenomenon that we talk about *money management*. In truth, successful use of money is much more a matter of *self management*. Navigating the consumer culture means navigating your inner obstacles. Reflecting on your relationship with money—your interactions, satisfactions, and discomforts—provides an excellent opportunity for self-observation. Investigating your inner world allows you to improve your interaction with money in areas where things are not going well.

One place to start exploring your inner world is to think about the "old tapes" that guide your ideas about money. These are messages that run in your thoughts or are buried in your subconscious mind. You may be aware of them, or you may not. They might be the family attitudes that you've picked up—money doesn't grow on trees; if you've got it, flaunt it; we must keep up appearances, even when money is tight; or…you name it. Since some of these old messages are deeply buried, it might take a while to figure out why you act in certain ways about money.

Perhaps one of my own stories will help you reflect on yours. At one point well into adulthood, I realized that I was avoiding having money beyond what it took to cover the basics. I'm an intelligent and educated person, so I had the means to earn more money, but it wasn't happening. I did some probing and uncovered the story behind this situation.

When I was a child, we lived in a rural area and my father worked away from home a good deal of the time. Although we weren't impoverished, we lived a modest life. Our house, as was usual at the time, didn't have a lock on the front and back doors. I realize now that my mother must have felt isolated and vulnerable, frequently being alone in the country with small children to care for. She would sometimes say, "It's a good thing we don't have much, because no one will rob us." I'm sure that was a comforting thought for her under the circumstances.

However, her apparently simple statement had a profoundly different effect on me. Hearing what she said, my child's mind concluded that it is dangerous to have money, that being poor is safer. Can you see how such a belief, carried into adult life, prevented me from having a comfortable relationship with money? Once that belief was conscious, though, I was able to reframe my viewpoint and am no longer hampered by that hidden belief.

Are there areas of discomfort that you experience in your relationship with money? This is where you get to play detective. What do you notice when you think about your dealings with money? Do you feel confident and in charge? Do you avoid thinking about it? Are you embarrassed that you can't "do better?" Is there a queasy feeling in the pit of your stomach?

Instead of thinking about money in a general sense, it might help to focus on specifics. What happens when you think about your credit card? Savings account? Investments? Income? Pay attention to your thoughts, but also to your feelings and emotions. Emotional reactions to money can include feelings of pleasure, satisfaction, fear, inadequacy, disgust, confusion, and immobilization. When you identify an emotion that isn't working in your favour, you have a chance to explore what's at the root of it. Bringing it to consciousness allows you to move past it.

The power of thought...

The way we think is important because it affects what happens in the world around us. Psychologists talk about this in a variety of ways. One is the *self-fulfilling prophecy*. Basically, this means that if you believe something will happen, then you unconsciously act in ways that will make it happen. Suppose you're preparing for a presentation and are worried about tripping over your own feet on the way up to the front; so worried, in fact, that you keep thinking about it. When your turn comes, what happens? You trip. By being so focused on that fear, you made it happen. That's an example of the self-fulfilling prophecy in action.

The following example of a self-fulfilling prophesy relates to money. Big lottery winners often lose, spend, or give away their windfall in short order. There are a variety of reasons for this, including a lack of financial knowledge and experience. For some winners, though, the reason is psychological. People who have never had much money before often have a self-image of being poor. When their newfound wealth contradicts that self-image, the subconscious takes action to rid them of the money in order to make the actual condition of life match the person's belief.

We all have beliefs about money. Some are constructive; some are not. Asking yourself questions can help you uncover your beliefs about money. Reflect on your childhood experiences, family attitudes, and peer influences; all of these can have a powerful effect on how you relate to money.

While childhood experiences are often not consciously remembered, they are powerful influences nonetheless. Preschool children are like sponges, absorbing all manner of things from what goes on around them. When children don't understand something, they often make their own sense of it. Many of these experiences and conclusions are filed in the subconscious, where they direct our subsequent behaviour without our being aware of the reasons for our actions. This was the case in the story I shared about my subconscious belief that having money was dangerous.

The tricky part with subconscious beliefs is uncovering them, since they are well buried. For me, the following informal method of meditation usually works. Identify an emotion or behaviour that isn't serving you well. Sit or lie quietly, eyes closed, breathing slowly and deliberately. This puts you in a calm state, and your mind may start to wander. Let the thoughts go where they like. Usually something will pop into your head that sheds light on the belief or situation you are investigating. It may not bring total clarity at once, but it starts an unraveling. Repeat the process over time to work through the layers of the experience.

Remembered experiences can be as enlightening as the unconscious ones. Think about traumatic experiences you've had with money. Did you lose some? How did you feel about that? Were you punished for losing it? Did you receive an allowance? Was your allowance withheld as a form of punishment? Were you rewarded for good behaviour with money? Did you receive gifts of money that you felt were unwarranted? Did you feel guilty because of that? In what other ways did emotions get mixed up with money in your early experiences?

Family beliefs can also have a lasting influence. Whether verbally identified or not, a culture around money exists in all families. Some use it freely and without thought because there is plenty. Others have little money and consider every expenditure with great care. Some believe their teenagers should not work because it's the time in their lives to enjoy themselves. Others believe that working is the best way for teens to learn to be responsible and contributing adults. Whatever your experience, you will better understand yourself if you consciously reflect on the money beliefs of your family.

The same is true of peer beliefs. We tend to think of peer pressure as a condition of our teen years, but we can be susceptible to it at any age. It could show up as the expectations of your coworkers about how you should dress and what car you should drive. It might be pressure to match the lifestyle of your friends or neighbours. Reflecting on peer beliefs and how they fit with your own values gives you an opportunity to grow, whatever your stage in life.

Maria Nemeth, author and life coach, says, "How you do money is how you do life." She defines financial success as "doing what you said you would do with money, consistently, with clarity, focus, ease, and grace."[1] In *The Energy of Money, she* helps people explore their relationship with money through a variety of activities. If you could use some help in dealing with your relationship with money, her book is recommended reading.

Once you gain insight into the misconceptions and hidden agendas that have been directing how you relate to money, you have the power to make other choices. You have authority over your actions. *You* are in charge, rather than your subconscious. Living consciously is where true power resides in your relationship with money.

Powerlessness...

We all need a sense of sovereignty over our destiny—that feeling of fulfillment that comes from being an active participant in what happens in our lives. The opposite is powerlessness, which is one of the most stressful of human conditions. If you have experienced powerlessness yourself, you'll know how debilitating it can be.

In any partnership—but particularly marriage or cohabitation—money can become the instrument of a power play. Imposing a sense of powerlessness on one partner is a common control tactic. This can be overt, but is more commonly expressed in subtle ways. Sometimes, it is an attitude that the partner earning more has the right to have the final say in decisions involving money. *Love & Money: A Life Guide for Financial Success* addresses this issue in Chapter 8, "Does Money Equal Power in a Marriage?" Author Jeff Opdyke, a personal finance reporter at *The Wall Street Journal*, offers a practical perspective that is recommended reading for anyone contemplating a living-as-one relationship. Using real-life examples, he identifies the ways in which disparity of incomes can cause relationship difficulties. Many of these revolve around feelings of power and inadequacy. He advises:

> If you see yourself or your partner struggling with issues regarding financial power in your marriage, then you must voice your unhappiness with the way money translates into power in your relationship and press for some measure of equality. Depending on the situation you're in and the ways in which money equates with power, your measure of equality can take many different forms.... a relationship of any kind "is not about who makes more or who works harder. It's about whether you both take responsibility for the family finances, sharing the pain of cutting back and spending money on things you both agree on."[2]

Freedom and conscious choice...

One of my favourite quotes is something I read long ago in *Adbusters Quarterly*: "The most secure prison is one in which the inmates think they're free, because then they can harbor no thoughts of rebellion or escape."[3] This is such an apt description of living in a consumer culture. We appear to have a lot of choice, and therefore tend to think we are freely making decisions. But are we?

True freedom comes from exercising autonomy over our lives. The consumer culture discourages that, preferring we adopt the cultural story about how to live. Our challenge is to detach ourselves from the cultural story and look at the illusions surrounding freedom and choice.

What has your experience been? Have the beliefs of the consumer culture simplified your life or made it more complicated? Has the use of credit given you freedom or put you in bondage? Have you found it true that bigger means better? Is there congruence between what the consumer culture promises and what you've experienced?

We don't need to live our lives according to outmoded ideas about consumption and economics. Instead, we can write our own stories. The choice *is* ours.

Defining value and worth…

Money plays a central role in the consumer culture, having become the primary means of organizing our social order and survival. Consequently, having money has its benefits. It provides us with comfort and security, and it opens possibilities. However, money is no longer just a medium of exchange. We have also given money the role of defining value and worth, not just of the goods we buy but of ourselves. It can happen so easily.

Value is defined, in one sense, as monetary or material worth. In practice, that translates into a thought such as "I paid a lot for my car, so it is valuable." Sometimes this idea is transferred to a related thought: "Because I drive this expensive car, I'm worthy and of value as a person." Such self-identification with the things we own leads to continual desire for more, bigger, and costlier items. In turn, we must find the means of funding this consumption, whether by working longer hours to pay for it or by purchasing on credit and thus going into debt.

How we define things goes a long way to shaping our world. What if we defined value differently—not as monetary or material worth but as worth measured by an item's usefulness or importance. Looking at value this way changes everything because it is not attached to money. When we no longer equate value with money, we are free to think in terms of enough. From that viewpoint, we have enough when what we have serves a useful purpose. This awareness empowers each of us to discern what is enough for us, and alerts us to the point at which we move from enough into excess. How does "enough" relate to power?

Here's a perspective from the New Road Map Foundation's financial integrity manual:

> Enough is a place of power and freedom—a launching point for cultivating the kind of fulfillment that money can't buy. We can go from a relationship with money that revolves around fretting and consuming to one that is oriented around creating and giving. That peak we strive for is a dynamic place. Maximum fulfillment comes from learning to recognize that feeling of "enough" and adjusting our actions accordingly. It takes certain skills and qualities
>
> - to reach enough
> - to recognize when you've reached enough
> - to stay near that peak of the Fulfillment Curve, without falling back into deprivation or down into gluttony[4]

It takes awareness and participation to exercise the power of living at the peak of our fulfillment curve, and this is a necessary part of navigating the pitfalls of the consumer culture.

Thinking of value in terms of life energy spent…

Another constructive way to think about value is to look at how much time it took to earn the money to buy a particular item or experience. The following description of how to do the calculation is paraphrased from *Financial Integrity: Transforming Your Relationship with Money.*[5]

$$\frac{\text{Adjusted income}}{\text{Adjusted job hours}} = \text{Real Hourly Wage (RHW)}$$

Adjusted income →

Adjusted job hours

"Adjusted Income" is: wages/salary plus value of job benefits received ***minus*** the expenses you have because you work (gas or transit fares, income taxes, work clothes, and others)

Adjusted income

Adjusted job hours →

"Adjusted job hours" is: actual amount of time spent "on the job" ***plus*** the time you spend on activities necessary to maintain the job (the hours spent commuting to work, shopping for clothes for the job, doing background research at home, and so on)

Once you've used the above formula to calculate your real hourly wage, the next step is to determine how much time you spend earning each dollar. Suppose your calculations reveal that your real hourly wage is $5.

In that case, each dollar costs you 12 minutes of your life.

Here's the logic: When you earn $5 per hour, that means you give up 60 minutes to get $5. Using a standard ratio formula, we can say that

If you earn $5 in 60 minutes,
Then you earn $1 in y minutes.

$$\text{Therefore:} \quad y = \frac{\$1 \text{ x } 60 \text{ minutes}}{\$5} = 12 \text{ minutes}$$

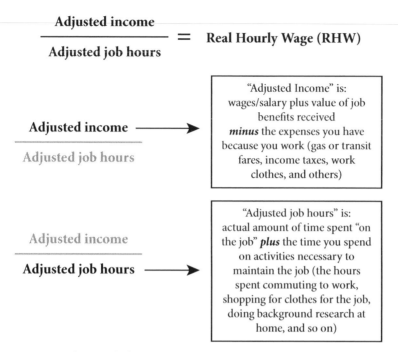

Those minutes are considered to be your *life energy*, because once you give them up, you can't have them back. This analysis gives you a realistic basis for looking at your expenditures and evaluating whether they are worth the amount of life energy you are spending on them. For example, if you buy something for $100, and each $1 costs you 12 minutes of work, then the item cost you 1200 minutes of life energy. That's 20 hours. Was it worth it? Sometimes seeing from another point of view is all it takes to shift what's happening in your life.

The fallacy of cheap...

Instead of thinking about life energy spent, some people view purchases in terms of how cheap they are. This approach puts attention on price rather than value. Price is a limited measure of the worth of something, as it doesn't take into account other factors, such as quality and usefulness, which contribute to true value.

It may seem that going for the lowest price saves you money, but that isn't necessarily so. If you buy shoes for $15 and they last three months, the cost is $5 per month. If you pay $70 for a good-quality pair that lasts two years, your cost is $2.50 per month. Instead of cost per month, it sometimes makes sense to calculate the cost per wearing. A party dress on sale for $80 sounds like a bargain. But if you wear it only once, it's an expensive purchase because it costs you $80 per wearing. Money spent on a classic garment that can be worn to a party and many more occasions gives you better value, even if the original purchase price was more than $80. It's all how you look at it.

Basing our decisions solely on price gets in the way of conscious spending because it's like wearing blinders: we don't see the deficiencies because we are dazzled by the low price. We don't remember that we already have three sweaters that are almost the same. We rationalize the poor fit by thinking, "But it's such a bargain, I just can't pass it up." We overlook the colour, even though we don't like it, for the same reason. But is it really a bargain? Clothes like this languish in our closets, seldom if ever worn, because they really aren't satisfactory; they don't suit us. The fact that they were cheap does not make them of value to us.

Thrift...

Thrift went out of style as we moved into the Era of New Consumerism, yet there was a time when it was a highly respected attitude. Thrift was seen as a measure of the skill of the woman who ran a household. In the Bags and Purses Museum in Amsterdam, I saw *chatelaines* from hundreds of years ago. A chatelaine was a clasp or hook that held a bunch of keys and was suspended from the mistress's waistband. These keys opened the larders and storerooms, and she had the status of being the *keeper of the keys.* It was an important role and not taken lightly, as the family's welfare and survival, in good times and bad, depended on her ability to use resources wisely.

Why did thrift become unfashionable? It seems to have coincided with the post-war pressure to consume more and more, when manufacturers and marketers wanted to maintain the economic momentum of wartime production. As a result, society no longer saw the value of cultivating an ability to use resources judiciously. In this way, we fell into habits of wastefulness and excess.

It has taken the prospect of environmental collapse, along with the worldwide economic crash of 2008, for people to once again consider the merits of thrift. I was in Ireland in the summer of 2009 and listened to a weekly radio program called "The Frugal Household." When a topic becomes a radio series, you know it's a common concern. Since then, there's been an increase in books and blogs about frugality and thrift.

Why bother?

Frugality and thrift are synonymous. *The Merriam-Webster Dictionary* defines frugality as "characterized by or reflecting economy in the use of resources." Yet it is common for North Americans to think disparagingly of thrift and frugality, equating them with being "cheap." This is a superficial view that does not reflect the subtleties and underlying motivation of true frugality.

Why bother being frugal? The economic collapse forced a lot of people in Ireland, and other parts of the world, to make better use of the money they had, as they coped with pay cuts or job losses. For those whose incomes weren't immediately affected by the downturn, there was still the threat that it could happen to them in the future. This led many to begin setting aside money as a cushion for what might lie ahead. Suddenly, being thrifty made sense.

How can a person practice frugality? By giving up wasteful habits and adopting thrifty ones. I could list dozens of thrifty habits, from turning off lights when you leave a room to taking your own lunches to school or work. However, it is the mindset behind these actions that is most important. A thrifty mindset is the desire to use wise economy in the management of money and resources.

In *The Five Lessons a Millionaire Taught Me*, Richard Paul Evans introduces the concept of the *millionaire mentality*. This was something he learned from a wealthy man who mentored him from the age of 12, when his father was severely injured and the Evans family was destitute. His book describes the mindset of wealthy people, and what he says may surprise you. It is highly recommended reading.

Contrary to common belief, the genuinely wealthy do not spend indiscriminately on whatever they want when they want it, just because they have the money. According to Evans, "Successful wealth builders understand that the world is designed to take their money,"[6] and the "millionaire mentality also knows that the average American has been brainwashed to consume and spend."[7] He identifies four key mindsets of the millionaire mentality:

1. The Millionaire Mentality carefully considers each expenditure.
2. The Millionaire Mentality believes that freedom and power are better than momentary pleasure.
3. The Millionaire Mentality does not equate spending with happiness.
4. The Millionaire Mentality protects the nest egg.[8]

Saving has been out of fashion...

Along with thrift, saving lost its place as a respected and sensible attitude. In "Hip Deep in Hock," published in *Macleans* at the end of 2004, author Steve Maich states:

> In 1985, the average Canadian socked away 15.8 per cent of his take-home pay. It was that savings cushion that allowed this country to bounce back from economic disasters like the 1987 stock market crash and the 1990 collapse of the residential real estate market. A decade later, the savings rate had slipped to 9.2 per cent of after-tax income. By 2003, the average Canadian saved just 1.4 per cent of his pay."[9]

From that low, the rate climbed back up to 4.8% in 2010.[10] However, financial experts recommend saving 20%, half of it for long-term savings for retirement and the other half for emergencies and fun things that we will be able to pay for in cash.

No doubt most Canadians would say that personal savings are important. Why, then, do we act differently? A big factor is our cultural conditioning to consume. Two unspoken cultural attitudes lie beyond the obvious pressure from marketing and advertising—first, that saving is a punishment and spending is a reward; and second, that we deserve and can expect instant gratification of our wants. Attitudes shape our behaviours, and both of these attitudes are powerful forces that encourage spending rather than saving.

Furthermore, conditions in this Era of New Consumerism make it very easy *not* to save because, if you don't have money to buy what you want, you can easily borrow it. That has changed somewhat since the banking crashes and "credit crunch" of 2008. However, credit is still much more available to you than it was to your great-grandparents. In their day, it was not possible to borrow more than you could afford, and you could only borrow for major items, such as a house and perhaps a car. You certainly couldn't buy small daily items, such as coffee and movie tickets, unless you had cash in hand.

This began to change in the 1970s, when credit cards became widely accepted and relatively easy to obtain. Borrowers no longer had to sit down with a banker and explain why they needed a loan. With a credit card, they could buy whatever they wanted without justifying the purchase to anyone, as long as they didn't exceed their credit limit and made the minimum monthly payments on time.

This created an entirely different mindset toward using credit. Whereas previous generations only used credit as a last resort and with some embarrassment, now it was seen as an easy solution to a lack of ready cash and quickly became a fact of modern life. This change in attitude has resulted in more and more of our incomes going toward interest payments on borrowed money rather than into a savings account. The millionaire mentality would consider this a very poor use of our earnings.

If we want to save, practicing thrift is a way to spend less money and have some available to set aside in savings. In good times, we might envision using those savings for trips and vacation homes. In tough times, our savings provide security and peace of mind, which are highly valuable when life is uncertain.

The first mindset of a millionaire is to carefully consider each expenditure. Richard Evans identifies key questions that a wealth-builder would ask before spending money:

1. Is this expenditure really necessary? (Or is it possible to get the same personal effect without using money or using less of it?)
2. Is this expenditure contributing to my wealth or taking from it?
3. Is this an impulse purchase or a planned purchase? Am I being pressured to make an expenditure I'm not certain about?[11]

These are powerful questions. They put you in charge of how and why you spend your money. They ensure that you are spending consciously within the context of *your* life. They prevent you from being a puppet of the consumer culture.

Think-abouts

He who pays the piper calls the tune.

Living consciously is where true power resides in your relationship with money.

Lives based on "having" are less free than lives based on either "doing" or "being." ~William James

The most secure prison is one in which the inmates *think* they are free...
~*Adbusters Quarterly*

Dealing with Money

Dealing with money used to be pretty straightforward. If you had none, you didn't buy things. If you had it, you spent a portion on what you really needed and saved some for the proverbial rainy day. Not so now. Credit cards, overdraft protection, lines of credit, and student loans have changed the playing field considerably. Most people don't intend to be irresponsible. The problem is that they just don't know what it takes to be financially responsible. What you learn here will help to rectify that.

Maintaining balance in uncertain times…

The world of money has become very complicated, to the point where many otherwise-competent people feel they need to hire financial advisors to assist with their investment decisions. The irony is that most of these advisors did not anticipate the big collapse of 2008. I recently heard a financial reporter comment that there are no experts anymore. I agree. If those who were supposedly "in the know" could not tell that a crash was on its way, is it likely they know how to avoid its effects? I wonder.

So it comes back to us to think about security, our ability to deal with uncertainty, and the strategies that might be most constructive in difficult times. There is no question that most people find uncertainty to be disconcerting and disquieting. The challenge of uncertainty is that you can't rehearse your response, since you don't know what will present itself. When dealing with money, you no longer know if the old rules apply or not. It depends on what happens and how events unfold.

One of the key attributes of people who cope well with uncertainty is an ability to maintain their balance and stability. The process of maintaining equilibrium is beautifully described by Frank Rivers in *The Way of the Owl: Succeeding with Integrity in a Conflicted World.* Using the metaphor of a mature owl in contrast to an inexperienced fledgling, he describes a number of qualities that help us skillfully navigate life. This is from the chapter entitled "Balance, the Ability to Adjust to New Conditions:"

> Gliding silently through the night air, the owl listens closely to the subtle messages from his inner ear, wings, and torso, making constant adjustments. The wind may be turbulent but his concentration remains focused. He makes tiny corrections with tail and wing tips, sculpting the air in every moment. His flight is a balancing act…The curious thing about balance is that while it must be sought, it can never be achieved. If everything stayed still, achieving balance would be relatively easy. We could simply measure the excesses and deficiencies and even them out. But since the world is always in motion, balance can never be complete and final. Like birds in flight, we always have to adjust for new conditions. Every state of equilibrium is provisional. No structure, process or relationship is completely stable. …Balancing is a high virtue, but it is not the only virtue. Sometimes the owl must go to extremes. Be balanced about balance.[1]

Life is a process of continual change. Every state of equilibrium serves for the time being, but nothing in life is permanent or static. We can't get things balanced and be done with it; we must continually respond to what presents itself.

Living lightly…

In our financial lives, one of the best ways to remain responsive to new conditions is to live lightly. One way to live lightly is to avoid burdening ourselves with debt. It's no coincidence that financial counsellors refer to people's "debt load." There is a heaviness to carrying consumer debt. When weighed down by debt, you lose your ability to respond to changing conditions.

A quick review of the two types of debt seems in order. Broadly speaking, all debt is divided into two categories—good (constructive) debt and bad (destructive) debt—depending on whether the loan is being used to purchase something that will appreciate or depreciate in value. Something that increases in value is constructive because it builds your overall financial worth.

Real estate and student loans are considered constructive debt. When you buy a house, for example, you can be fairly confident that its value will increase over time. The theory is that this increase in value will offset the interest that was paid during the length of the mortgage. That being said, old assumptions have been shaken by the 2008 economic crisis and "mortgage meltdown." So, although it has historically been true that housing values have gone up over time, there is no guarantee that this will continue to be the case.

Consumer goods and services are bad debt because they are worth less today than they were last month. You would take a loss if you sold your CD collection, computer, or car (unless your car is a collector's item, but that is a different matter). When you take a vacation or attend a concert using money borrowed on a credit card, the experience is going to be over before you have paid for it. Not only that, it will cost you close to 20 percent extra because of the interest you pay. Your life becomes very expensive when lived on borrowed money.

The thinking that traps us...

Why do people fall into the credit trap even though it costs them so much money? Imagine two people with exactly the same income. It would seem they both have the same amount of money to spend. However, they don't because Pat uses credit and Chris doesn't. Each month, some of Pat's income goes to interest charges, reducing the money Pat has to spend on goods and services. On the other hand, Chris's salary is not eroded by interest payments and the full amount is available to spend. The following diagram shows the effect of interest on incomes that started out the same.

Income Erosion From Paying Interest

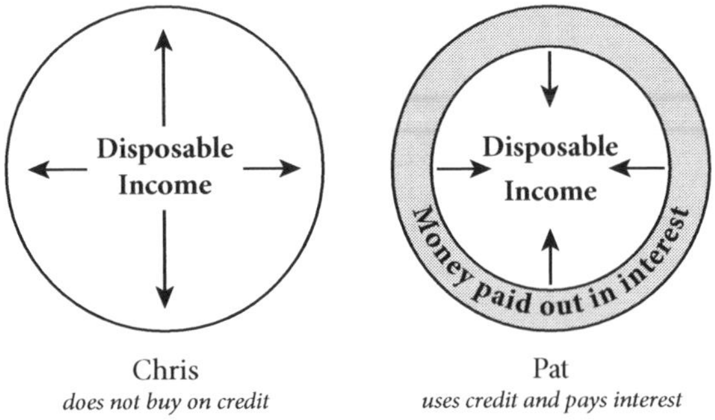

There's a psychological factor at play here. Pat, being aware that Chris earns the same salary, expects to be able to buy as much as Chris does. Pat does buy as much as Chris…but by using credit and paying interest. Over time, Pat's disposable income shrinks as credit payments increase, but expectations don't change. At some point, Pat may experience a financial crisis, such as a job loss or an inability to make the interest payments, and will find there is no resilience in the situation. Drastic measures may be required.

It is not uncommon for financial counsellors and bankruptcy trustees to encounter clients with six or eight credit cards charged to the limit, and the individual can't manage even the minimum payments for all of them. Some people attempt to solve this with a consolidation loan which, in itself, is a very tricky business and is only helpful if used with finesse.

Debt consolidation: a solution or a bigger problem?

You can only make skillful use of something when you fully understand how it works. Unfortunately, consolidation is rarely understood by people using it, and, as a result, they find themselves deeper in financial trouble instead of improving their situation.

To consolidate means to bring several items together into one. When applied to loans, *consolidation* means that a person ends up with one large loan instead of several small ones. The consolidation loan is taken out in an amount sufficient to pay off the balances of existing debts, whether they are credit cards or personal loans. Those original debts no longer exist, and the borrower makes only one monthly payment on the larger debt—the consolidation loan. It sounds innocuous, and you might wonder what the harm is. Let's have a look:

1. You risk losing the security you pledged in order to get the consolidation loan. If you have equity in your home, you may be asked to use it to secure your consolidation loan. Indeed, this may be the only way to get the loan if your credit rating is poor. The pledging of your security greatly reduces the lender's risk and significantly increases yours. If you fall behind on your loan payments, you could lose your house.

2. For the borrower, consolidation loans are usually expensive loans. People frequently pay higher interest rates on their consolidation loans than they did on the original loans. Because of the higher rate, more is paid in total interest over the life of the loan.

3. You could get caught in the "low monthly payment" trap. When consolidating, it seems appealing to negotiate lower monthly payments to further reduce the financial pressure. It sounds like a good idea until you consider the implications: it keeps you in debt for a longer time because you are stretching out the debt and therefore paying more in total interest. Imagine a 60-month (5-year) loan of $5000 at 8% annual interest with monthly payments of $101. It's tempting to reduce those payments in half, to $50 a month, in order to have more money to spend now. However, with those reduced payments, it takes 165 months (i.e., 13 years and 9 months) to pay off the loan. The repayment time has been increased by 8 ¾ years. Not only does this increase the length of your indebtedness, but you pay considerably more in interest. The total paid over 165 months is $8260. Since the

loan was $5000, the interest portion is $3260 ($8260 – $5000). The interest adds 65% ($3260/$5000 × 100% = 65%) to the cost of whatever was purchased with that loan. It is no wonder some people feel they can never get ahead.

How does this happen? Why would anyone go for the lowest monthly payment when it is so obviously a poor financial choice? It's a combination of two factors. The first is lack of information; no one has told them what I've just explained. The second is encouragement by the lenders. Consider this wording from the website of a Canadian bank in their section about car loans: "Lower [your] monthly payments by taking up to 8 years (96 months) to pay off your loan, giving you maximum flexibility."[2] They make it sound very attractive and don't explain the implications of choosing the longer loan period.

At that bank, the minimum car loan amount is $5000 and there is no mention of the total amount of interest paid on it. I thought it would be revealing to find out, so I put the figures into an online interest calculator. Assuming a loan of $5000 at 8% interest, those extra three years cost $702 more in interest. (The 5-year loan costs $1083 in interest, whereas the 8-year loan is $1785) If you don't think to ask the question, you could easily and innocently fall into the interest trap.

Apart from the extended repayment period and higher total interest, there's another trap to lower monthly payments. It is not uncommon for people who have just lowered their monthly payments to buy something new because they feel they have money to make payments on something else they've been wanting. The thinking flaw is obvious when it's spelled out like this, but financial counsellors see many people who live their lives this way.

In contrast, skillful use of consolidation demands a good measure of self-mastery and discipline. *Consolidation might work to your advantage, but only if you use it with finesse.* If you were able to get a consolidation loan with an interest rate lower than that of the existing smaller loans, and if the monthly payment on the consolidation loan was at least as much as the total of all the monthly payments on those existing loans, then and only then would a consolidation loan make sense. Unless borrowers know this, they find themselves on a slippery slope of repeat performances, once they take that first consolidation loan.

When you make destructive financial decisions, nobody intervenes until you are so deeply in debt that you can't carry the load any more. It's up to you to take responsibility for your own financial well-being. Think. Ask questions. Apply common sense. Don't be pressured into decisions until you are sure you have the full range of information you need. Remember that lenders have a vested interest in your taking a loan for as long as possible because that's how they make the most money.

It's a basic principle of finance: *The lower the monthly payment, the longer it takes to pay off the loan and the more you will pay in total interest.* Once you understand that concept, turn it around. Then you can see that the *higher* your monthly payments, the *shorter* your loan, and the *lower* the total amount of interest you will pay. If you must take a loan at some point in your life—perhaps to buy a house or car—remember this principle. With a large loan such as a mortgage, you can save tens or even hundreds of thousands of dollars in interest by paying off the loan in the shortest time you can manage. When you repay lenders as quickly as possible, you are beating them at their own game and being financially responsible to yourself.

Is bankruptcy the answer?

Very early in my teaching career, I learned the realities of bankruptcy from one of my students. He was a single father of four young children. We had been talking about the ins and outs of bankruptcy: it stays on your credit file for six years (14 if it's the second bankruptcy); you will likely have to pay cash for everything during that time because lenders will be reluctant to give you credit; it costs money to file for bankruptcy because there is a fee to be paid to the trustee; you must account to the trustee for all your income and expenditures while the bankruptcy is in progress; you can only keep a specified minimum of your assets and the rest are sold to generate funds to be used in repaying your creditors.

This young man was in the midst of bankruptcy proceedings at the time. He confirmed what we'd been discussing and added a few details. However, what really stuck with me was the poignancy of what he found most difficult about declaring bankruptcy—having to tell his children that it was not possible to buy them what they wanted for Christmas that year.

Personal bankruptcy—much more common now than it was even 20 years ago—is not an easy solution to financial problems. Apart from the psychological stress, there are stringent financial requirements during the bankruptcy process. Individuals with income above a specified monthly minimum must pay a portion of that "surplus income" each month toward repayment of creditors. A person may be in the bankruptcy process for anywhere from nine to 36 months, depending on the individual situation.

Bankruptcy is not to be taken lightly, but is sometimes the only sensible course of action for people who would be unable to pay off their existing debts within a reasonable time, even if they were to cut their monthly expenses to a bare minimum.

How does one get to that stage? Surprisingly easily. The following story comes from an article in *Macleans*.[3] While Jonathan Rabbat was in university, he paid for his expenses with credit cards. At the time of graduation, he had four cards on which he was making the minimum payment each month. He moved from Montreal to Toronto to look for a job, while he lived on cash advances from his cards. The job he found paid less than expected, so after a few years he quit and started in business for himself in hopes of generating a higher income. A year and a half later, he was living in an apartment with nine other people, trying to keep his expenses low enough to stay financially afloat.

It wasn't working, and creditors were continually hounding him, so he made an appointment with a financial counsellor. By then, he was $45,000 in debt and had barely enough income to survive. The counsellor's assessment determined that he was clearly a candidate for bankruptcy. At the time his story was written, he'd been through the process, and his situation had completely turned around. His debts had been cleared in the bankruptcy proceedings, so he was starting with a clean slate. He'd found a job that provided sufficient income for him to live in an apartment on his own. He had a *secured credit card* (i.e., one *guaranteed* by funds he had deposited with the bank) in order to rebuild his credit rating. And most of all, he had peace of mind. His concluding statement was "Now I owe nobody. I'm a free man."

What about financial counselling?

Sometimes we can solve our problems ourselves, and sometimes we need another point of view. When it comes to money problems, financial counsellors can provide an outside perspective that is often very helpful.

Financial counsellors assist with the daily practical issues of money—cash and debt management, budgeting to save for major purchases and retirement, and clarifying goals and values. Sometimes you'll find a not-for-profit agency that offers these services; other times, the counsellor is running a for-profit business. *Financial advisors* focus on estate planning, investments, and retirement savings; they frequently work for investment companies.

Charges for financial advice may be in the form of a fee for service provided, or commission on financial products sold to you. The commission route is less obvious because the fee is lumped in with your investment, and you might actually think the advisor is providing a free service...unless you ask. A commission seller works for the company whose products are being sold and is paid a percentage of sales made. The commission is part of what you pay to buy the investment. The main criticism about taking your advice from commissioned sellers is that they have a conflict of interest.

Conflict of interest exists when there is a conflict between the private interests and the official responsibilities of a person in a position of trust. When you engage a financial advisor, you are entrusting that person with your financial well-being. The conflict exists when the advisor's private interest, which is to produce personal income, is tied to the recommendations being made to you. If a seller receives a commission for his or her recommendations, that should be declared at the beginning of the consultation. If you are unsure how the advisor is being paid, don't be afraid to ask. It's both your right and responsibility to obtain full disclosure.

Fee-only advisors and counsellors are independent professionals who charge either by the hour or a flat fee, which is determined in advance for a particular project (developing a budget plan, for example). Because they are not dependent on selling products to earn their income, fee-only advisors are more motivated to look at the big picture of your financial situation rather than focusing strictly on investments. When they recommend products, they can select from the full range of what's out there rather than just from their employer's particular offerings. In these ways, you may get a more personally tailored plan by consulting an independent advisor.

Agencies that provide credit counselling may also charge fees, but the fees are usually minimal, as these not-for-profit organizations also receive funding from other sources. One thing to watch for is businesses that imply they are non-profit agencies when they are not. You'll want to be aware of this so you are alert to any biases.

Think-abouts

Debt is the new slavery.
~Professor Sut Jhally

We can make things work better by recognizing what the real problem is and by being willing to make changes. Both of these are simple steps, but not easy. Does that mean "simple" and "easy" are not the same?

It has been said that ready access to credit decreases your freedom. What do you think? Do you agree or disagree?

Today there are three kinds of people: the have's, the have-not's, and the have-not-paid-for-what-they-have's!
~Earl Wilson

Today we are only as free as our purchasing power permits. ~Jacque Fresco

Taking Your Situation in Hand

Counselling can be helpful, but you may prefer to resolve your situation on your own. The first step is to recognize there is an issue with how you are handling your money. What are the clues? Basically, you're looking for indications of living beyond your means (i.e., spending more than you earn).

This can show up in a variety of ways. Perhaps your money runs out before the month does, and you find yourself borrowing small amounts from family or payday lenders to make it through to your next paycheque. Perhaps you don't have the money to pay off your credit card in full when the bill arrives, and you resort to making the minimum payment. Perhaps you have stopped making payments to one or several creditors and are receiving phone calls from bill collectors demanding the money.

To turn the situation around, two things are required: first, reduce your cost of living to within your means, and second, repay the outstanding debts. Here's how to work your way through this, if you want to do it without outside help.

Track your expenditures and income...

Start by logging your expenses and income. Keep track of everything you spend and earn over a one-month period—and I do mean *everything*, tedious though that may be. When it comes to expenditures, it's the little things that often do us in—the daily lattes, bottled water, muffins, lottery tickets. Financial author David Bach calls this the Latte Factor and describes it this way on his website:

> The Latte Factor® is based on the simple idea that all you need to do to finish rich is to look at the small things you spend your money on every day and see whether you could redirect that spending to yourself. Putting aside as little as a few dollars a day for your future rather than spending it on little purchases such as lattes, bottled water, fast food, cigarettes,

> magazines and so on, can really make a difference between accumulating wealth and living paycheck to paycheck. We don't even realize how much we're actually spending on these little purchases. If we did think about it and change our habits just a little, we could actually change our destiny.[1]

Once you've tracked all your expenses for a month, put the figures into appropriate categories: clothing, entertainment, food eaten out, rent, utilities, personal care, gifts, etc. Total each category, and then add those totals together to see how much you spent overall. When you buy something using your credit card, immediately record the amount as money spent, so you will have the funds on hand to pay the bill in full when due.

Record income as well, noting amounts at the time they are received and totalling them at the end of the month. It's important to differentiate between *regular* and *extraordinary* income. Regular income is predictable—your biweekly paycheque, your monthly allowance, the amount you pay yourself each month from the savings you had set aside last summer to cover your expenses during the university semester. These are amounts you can count on, and they are the basis of your planning. *Extraordinary income* would be lump sum payments, such as gift money, inheritance, loans, and scholarships. Keep track of them in a separate income category because you won't be receiving them every month.

If you have *variable* regular income, such as tips, base your spending plan on the *lowest* amount you receive in a month; then any extra will seem like a bonus. This puts you in a much stronger position than those who make plans using an overly optimistic value for tips and then find themselves playing catch-up when they receive less money than they expected. The same applies if you work a variable number of hours, which is the reality for most part-time workers these days. Base your plan on the lowest number of hours you work each week, not the hours you hope you will get.

Once you have a figure for total monthly expenses and income, compare them. Are they the same? If they are different, determine which is more—income or expenses. If expenses are more, you are living beyond your means. Living *within* your means is simply a matter of not spending more than you have. It's a common-sense concept that became clouded once credit came into widespread use.

Then and now...

At one time, people really couldn't spend beyond their means because they paid for everything with cash or a cheque written on their bank account. There was no overdraft protection, so a person had to be sure there were sufficient funds in the account to cover a cheque before writing it. An NSF (non-sufficient funds) cheque was serious business, and there were stiff financial and legal penalties for obtaining money under false pretenses. The only way to borrow money was to apply for a personal loan and make a case to the manager about why the money was needed and how it would be paid back. This sort of system provided a structure that kept most people out of financial trouble.

Today, that structure does not exist, and the onus is on you to look after yourself and your financial well-being. Although NSF cheques are still illegal, banks offer overdraft protection in which they lend you money to cover cheques beyond the amount of your own money in your account. This, they say, is to help you avoid the potentially embarrassing situation of having a cheque bounce. They also offer personal lines of credit, so you have easy access to borrowed money without having to explain and justify your purchases. And, of course, credit cards serve this function as well. There is no one monitoring your daily use of credit, and there is no structure to keep you from spending beyond your means. Literally, the buck stops with you.

The biggest favour you can do for yourself is to cultivate your innate common sense. Common sense tells us that it is unsustainable to spend more money than we bring in. Yes, we can do it for a while. But sooner or later the whole thing will collapse like a house of cards. Without a stable structure, how could it be otherwise?

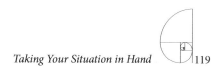

Building a stable financial structure for your life...

There is a lot of unreality and magical thinking surrounding money. Why else would people (and governments) think they can continually spend more money than they have? To make it seem more real, I'm going to use the analogy of constructing a house as a model for building a sound financial structure.

A house starts with a foundation. The foundation for human life is adequate food, shelter, clothing, and transportation.

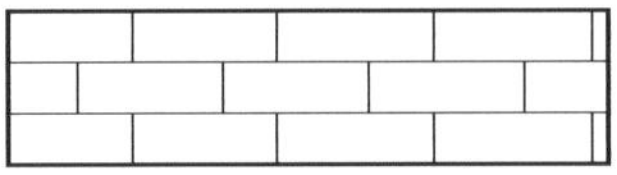

FOUNDATION
Adequate food, shelter, clothing & transportation

The word "adequate" is significant. In terms of basic survival, no one needs steak, lattes, designer clothes, and a new car every two years. Many people find these lovely to have, and I'm not saying we shouldn't. However, they fit elsewhere in the picture. How much we can spend on these lovely extras is determined by the amount of money we have. The more money, the more there is to cover the basics and still have some to spend on luxuries.

The lovely extras, niceties, luxuries—or whatever else you choose to call them—are the walls of your financial structure. They create the boundaries and contribute to your quality of life. The height of the walls will depend on how much money you have left after paying for the foundation.

If there's not much left, then the walls will be short. If there's a lot of money remaining when basics have been paid for, the walls will be higher, as shown in the next diagram.

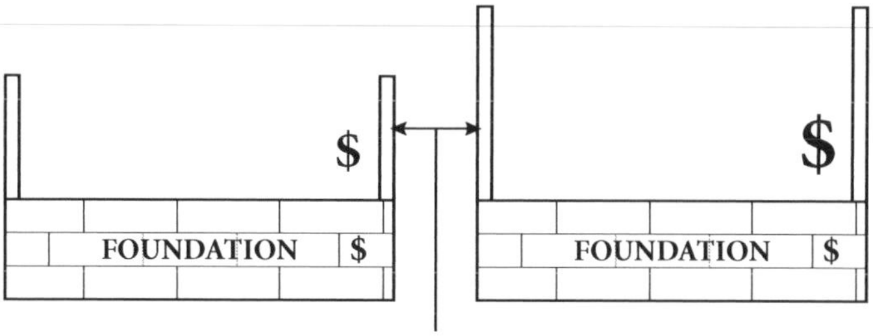

But foundation and walls do not make a house. Without a roof, you are at the mercy of the elements. The same is true of your life: you need to have financial protection measures in place, so you aren't at the mercy of the unforeseeable and the inevitable. These protective elements include an emergency fund, insurances (life, health, and property), and long-term savings for income replacement when you are retired.

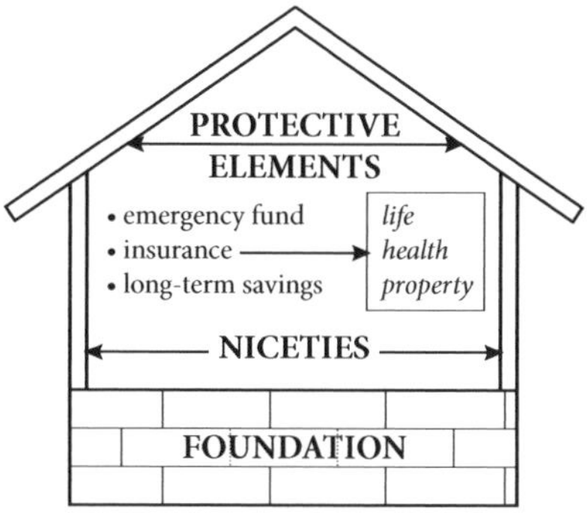

These protective elements are as important as the foundation and walls. They are the buffer between you and the financial costs of the unpredictable. An emergency fund allows you to avoid going into debt when something unexpected happens. Insurance covers catastrophic costs that could cause financial hardship or bankrupt you if you had to cover them yourself. Long-term savings allow you to live comfortably when you are no longer working to earn an income.

Spending all your money on luxuries leaves you exposed to the risky elements of life. The sensible solution is to divert some money from luxuries and niceties to make sure your financial house is snug and secure.

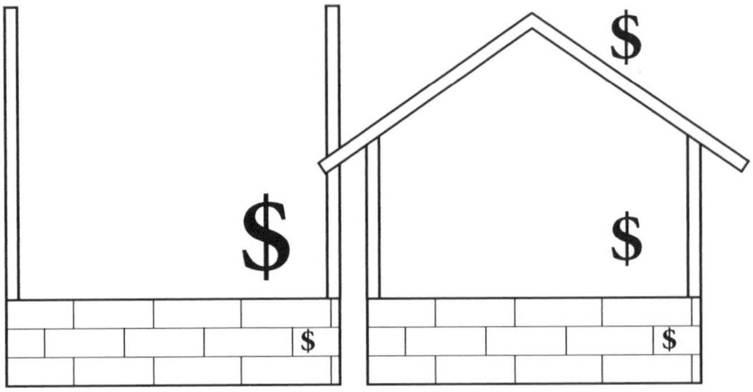

If you don't like living with the resulting short walls, then find a way to generate more money so you can increase the height of the walls without compromising the roof. Then you can be snug, secure... and happy.

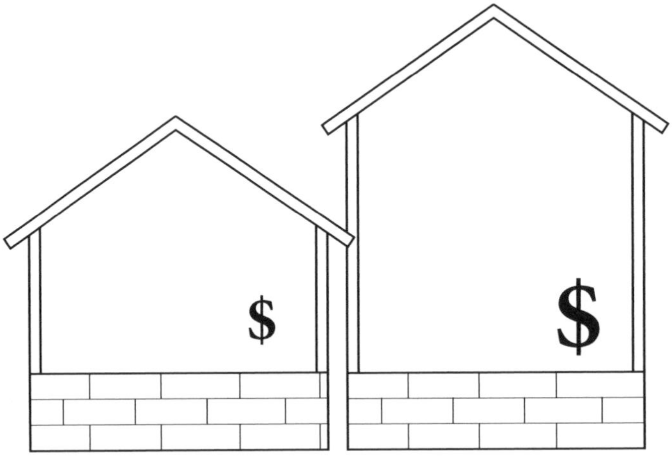

Plan to pay yourself first…

To build a satisfactory house you need some sort of plan, and the same is true for the financial structure of your life. Many financial advisors suggest that you *pay yourself first*. Imagine a lineup of all the people/companies who you give money to each month—your landlord, the electric company, the bank for your credit card payment, your cell phone provider, and so on. Where do you want to be in that lineup? Do you want to be at the end, getting what's left over, if indeed there is any money left over? Or do you want to be at the front of the line, receiving your payment first? It *is* a choice.

How would that look in practice? To pay yourself first, you set aside a percentage of your income in a savings account or investment *before* allocating money to everything else. The Wealthy Barber advises the young people consulting him: "Invest ten percent of all you make for long-term growth."[2] The best way to pay yourself first, he tells them, is to have the 10% automatically taken from their paycheque when it's deposited and transferred to an investment. He assures them that they won't miss the money because they didn't even see it.

You might think paying yourself first is impossible because you just don't have enough money to spare 10%. Perhaps you truly do not. But people can do surprising things when motivated. I learned this long ago when I was teaching a money management course in a job retraining program. One of the participants was the mother of three preschoolers, living on an income of $800 a month—a very small amount even back then. She was adamant about building an emergency fund and put aside $80 each month without fail. To her it was crucial to build up her financial resilience, so unexpected expenses wouldn't propel her into the downward spiral of debt. She had been there once and knew first-hand the level of stress that debt causes.

It was a challenge for her to forego spending that $80 each month, but she rose to it admirably. I was impressed with the long list of thrifty practices she described. She knew how to mend clothes, not waste food, access free entertainment for her children, and shop at thrift stores. She was not embarrassed to let her extended family know that hand-me-downs were welcome. It was clear she had a sense of confidence in herself and her vision for her family, and she was not about to squander the resources at her disposal.

Living within your means and setting aside money for long-term growth isn't easy in a consumer-based culture. Finding the motivation is up to you. Why would you bother?

- Perhaps to become independent of your parents.
- Perhaps for the satisfaction of knowing you can look after yourself.
- Perhaps to give your children a secure life.
- Perhaps to set yourself up financially to have options in the future.

Freedom is the motivator for young Canadian author and speaker, Lesley Scorgie: "Money is important because it builds a path to freedom. Without it, your choices can be limited. With it, you can pursue your dreams. Wealth is no longer just about money. It is about freedom."[3] When she was seventeen, Lesley appeared on The Oprah Show. The theme was teenagers on track to be millionaires by the time they were 25. Clearly, she had a vision of what she wanted to do and knew why it was important to her.

Getting debts paid off ASAP...

In your self-directed program to take your financial situation in hand, thrift is an important first step. By reducing waste and unnecessary expenditures, you increase the amount of money you have available to do what's most needed, whether it's to build your emergency fund, to start a long-term savings plan, or to set some aside for a down payment on a house. If you have outstanding debt, such as a car loan, personal line of credit, or a credit card balance, swift repayment of that debt should be a high priority.

Why? Paying interest on consumer goods and services makes no sense at all because you are still paying for them long after they've been worn out and used up. It takes so long to pay off the debt because most of each month's minimum payment goes to interest, and very little actually pays down the amount you borrowed. As a result, it will take many, many months and sometimes years to finally get the last bit paid off. If you are in this situation, you need a strategy to short-circuit the cycle of paying for years and years.

Power paying is your way out of the debt trap. To do this, you make minimum payments on all debts to keep yourself in good standing with your creditors. Plus, you apply a consistent amount of "extra money" to one of the debts every month until it is paid off. When that debt has been retired, you take all the money you'd been paying toward it and apply that full amount to another of your debts. Because the monthly sum paid will now be substantial, you'll pay off that second debt even more quickly. Once it is paid off, you focus on paying off the third with even larger monthly sums—hence the term *power paying*. Some people refer to this as "snowballing" your debt repayment. If you would like to see this explanation in chart form, refer to the resources section of my blogsite at www.TheUncommonGuides.com.

How can you generate extra money to put more toward paying down your debts? You can either earn more income (second job, increased hours at existing job, selling some of your excess belongings, etc.) or reduce your current expenses so you can divert a specified amount of your existing income to debt repayment. If you can do both—that is, cut expenses *and* increase income—you will have even more money to put toward the repayment project and will complete it more rapidly. The sooner you've paid off your debts, the sooner you'll have money available to put toward goals other than paying for old purchases.

In some instances, you may find that you just cannot manage to make the full monthly payments to all your creditors, despite having pared down your expenses and increased your income as much as possible. You could try negotiating with your lenders to accept reduced payments. Sometimes they will even waive part of your outstanding balance if they see you are taking responsibility for dealing with the situation. It doesn't hurt to ask.

If putting together such a proposal seems a daunting prospect, you can engage a credit counsellor at this stage to assist you. Depending on the services available where you live, you could get help ranging from assistance in constructing the plan, to contacting the creditors with the proposal, to providing mediation services to make sure your payments reach the creditors. In some instances, a credit counsellor will also assist you with court proceedings to require the lenders to accept reduced payments. In Alberta, this process is called Orderly Payment of Debts (OPD) and is administered by Money Mentors, a not-for-profit financial counselling and money-coaching organization. This program, offered in only a few provinces, can be a viable alternative to filing for bankruptcy in some situations. According to the Money Mentors website, "Through the OPD program, you can repay your debts in full and your interest rate drops to 5%. And yes, the collection calls will stop too."[4]

Another alternative for resolving debt issues is filing a Consumer Proposal, which is done through a bankruptcy trustee but is different from bankruptcy. A Consumer Proposal may be the preferred option when you can afford to repay some or most of the debt but need more time or want to protect your wages from being garnisheed. When a Consumer Proposal is accepted by creditors, it is a legally binding agreement during which no more interest accumulates on your debts and the creditors cannot take you to court. Your assets are taken into account when determining whether a proposal is a viable option for you, but the proposal process allows you to retain assets. This is unlike bankruptcy, in which certain assets must be forfeited to generate money to repay your debts. And whereas bankruptcy remains on your credit record for six years, a proposal is on your file for only three years.

Consumer proposals and bankruptcy are both good options in cases of unmanageable debt. Determining which is the best alternative depends on a skillful assessment of all the factors at play in a particular situation. Licensed bankruptcy trustees are a trustworthy resource for helping you make this assessment: they specialize in this area of financial management, and are governed by strict regulation. Beware of unlicensed agencies, many of which advertise online and prey on people's vulnerability and desperation. They are not regulated or monitored, and charge very high fees which are often taken from payments that the debtor thinks are going to reduce their debt. To find a licensed bankruptcy trustee in your area, consult the Yellow Pages in print or online.

Financial security in uncertain times...

Let's step back, then, to take a big-picture look at what we can do to create financial security when we're not sure what's going to happen next. The following four actions are fundamental.

1. **Do not incur bad debt**. Bad debt is destructive because you are paying interest on goods and services that are depreciating in value. If you already have some of this kind of debt, pay it off as quickly as possible. *Start thinking differently about purchases*: If you want to buy an item—even something as large as a computer or a car—start saving so you can pay cash. That way, you will avoid paying interest for it.

2. **Create an emergency fund**. This should be a savings account that gives you ready access to the fund when you need it, but is not attached to your debit card. This strategy will ensure you do not spend this money on impulse. An emergency fund may seem entirely unnecessary if you are a parent-supported student whose emergencies are taken care of by the adults in your life. However, imagine yourself in your first job, having worked for two years and then being let go during a company downsizing. How would you survive without running back to your parents? That's where an emergency fund comes in. If you have money in the bank, you'll have the security of knowing there is time to look for another job. You won't have to wonder how you will pay the rent; nor will you need to run up debt using your credit card to buy necessities, such as food and gasoline. For many years, financial counsellors recommended that an emergency fund be equivalent to three months' expenses. Now that times are more uncertain, they suggest it be enough to cover six or even eight months of living expenses.

3. **Consider your lifestyle.** Are you bogged down by myriad possessions that you don't really care about? Do you know exactly what you have and where it is? Paring down your possessions to the essentials can be challenging but also liberating. I once met a woman who was struggling with how to reduce her ever-growing supply of belongings, so she could be more mobile. One day she triumphantly announced that she would keep only that which she could "care for exquisitely." What a wonderful way to determine when enough is enough.

4. **Be cautious and reasonable when undertaking good debt.** Even though debt for an appreciating asset is referred to as "good" debt, it is not immune from pitfalls. Buying a home is a good example. Perhaps house prices are inflated, and it isn't really a good time to buy right now. Perhaps you live in a town or city that has lost its economic vitality, with the result that property values will likely go down over time rather than up. Give careful consideration before buying a house because buying in the wrong place or at the wrong time can cost you money rather than improve your financial position. If you plunge ahead, keep your mortgage as small as possible by managing your expectations; you don't need your dream home on the first go-round. There is something satisfying about starting modestly, learning what you want (and don't want) in a home, and moving on to the next one when you're ready. The advantage of this approach is that you keep your monthly payments reasonable, and you don't join the legions of "house poor" people who spend so much on monthly housing costs that they can only fund the rest of their living expenses by running up debt on their credit cards. Ironically, the interest they pay on their credit cards negates the financial advantage they might have gained from buying the house.

The security gained from taking these steps represents an enormous degree of freedom in the sense of independence, having options, and not being under the power of others. Genuine freedom is not simply doing what you want. Paradoxically, freedom requires discipline—the willingness to do what we must. This is mastery of ourselves and is what makes us genuinely powerful.

Moving forward...

As you move into a career and independent living, life requires you to engage in the mechanics of handling money in both small and large ways—budgeting day-to-day expenditures; using credit; buying a house; investing money in term deposits, RRSPs, mutual funds, or the stock market; making a will; buying insurance. The next few chapters provide an overview and context, focusing on a basic understanding of the principles and issues involved. At some point you'll need more information. When that time comes, check the resources section of my blogsite at www.TheUncommonGuides.com for more useful information.

As well, there are many books, websites, and blogs that cover money-related topics in detail. Look in the money management and personal finance sections of libraries and bookstores. One caution—financial regulations about matters such as taxes vary from one country to another. When you're reading a foreign financial book—of which there are many good ones—read it for the principles it presents but don't take action until you check out the laws in the country where you live. Knowledgeable Canadian financial writers include David Chilton, Gordon Pape, Ellen Roseman, Lesley Scorgie, and Gail Vaz-Oxlade, among others.

Think-abouts

If money is your hope for independence, you will never have it. The only real security that a man will have in this world is a reserve of knowledge, experience, and ability.
~Henry Ford

If a person gets his attitude toward money straight, it will help straighten out almost every other area in his life.
~Billy Graham

Loss of freedom.
Loss of cash flow.
Loss of time.
Loss of opportunities.
These are the four major effects of debt.

Impact of Your Generational Era

Many things affect how you deal with money, including your personality and family upbringing. Less obvious, perhaps, is the impact of the year you were born. Without doubt, social conditions at any time in history shape the generations born into them because of their unique formative experiences. A dramatic example is the generation that grew up during the Great Depression, which began in 1929. Often called the Dirty Thirties, it was a time of hunger and desperation for many. Family fortunes were devastated when the stock market crashed. People were left homeless when their mortgages were foreclosed because they couldn't make the payments. Mothers struggled to feed their children, while their husbands looked for non-existent work. People were known to get by on one meal a day. Sometimes that meal consisted only of "soup" made by ordering a cup of hot water in a restaurant and stirring in a bit of ketchup from the bottle on the counter. Welfare, food banks, and homeless shelters were pretty much non-existent, so people had to fend for themselves.

Living through the Great Depression…

Think for a moment of someone you know who lived through the Depression. If you can, imagine yourself in that situation. How would this experience affect your attitudes and behaviours concerning money and possessions?

A common outcome was a strong tendency toward "saving for a rainy day" because people had seen how vulnerable they were when they didn't have financial reserves. Wastefulness became unthinkable for many; if they thought there was even a bit of flavour left in a tea bag, they would save it to use again another day. The ultimate in these behaviours is illustrated by my friend's grandmother, who had a full box labelled "string too small to use." Depression survivors also came to value education, seeing it as a means of being able to earn a good income; as a result, they sacrificed whatever it took to make sure their children were educated.

Oddly enough, or perhaps quite understandably, some people reacted in completely the opposite way when the tough times were over. Their attitude was "I did without when I had to. Now that I have money, I'm going to spend it!" The point of being aware of the effect of social conditions is not to decide who is right or wrong. Rather, it's a means of giving context to behaviours you might observe in people you know. If your great-grandmother hangs up used tea bags to dry and writes her grocery lists on old envelopes, perhaps now you will view those behaviours with greater insight.

For a relevant and readable commentary on the values, attitudes, and behaviours arising from changing social conditions, I like *Live Well on Less Than You Think* by Fred Brock. He describes generational groupings based on the 1997 book *Rocking the Ages: The Yankelovich Report on Generational Marketing*. Their research broke out three major groups—the Matures, the Baby Boomers, and Generation X. The group I've just described is the Matures, who were born before 1946.

Growing up in the Golden Age…

Now let's turn our attention to the generation that grew up in the 1950s and 60s. The Great Depression was past, ended by the high level of economic activity that resulted from World War II. When the war was over in 1945, economic activity was redirected to the production of consumer goods. In North America this resulted in what some refer to as the Golden Age of the Economy—an era that lasted until about 1975. During this time, work was plentiful. New graduates had their pick of several job offers in their field. People who had jobs were certain they would continue to be employed unless they did something really irresponsible or stupid. People who achieved management positions knew they were set for life and would retire with secure pensions.

Take a moment to think about growing up in those social conditions. Prosperity and certainty were the themes, and this created a completely different set of attitudes in this generation, which we have come to know as the Baby Boomers. Born between 1946 and 1964, Boomers are generally considered to be materialistic, individualistic, spoiled by their parents, and inclined to put their attention on present pleasure. Their mottoes of "I deserve it." and "The future will take care of itself." are quite a contrast to the children of the Great Depression.

Generation X…

Generation X is the next grouping, born between 1965 and 1978. Fred Brock describes Gen X as having a strong sense of reality, seeing the need to take responsibility for their financial futures and having the willingness to reinvent their lives as necessary. Flexibility, adaptability, and resourcefulness are characteristics they share. According to Brock, one notable feature of this generation is the tendency to form households and become parents at a later age than did previous generations.

His observation about the postponement of parenting has been verified in a recent study by the American Center for Work-Life Policy.[1] It found that 43% of Gen X women do not have children, despite being between the ages of 33 and 46. The researchers attribute this to factors such as extreme work schedules due to career ambitions, high college-related debt, several economic downturns, and the mortgage crisis. They point out that these economic factors make Gen X the first generation not to match its parents' standard of living. From another perspective, they found Gen Xers to be resilient and skilled at handling change, probably because of all the bumps they have experienced during their adult lives.

What now?

There is yet no clear-cut picture of the youngest group of adults, variously called Generation Y, Millennials, Generation Next, the Net Generation, and Echo Boomers. Born after 1978, these young people are a product of the New Era of Consumerism described by Juliet Schor.

Many have been raised by over-protective older parents who are often highly involved in their children's lives, even as these children move into adulthood. Their method of parenting has been called "bubble-wrapping," and they are sometimes referred to as helicopter parents because of their tendency to hover. These children have received lots of praise and no criticism, sometimes to the extent of being unrealistic. They also grew up with an overabundance of consumer goods, purchased by their parents with the use of credit. This has resulted in no sense of limitation based on income and has left them with a deep sense of entitlement. This newest generation of adults does not exhibit the qualities of realism and independence that were characteristic of the Gen Xers before them.

This new generation is also the first to grow up being completely connected to technology right from the beginning. The impact of this is of interest to Don Tapscott, a member of World Economic Forum and Adjunct Professor in the Rotman School of Management at the University of Toronto. In a 2008 article in *Businessweek*, Tapscott offers a perspective on technology as it relates to generations, observing that the Net Generation is uniquely positioned to change media, politics, and the culture:

> The medium that boomers grew up with, broadcast TV, helped to create our consumer culture. The fixtures of suburban life—the SUVs, the expanding floor size, the family room off the kitchen—were created by and for boomers. The many ways that we organize ourselves at work and in our civic lives are based on models that were defined or reinforced by the dominant demographic, the boomers. Their influence is so powerful we hardly notice it.
>
> But now, these old ways are starting to be shattered by the new Web and this new generation. The new Web, which lets people contribute to knowledge and not just consume it, is revolutionary.... As students, children, and consumers, Net Geners are pressuring schools, families, and markets to change. As knowledge workers, educators, government leaders, entrepreneurs, and customers, they will be an unstoppable force for transformation.[2]

Before leaving the subject of generational influence, I think it's important to reiterate something that Fred Brock says: "It should be noted that while generational stereotypes are broadly accurate, it is, of course, wrong to generalize excessively about large groups of people. Generation is not destiny. We are all individuals, and we are all different."[3] Nevertheless, there is enough evidence of generational trends for us to pay attention. For one thing, knowing your grouping helps you understand one aspect of why you are the way you are. In your quest to become more conscious, this knowledge is one of the puzzle pieces. Another is awareness that manufacturers target their advertising toward the common characteristics of generational groups. When you know that, you can assess their pitches with greater clarity, deciding on the life you want rather than reacting as part of a stereotype.

We can also learn from the experiences of those who went before. Fred Brock, born just before the baby boom, shares the two main lessons he learned. The first lesson is what he describes as the terrible effect of debt (which he sees as the Baby Boomers' greatest weakness) and how liberating it is to pay off debt or get it fully under control. The second lesson is the importance of cutting expenses to increase income. "We just need to develop armor and smarts against commercial forces that lure us to spend…"[4] I couldn't have said it any better.

Think-abouts

Each generation imagines itself to be more intelligent than the one that went before it, and wiser than the one that comes after it. ~George Orwell

Isn't it a shame that future generations can't be here to see all the wonderful things we're doing with their money? ~Earl Wilson

Every generation laughs at the old fashions, but follows religiously the new. ~Henry David Thoreau

Issues in Your Relationship with Money

I don't suppose anyone deliberately sets out to make a mess of his or her financial affairs, but it happens. There are some fairly typical patterns of dysfunction, so let's have a look at them and think about strategies that might put you in charge of yourself and your money, instead of vice versa. Common issues in a relationship with money include:

1. Letting money disappear
2. Not getting around to saving
3. Never getting ahead
4. Paying unnecessary interest and fees
5. Thinking like a wannabe
6. Being driven by subconscious attitudes and fears

First Issue: Letting money disappear…

If your money disappears as fast as (or faster than) you can earn it, then you need a strategy to put yourself in charge. The first step is tracking your money, so you know what you have and where it is going. Research shows that people who actively manage their money "(1) report more money in savings and investments, (2) carry lower credit card balances, and (3) have fewer maxed-out credit cards."[1] Active money management is more than using debit and credit cards for spending, or looking at bank and card statements periodically. When you are actively managing your money, you monitor how much is coming in and where it is going in relation to the spending plan that has been established.

There are numerous e-tools available to help you, including budgeting programs, downloadable Apps, and online spending reports through your financial institution. If you think they might work for you, take the time to explore different options. Read online reviews, and talk to people you know about what types of tools they use.

However, your monitoring process doesn't have to be that complicated or fancy. In fact, it might be better if it isn't. Canadian financial writer and television personality Gail Vaz-Oxlade describes her system: "Manually looking at the numbers at least twice every month makes me account (and holds me accountable) for where my money has gone. I think shortcuts are just ways to ignore what's really going on. My way takes more time, but there's no foolin' it."[2] The most important thing is to find a way to regularly stay on top of what's happening with your money and to be consistent so you get a view over time.

The challenge in this era of intangible money and digital recordkeeping is the element of unreality about it all. For some people, it helps to use a system that makes their money more real. This could involve printing out paper records and putting tick marks beside figures as they verify them. It might involve managing some of your cash flow by using envelopes, jars, a cheque book, or a manual record of certain categories.

The envelope system

I was surprised to learn from one of my students that this old method of managing cash flow has recently resurfaced. This is an easy way to keep track of spending, especially in categories where it is easy to overspend.

Decide how much you will spend in each category during a particular time period—usually one or two weeks—and put the money into a labelled envelope. You can spend in that category as long as there is money in the envelope. When the money is gone, you stop spending until the next time you refill the envelope. If you receive a paycheque every two weeks, then it makes sense to put a two-week amount in your envelope and replenish it on your next payday. People usually find it easier to work with a short time period, such as a week or two, rather than a month.

The magic jars

The magic jars are a variation on this theme, developed by Gail Vaz-Oxlade. You may have seen her television program, *Til Debt Do Us Part.* Under her guidance, heavily indebted couples reverse their financial situation and, in the process, reduce the stress on their relationship.

Her method involves implementing a very strict budget to free up money to pay down debt. She has found that people are much better at sticking to the budget when they can see what is available to spend and when it is gone. Her magic jars are clear glass jars, labelled as to category, and filled with the allocated money at the beginning of each budget period. She reports that not only do couples usually live within the allowed amount, they often have some left in the jar at the end of the budget period.

A cheque register

This is a retro idea that works for some people because it is an easily portable way of keeping immediate track of how much money they *really* have. You may think you get this information by looking at your bank account online—but one crucial thing is missing. Your online record *does not show what will be coming out later* (e.g., automatic payments and charges on your credit card). It only shows what you *did* spend. This deficiency is precisely what can get you into financial trouble, leaving you short of money before the next paycheque.

The cheque register is a small record book your bank provides along with blank cheques for your account. You may never have ordered any cheques, since debit, electronic transfers, and automatic withdrawals cover most situations. However, your bank will still provide the cheque register at no charge. You need only ask.

Start by recording the balance in your account on the first line (see example that follows). Each time there is a deposit or you make a withdrawal (either by cheque or debit card), record the amount and calculate the account balance. No surprises there; that's standard record-keeping procedure. But there are two additional things to do. First, record any automatic withdrawals that will occur in this pay period, even if the amounts haven't actually come out of the account yet.

Second, record the amount of each purchase made on your credit card *on the day you make it*, and then subtract that amount from your account total. I know it doesn't actually come out of your account at that moment, but subtracting it from your balance ensures you have money allocated to pay for it when the bill arrives. That way, you'll never end up paying interest because you didn't have enough money to pay the card balance in full when it was due.

If you are oriented toward electronic record-keeping, you might prefer to use a spreadsheet or budgeting program rather than a handwritten record book. Make sure it incorporates a means of accounting for credit card purchases at the time they are made and for upcoming automatic withdrawals. The system you choose should also keep you on top of the process on a daily basis. If you wait until the end of the month and then discover you've overspent, it's too late to do much about it.

NUMBER OR CODE	DATE	TRANSACTION DESCRIPTION	PAYMENT AMOUNT	✔	FEE	DEPOSIT AMOUNT	$ BALANCE
	Sept 10	Initial amount	$			$	116 00
	Sept 15	Pay cheque				321 60	437 60
Debit	Sept 17	Co-op	78 60				359 00
Master Card	Sept 21	Bay - sweater	49 99				309 01

It's important to note that this method assumes you will not be living on your **overdraft**. Overdraft allows you to spend more than you have. When you do, the bank lends you the amount you overspent and charges you interest for doing so. As soon as any money is deposited into your account, the bank reclaims the amount it advanced you as well as the interest you owe for borrowing it.

Without overdraft "protection," the bank will refuse debit withdrawals and will not honour cheques for which there are insufficient funds. With overdraft "privileges" they will allow those withdrawals and cash all cheques. When you think about it, overdraft protection is simply a means by which banks give us license to be sloppy in our money management. And when we are, they benefit by collecting money from us in two ways—monthly fees we pay for the service, and interest that is charged when we use it. Where's the sense in that?

Besides, living on overdraft becomes an ever-spiralling trap. You overspend without immediate consequences, such as the embarrassment of having a debit purchase refused. That seems to put you ahead of the game. But when your next paycheque is deposited, some of it is automatically drawn into the financial hole created by the overdraft plus interest. That leaves you with insufficient money to cover your expenses for the next pay period, so you bail yourself out using your overdraft again. This sounds innocent enough, but over time you actually have less money to spend because of the interest you are paying to the bank. After using overdraft for a while, most people conclude that it makes no financial sense because it drags them down rather than helps.

The subtraction system

This method is a pencil-and-paper means of doing what the envelopes and jars do. It's a chart that tracks expenditures in your budget categories. As shown in the illustration, the number at the top of each category is the amount allocated for the designated time period. It is entered into the top left corner of the first square in its column. When you spend from a category, that amount is recorded in the lower right corner of the square. You then calculate how much remains to be spent, and record that in the upper left portion of the next square in that column. Using this method, you only have to glance at the upper left of the last square of each column to know where you stand in each category. For example, the Eating Out category in the illustration shows that the budgeted amount is

$50. The first expenditure was $10, leaving $40 available for spending. The next expenditure was $12, so the category has $28 left. Nothing has been spent on entertainment, and there is $15 left to spend on clothes.

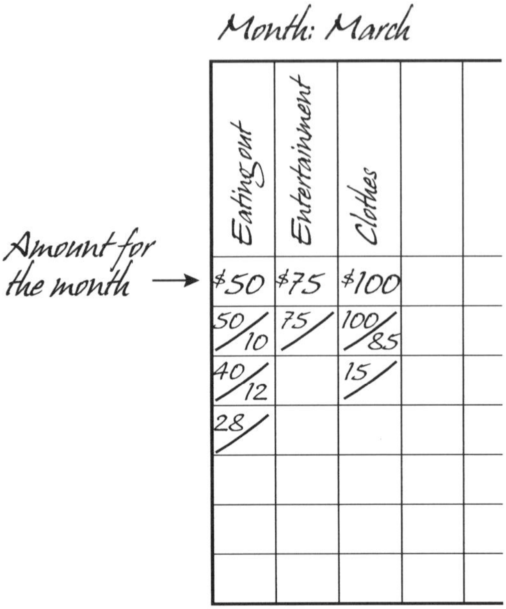
Month: March
Eating out
Entertainment
Clothes
Amount for the month
$50
$75
$100
50/10
75/
100/85
40/12
15/
28/

This subtraction system was developed by my colleague Faye Forbes Anderson, a financial counsellor who came up with this approach to assist clients who were frustrated with their finances. She says, "I used it with almost all of my clients for many years—sometimes just for a few expense categories (irregular expenses, food…), sometimes for all debit card expenses. And although I generally encouraged clients not to mix payment methods if they wanted to keep their processes simple and successful, this was the only way I could think of for addressing mixed methods of paying (some cash, some cheques, some credit cards, some debit cards) for certain expenses."

Second Issue: Not getting around to saving...

Many people just don't get around to saving. They intend to transfer money into their savings account each month, but just don't get to it. The antidote for that is shockingly simple: *Set up a system so that savings happen automatically.*

It's easy to set up an automated saving system. You need only complete a preauthorization form at your financial institution in order to have money transferred automatically from your chequing account to savings. Of course, this strategy assumes that you already have a savings account. If you don't, open one. If you continue to keep all your money in a chequing account that is readily accessible by debit card, you'll likely never accumulate wealth. Without a savings account, you are making it much too easy to spend everything you have. The preauthorized payment strategy can also be used to purchase an RRSP, which is a Canadian retirement saving program with income tax benefits. We will cover more about RRSPs in a later section.

Purchasing a Canada Savings Bond (CSB) through a payroll savings program is another way to ensure that you save regularly. You decide how much you want to contribute each pay period. Your employer deducts that amount and submits it to the program. Because the money comes off your pay before it is deposited in your bank account, you likely won't even miss it. A payroll savings program is a good means of paying yourself first.

Third Issue: Never getting ahead...

Despite good intentions, some people just never get ahead when it comes to money. They want to, they think about it, they wonder what they should do, and they never take the next step. With multiple complex options facing them, deciding what to do with their money seems so daunting they don't know where to begin. Or they get started investigating the options and become overwhelmed. In either case, they end up doing nothing.

Research has shown that we can experience paralysis when faced with too many options, whether we are buying something or putting our money into an investment. Psychologist Barry Schwartz, author of *The Paradox of Choice*, provides insight into why this happens. In an article published in *Scientific American*,[3] he describes how decision-making varies depending on personality. Someone who has high expectations works hard to make the best possible decision and is disappointed when it turns out to be less than perfect. That person may attempt to escape disappointment by not making any decision at all.

Opportunity cost is also a factor in decision-making. When you decide on one option, you give up the benefits you would have gained from another. For example, if you decide to buy a Canada Savings Bond at a fixed interest rate, then you have given up the potential capital gains you could have achieved by playing the stock market. If you decide to put your money in a particular mutual fund, then you give up the potential earnings from any of the other funds in the class you are considering.

Psychologically, there can be a sense of loss for the option given up. If there are many options and there is loss associated with each, the total can be enough to cause a great deal of dissatisfaction and discomfort. The degree of opportunity cost that individuals experience depends on their psychological make-up. Perfectionists find decision-making most immobilizing. Those who are inclined to look for solutions that are "good enough" will consider fewer options and have fewer opportunity costs to subtract. The following recommendations from Schwartz's article are good advice for those of us bogged down in decision-making. If you'd like to hear more about this, I recommend his excellent 20-minute video on YouTube.[4] What I like about his advice is that it makes common sense:

> **Choose when to choose.**
> We can decide to restrict our options when the decision is not crucial. For example, make a rule to visit no more than two stores when shopping for clothing.
>
> **Learn to accept "good enough."**
> Settle for a choice that meets your core requirements rather than

searching for the elusive "best." Then stop thinking about it.

Don't worry about what you're missing.
Consciously limit how much you ponder the seemingly attractive features of options you reject. Teach yourself to focus on the positive parts of the selection you make.[5]

You may not be saving money because you can't decide where to put it. In that case, do something rather than nothing. Make your best decision for the moment, and implement it. You can always adjust when circumstances change or you learn of a better way. You need to start with some basic information, so here's a brief summary of savings vehicles, those places where you might put your money once you have started paying yourself first.

Open a savings account (or two)

As well as a chequing account, a savings account is a basic requirement. It's the first stop for money you want to keep out of immediate reach. When opening a savings account, you want one that pays interest. Currently, rates are so low that this may not seem to matter, but you'll have the system in place and will benefit when rates go back up.

It's a smart move to set up this account without debit card access. If you really need money from it, you can make a personal withdrawal or an online or telephone transfer. This approach gives you breathing space—a moment of consciousness to think about whether withdrawing from these savings is what you *really* want to do.

Your savings account is an *emergency fund*. It's a back-up resource for times when the unexpected happens—an airline ticket to attend a funeral, a major vehicle repair, or loss of your job. Given the current economic climate, it is prudent to build this account until it has the equivalent of six to eight months' living expenses (rent, utilities, food, loan payments, and anything else that would be required to keep your life going while you were looking for another job).

Let's be clear, though, that vacations and oil changes are not emergencies and should not be paid from this account. They are *irregular expenses*, in that they occur only occasionally during the year. However, they are predictable and therefore cannot be considered emergencies.

The best way to plan for irregular expenses is to have a second savings account designated for this purpose. Deposit money regularly in this account, based on the anticipated total of your irregular expenses. For example, over the course of a year, you would need $2400 to cover the following irregular expenses: vacation $1400, car maintenance $400, Christmas gifts $600. If you deposited $200 into your irregular expense account each month, you would have money available when you need it. The foolproof way to make sure this happens is to arrange a pre-authorized monthly transfer from your chequing account to the irregular expenses account. The transfer should be scheduled to occur the day after your paycheque is deposited into your chequing account.

You may be wondering if it's necessary to have another account. Can't you just keep your money for irregular expenses in the same account as your emergency fund? You can, if you are clear about how much you have in the account for each purpose and are disciplined enough to live by that. Most people find it simpler to open a separate account.

Other savings vehicles to consider

Eventually, your emergency fund will reach your target amount, if you regularly make reasonable deposits. Then what? You might decide to put money into a certificate of deposit in your bank. In Canada, these are called *guaranteed investment certificates* (GICs) and *term deposits*; U.S. books on personal finance refer to them as CDs, *certificates of deposit*. With investment certificates, the money is committed for a predetermined length of time, and your reward for keeping it there is a specified percentage in interest.

Usually, there are penalties for withdrawing money early from a certificate, and sometimes you simply can't access it until the term is up, so take this into consideration when deciding which best suits your situation. For example, a student looking for a place to put loan money until the tuition payment is due in three months shouldn't lock it into a one-year GIC. These investments also don't work if you're looking for one that you can make deposits to every month, as GICs are structured for a one-time deposit that is typically a minimum of $500 or $1000. However, you could make monthly deposits into a savings account until you have the minimum amount and then buy your GIC.

Treasury bills, often referred to as T-bills, are in a category called money market funds. They are short-term investments that pay a relatively high interest rate but are not particularly accessible to small investors because of the high minimum required.

Fourth Issue: Paying unnecessary interest and fees...

Whenever you pay out interest and fees, they are direct costs to you. Avoid them except in carefully considered circumstances. Credit cards are the most common means by which people pay out interest. They can be a great convenience, and there are some transactions, such as reserving a hotel room and renting a car, that require a credit card. But there is no requirement that you play into the lenders' hands and incur interest charges. All credit cards have a period of a few weeks' grace before interest is charged. *You can avoid paying interest simply by paying the bill in full before the due date.*

Facts about credit card interest

The interest structure of credit cards is set up for the lender's benefit, not yours. Here are some important things you should know. This is not an exhaustive list, but highlights some key points to get you thinking about how to use your credit card with finesse.

1. **The no-interest grace period applies to purchases, but *not* to cash advances or credit card cheques.** Credit card cheques are simply a cash advance in a different form. When you take a cash advance on your

credit card, the interest calculation starts immediately. If you check your statement, you may find that the cash advance has a higher interest rate than your purchases. Best advice: Set up your finances so that you don't need to resort to taking cash advances on your credit card. In your mental notes to yourself, put it in the "unthinkable" category.

2. **You don't pay interest if you pay the outstanding balance *in full.*** Why did I emphasize "in full"? Well, here's the shocker. If you pay anything less than the full balance, you are charged interest on every purchase on that bill going back to the date each purchase was made. I learned this the hard way during a period in my life when money was particularly scarce. Even then, or perhaps I should say especially then, I used my card only as a convenience and paid it in full each month. However, a month came when I didn't have quite enough to cover the balance, so I confidently paid all but $20. That way, I thought, I'll only have to pay interest on $20, which isn't so bad. Was I ever naive and mistaken. A large sum of interest appeared on my next statement, which I discovered was the interest on *everything*, not just the part of the balance that my payment hadn't covered. My next surprise came when there was also some interest to be paid the month after that, despite the fact that I did not use the card to buy anything else in the meantime. This certainly taught me a valuable lesson, and you can be sure it didn't happen again.

3. **If you are working on clearing an unpaid balance off a card, the first thing you need to do is stop using the card.** As long as you are making new purchases, you will pay interest from the first day of each purchase and—I'm not kidding—it is like getting sucked into quicksand. Trust me; you don't want to go there.

Late fees and penalties are just a "stupid tax"

One of my sons travelled for a couple of years and occasionally ended up paying too much for things because he didn't know the local customs, or because he wasn't paying attention. When telling these stories, he referred to it as a "stupid tax," that is, the price for being stupid. That's what late fees and penalties are.

In this category you could include penalties such as late fees for not returning movies and library books on time, not paying rent on time, or being late in paying your utility bill. Individually, these are usually small amounts. But over time they add up to a sizeable price to pay for inattention and disorganization.

Fifth Issue: Thinking like a wannabe…

Many people have issues with money because they think like a "wannabe": they wannabe like the rich and famous—or at least how they *perceive* the rich and famous to be. They see that the wealthy drive expensive cars, wear designer clothes, travel frequently to luxurious places, and live in extravagant houses. The person who wants to be like them emulates these externals—the lifestyle markers they can see.

Applying the millionaire mentality

What is more significant, though, is what you can't see—the underlying values and attitudes that got the wealthy where they are. This is the millionaire mentality described by Richard Evans—building wealth by reducing expenses and increasing income. Then, when there is a solid financial base, they are free to spend on luxuries.

The wannabe does just the opposite, squandering assets to buy the visible signs of a lifestyle he or she can't afford. As Juliet Schor discovered, this is the basis of the debt issues experienced by many Americans.

If people were to adopt a millionaire mentality, how would it show up in their lives? Let's first consider reducing expenses. There are many ways of reducing expenses, including purchasing used goods instead of new ones. When you purchase a new vehicle, as soon as you drive it off the dealer's lot, it's worth substantially less than what you paid for it. Depending on the brand and model, it could be worth 15 to 30% less. This is referred to as depreciation. Depreciation reflects the fact that you buy a car at a retail price but as soon as you take ownership, it is only worth the wholesale price (the price the dealer would be willing to pay to buy it back from you). A vehicle depreciates considerably in the early years. If you always buy new cars and replace them every year or two, depreciation will cost you a lot.

However, you can benefit from depreciation by purchasing a used vehicle that is two or three years old with low mileage. It will be new enough to still be in good condition, and the first owner will have taken the major loss on the depreciation, so it will cost considerably less than the original purchase price. Many people find that this is the best way to get a reliable car at a reasonable cost. Of course, as you would when making any large purchase, you must do your research: check the *Lemon Aid* guides, find out from the motor vehicles department if there are outstanding liens[6] on the car, compare prices, and have a mechanical check done. You will also want to ask yourself and the seller why the car is being sold, because you don't want to buy someone else's mistake. Nevertheless, there are many reasons that people sell next-to-new cars. Some are simply willing to pay for the status of having a new car every year or two; let them pay the depreciation, and you can be the financial beneficiary.

You can also save a lot by buying used clothing. Remember this when you have children. As well as online and through garage sales, used clothing is sold primarily through two retail channels—consignment stores and thrift stores. In Canada, the difference between them is how the stores obtain the goods and what happens to the profits. Thrift stores have no acquisition costs because the items they sell have been donated to the store. Consignment stores are in an entirely different position. When a garment is sold, the former owner is paid a percentage of the proceeds, and the store keeps the remainder for its services in displaying and selling it. Consignment stores are private businesses, whereas thrift stores are operated by not-for-profit organizations for fund-raising purposes.

From the consumer perspective, which one will have cheaper items? Which one will have more out-of-style garments for you to sort through to find the good stuff? Thrift stores. That's what makes treasure hunting at thrift stores good sport for some people. Both of my daughters-in-law have made excellent clothing buys in thrift stores, and I can assure you that no one would look at either of them and think, "Hmmm, she's wearing clothes from a thrift store." One of them has bought used clothes for her four-year-old daughter from the time she was born. Her philosophy is to search out brand names and to never pay more than $5 for an item of kids' clothing. I've seen these clothes. They look brand new, and I think she's very clever to let someone else pay the depreciation on them. Not only that, she has a plan to recoup her money by eventually reselling these items at a community sale. Here are some of her comments about thrift store shopping:

- There is a strategy to thrift store shopping: shop in affluent areas, and be open to the possibilities of what can be found at a thrift store. Some items are in fact new and still have the store tags on them.
- Ask yourself the following questions when looking at items at a thrift shop: Do I know the retail value of the item? How much could I get it for on a really good sale in a retail store? Is the thrift store price therefore "thrifty" when compared to a good sale or clearance price?
- Change strategies as necessary. It has recently become apparent to me that newborn to 24-month clothing is abundant at thrift stores but larger sizes are less so. With less selection in my daughter's current size, I'm shifting my attention to watching for deep discounts in good stores. Since I'm in the habit of being aware of regular prices, I know when a discount is worthwhile.
- You can buy more than clothes at thrift stores. We've also made excellent purchases of furniture, art, small appliances, and jewellery. My husband

found an unused electric coffee maker for $5; new it costs $99. He also bought a painting for $3. By doing a bit of Internet research, I found information about the artist and learned that this painting would sell for about $400 at auction. Another day, he found 18 more pieces of our wedding china, still in their original boxes. To give you an idea of some of our savings, here's a list of what he found on a recent trip to one of our favourite thrift stores. The new prices in the following chart are our best estimates and are included to underline how important it is to have an idea of what regular prices are; it's the way we know if a used item is actually a good deal or not. The used prices show what the price tags said, and everything was 50% off the tagged prices that day. As you can see, we saved $601. That's why we think of thrift store shopping as treasure hunting.

Comparison of New and Thrift Store Prices

	NEW	USED
Christmas tree stand	$14.00	$5.00
Kids watch	$22.00	$5.00
Gum boots – kids	$20.00	$3.00
Gum boots – adults	$45.00	$7.00
Rollerblades – adults	$229.00	$20.00
Massager	$264.00	$4.00
Bodum coffee press	$30.00	$2.00
		-50% sale
	$624.00	**$23.00**

Good value or false economy?

Keep in mind that shopping at thrift stores won't guarantee that you'll make good buys. I've known people who will purchase almost anything at a thrift store because it's cheap. Frequently, these are things that are of no use or are just plain ugly, so they end up shoved in a cupboard or closet. The fact that they were cheap did not make them good value.

I've seen the same thing happen with items on sale. People seem to think they are saving money by getting things for much less than the original price, but this is actually a *false economy.* Purchasing eight T-shirts for $5 each is a waste of $40 if you don't wear them because you don't really like the colours or they shrank in the first washing. You would have been better off spending the money on one well-made shirt in your favourite colour. Also consider a cost per usage approach. If you buy a pair of jeans for $80 and wear them once, that is $80 per use. However if you wear them 80 times over a year, that is $1 per use.

The way to get good value from sales and thrift shops is to ask yourself, "Would I be willing to pay full price for this if I had plenty of money?" If not, then clearly there's something about it that doesn't suit your needs and tastes, so why would you spend *any* money at all on it? Adopting this mindset, which is the *attitude of discerning shoppers*, will save you money by keeping you focused on good value rather than cheap price.

That thought brings me to the other aspect of the millionaire mentality, and that is looking for ways to increase income. Never overlook the possibility of reselling things you bought and no longer use, whether textbooks, clothes, music CDs, or sports equipment. You may only get one-quarter or less of what you paid, but this is a case of something being better than nothing. Besides generating some money, you'll be putting your unused items in the hands of people who will appreciate them, as well as reducing clutter in your living space.

Sixth Issue: Being driven by subconscious attitudes and fears…

Buying used items doesn't appeal to everyone. Some won't even consider them. Others will buy only a certain type of goods, such as furniture, while insisting that all clothing must be brand new. Some people can give you a list of reasons to explain their behaviours; others just know where their bottom line is when it comes to shopping used.

How do *you* feel about buying used items? Logic tells us it's often the financially sensible option, yet our actions are influenced by much more than logic. That's why economic theory about rational consumer behaviour really can't explain much of what goes on with people and their money. We spend it in irrational ways because of subconscious feelings and beliefs.

The way to address irrational behaviours is to uncover these feelings and bring them into awareness. This is the first step to freeing yourself from reacting on the basis of these unconscious impulses. Imagination can help uncover them, as in the following example. Imagine that you just bought a used table and chairs at a thrift store and are telling a friend about them. Would you describe them as old, used, vintage, retro, or antique? If it was one of the last three, why was that? Most people would say that "vintage," "retro," and "antique" imply a certain cachet, that they suggest the item is more than just old junk. The item's history gives it some interest and prestige, and therefore makes it seem worthy of them.

Now turn your imagination to *where* you might make the purchase. Besides thrift and consignment stores, used items can be bought in many places, including second-hand stores, junk shops, architectural salvage shops, garage sales, church rummage sales, estate sales, antique stores, and auctions. Where *wouldn't* you shop, and why? Maybe you know the reason, but perhaps not. Unconscious beliefs are often elusive—that's why they have managed to stay unconscious.

If you don't know why you are reacting negatively, explore it a bit. Think more about one of the places where you wouldn't shop. Think about why you wouldn't shop there. Then pay attention to the feelings in your body. Do you get a knot in your stomach? Do you feel as if you can't breathe properly? Do you feel a vague discomfort that you can't identify? When you find such a spot, gently put your attention there, breathing deeply and perhaps closing your eyes. Be still, and see if any insights come to you. You never know what underlying beliefs might surface.

Words are powerful and often evoke emotional reactions. Exploring your emotions can help you gain insight into unconscious feelings and beliefs that are driving your decisions. The good thing about such an exploration is that you are not committing yourself to doing anything one way or the other. You are just finding out what's what. Once you have a picture of the reality, then you are in a better position to make a decision. You may decide to continue doing what you have been doing, but now it is a conscious decision—and that puts you miles ahead of where you were when you were a puppet of your unconscious mind. When you make a conscious decision, *you* have the power.

Themes that drive us

Deeply buried feelings and beliefs are our own; they are unique to each person and the influences of the life he or she has led. Yet, there are themes that run through these beliefs. One theme is specialness: "I'm special (or my children are special) and only the best (i.e., most expensive) is good enough." It follows, then, that used items just will not do and aren't even considered as an option for someone who feels this special.

One of the most common unconscious beliefs is some variation of the following: "If I can't afford new, then it shows I'm not successful." For someone whose income isn't enough to afford the new item, this belief leads the person to ignore the reality and buy new by whatever means of credit can be accessed. Between the high purchase price of new items and the interest paid over years and years, the financial burden becomes huge. And the result is typically a feeling of never being able to get ahead, despite extra effort and hours spent working. The irony is that the person still does not feel successful, despite having bought only new consumer goods.

This can be devastating to intelligent and otherwise-competent people. They find it difficult to reconcile because the lack of progress doesn't fit with their image of themselves as capable and competent. One coping mechanism is denial—not acknowledging the reality of the situation even though the evidence is there.

The biggest challenge in dealing with unconscious beliefs is recognizing them. Nothing changes until we shine a light on those attitudes that lurk in the shadows and cause us to behave in ways that puzzle us because they don't make any sense. One of my favourite strategies is to ask myself questions about what's going on. If I were feeling that my finances were in a mess, I might start by asking,

"Why is my financial life so chaotic when I'm an intelligent and sensible person?" Asking insightful questions of yourself paves the way for answers to appear, and usually those answers lead to more questions. After a while, a picture emerges about what is *really* going on.

If chaotic finances are your situation, don't waste energy berating yourself. Although a chaotic life is difficult to sustain, it's not a bad thing in the short term because the situation is unsettled and therefore ripe for change. In terms of systems theory, physicists explain that a system exists in a basin of attraction. Chaos occurs near the edge of the basin of attraction. If there is an impetus toward change at a crucial moment, the system leaps into a new basin of attraction and establishes a new way of being. A surprisingly small disturbance, which they refer to as a perturbation, can initiate this leap. The questions you ask and the answers that come to you can be that necessary impetus for change.

Four steps toward change

1. **Increase your awareness.** The first step is to explore the issue by using your imagination and asking yourself questions. You are not passing judgment on yourself or committing to a course of action at this stage. What you are doing is uncovering unconscious feelings and beliefs so you can examine them from your present perspective.

2. **Ask yourself if the belief or feeling is serving you well.** Usually we created these beliefs at a very different stage of our development, and often they were a survival tactic. When they worked, we held onto them. Sometimes after uncovering one of these beliefs, you decide that you're not going to take any action at the time. You know what's driving you, but you aren't interested in changing things right now. There can be many reasons for taking this position and, after all, it is your life. If that's where you're at, it probably won't hurt to just tuck it in your mental parking lot until the time is right for making a change.

3. **Let go of the outdated belief.** For change to happen, you need to let go of the old belief that is no longer working, so you can befriend a new one. It's a two-part scenario, because there is no mental space for a new belief if the old one is still firmly in place. In your exploration of ways to do this, you'll find that there are many techniques for letting go. I have found EFT (Emotional Freedom Technique) to be both simple and readily accessible. For a free manual and demonstration of the process, go to EFTfree.com. In the manual, the use of EFT is described this way:

   > EFT allows us to release and transform the way uncomfortable feelings... may be affecting our experience. EFT can also be used to help transform the thoughts and beliefs behind our emotional experiences.... As we begin to notice, acknowledge, and transform how we carry our emotions, we begin to see how this may be contributing to...challenges in our lives. By using EFT, we can reconnect with a renewed sense of wellbeing as well as change the way stress affects us. ...Developed by engineer Gary Craig and inspired largely from the work of Dr. Roger Callahan, EFT is easy to learn and flexible enough to be used by anyone.[7]

4. **Install a new belief.** Once you have found the unconscious belief and let it go, you can install one that is more constructive. If you aren't immediately clear about what that new belief would be, go back to your imagination. Explore possibilities and play with ideas by asking yourself "What if...."

The freedom of being conscious

Making a change can seem threatening. The advantage of this process is that you are just exploring. You are not saying there is anything you will change; you are just checking out a variety of options. I've found it useful to explore possibilities at various points in my life. It has given me the freedom to think about how I might approach a situation when I really don't know what to do. By playing with ideas, I have followed threads of thought I'd have normally ignored. And I have ended up in places and doing things, that hadn't previously been part of my mental picture.

Think-abouts

That money talks,
I'll not deny.
I heard it once.
It said, "Goodbye."
~Richard Armour

Many folks think they aren't good at earning money, when what they don't know is how to use it.
~Frank Howard Clark
author

How often do we stand convinced of the truth of our early memories, forgetting that they are assessments made by a child? We can replace the narratives that hold us back by inventing wiser stories, free from childish fears, and, in doing so, disperse long-held psychological stumbling blocks. ~Benjamin Zander

Be honest with who you are and what you have.
~Suze Orman with Oprah

Growth of Money

Before we look at the other places you might put your money, this seems a good time to talk about the growth of money from a variety of viewpoints. What we're looking at, in its broadest sense, is investing. To *invest* is to put your money where it can be expected to produce a return. The return will be one of three types: interest, capital gain (loss), or dividends. The type of return becomes important when considering the tax implications of your earnings, so we'll come back to this again later.

Characteristics of investment...

We can think about investments in terms of their characteristics: risk, return, liquidity, and term. These are important considerations when deciding where to put your money in any particular circumstance.

Risk relates to the degree of security of your investment. Generally, we think of risk as the chance of losing part or all of the money you put into your investment; some are more secure than others. By this criterion, putting money into a GIC in your bank is less risky than buying shares on the stock market. However, there are also varying degrees of risk within an investment category such as the stock market. Shares in a company exploring for gold are much more risky than shares in a Canadian bank. Sometimes you can afford to take more risks than at other times, and this should be considered when making financial decisions.

Return is what you get back when you put your money to work out in the world. Return is directly proportional to the degree of risk. A low-risk investment pays a lower return; in a sense, that is the price you pay for making a more secure investment. That's why bank accounts pay the lowest interest of all investments. High-risk investments offer the potential of a higher return as a means of attracting investors, who need an incentive to take that higher risk. It is important to note, though, that "potential" only means it *might* happen. With riskier investments such as stocks, there is no guarantee of a gain. Indeed, you might lose money.

Liquidity is the third characteristic of investments. Liquidity is the degree to which the investment can be cashed (or liquidated) without loss of principal. Principal is the amount you put into your investment. With a bank account or GIC, you always get back your principal plus any interest that has accumulated.

On the other hand, when you buy real estate, the value varies depending on market forces. Sometimes it goes up and sometimes down. If you sell your real estate investment when prices are down, you might recover less than you put into it. In other words, you will have lost some of your principal. Therefore, real estate is less liquid than a GIC. It doesn't mean it's a bad investment; it just means that you don't want to put money there if you can't hold onto the investment until the market goes back up. The same is true of buying stocks, which are similarly subject to the vagaries of the market.

How does it help to know about liquidity? From a practical perspective, it reminds us that it's not a good idea to put emergency savings or student loans into the stock market. Any money that you need to access readily should be put into highly liquid investments to protect your capital. Illiquid investments, such as stocks and real estate, are best suited for money that you can leave there for as long as it takes to make a profit.

There is an inverse relationship between liquidity and return: when liquidity is higher, return will be lower. Reduced return is the price we pay for the guarantee that we will not lose our principal. Sometimes this is a good trade-off.

Term, the fourth characteristic, is the length of time your money is locked into an investment. There is no term associated with your bank account: you can take money out whenever you like. GICs are another story. Term is a basic part of the purchase agreement. Usually terms are from one to five years, and the money is locked in to varying degrees. In some cases, you forfeit part of the interest if you cash it in before the term is up. In other cases, the money is very tightly locked in and will only be released early if the certificate-holder dies.

Thus, it's important to be clear about conditions related to the term of any investments you purchase.

Term is generally directly related to return—the longer the term, the higher the return. The lender has to offer a higher interest rate to entice you to lock in your money for a long time. If a five-year GIC only paid the same as a one-year GIC, why would you bother tying up money for a further four years?

In my experience, there was one notable exception to this direct relationship between term and return. In the early 1980s in Alberta, interest rates literally shot up overnight. Because of this volatility and the accompanying uncertainty about whether rates would continue to climb or drop back down, banks were reluctant to issue longer-term certificates. They didn't want to be locked into paying out high interest on five-year GICs, if interest rates dropped again. They completely changed their approach and encouraged investors to buy short-term GICs by offering highest rates on those certificates. Once the situation stabilized, the assignment of interest rates returned to the usual pattern of higher rates for the longer term.

Factors affecting the growth of money...

There are several factors that affect the growth of money. Knowing about them gives you an advantage when you make your financial plans and decisions. Four significant factors are:

1. Time
2. Taxes
3. Inflation
4. Type of investment

Growth factor #1: The impact of time on our investments…

David Chilton, author of *The Wealthy Barber,* was asked in an interview by CNN Money's Wall Street correspondent Jordan E. Goodman: "What is the most common money blunder?" Chilton's reply:

> Procrastination. People get serious about saving far too late. I like the example of the twins. Beginning at age 22, one invests $2,000 a year for eight years and then never sets aside another penny. The other waits 10 years and then invests $2,000 a year for the next 33 years. At age 65, assuming they earn 8% a year, they both end up with the same $347,000. People underestimate the power of compounding.[1]

Compounding is essentially about earning interest on interest. In an investment, it means that you leave the interest in the account and when the next round of interest calculations are done, the previous interest is included as part of the principal on which those calculations are based. The amount you end up with varies, depending on the interest rate. But the compounding process is always the same. Numerically, *compounding interest* would grow as shown in the chart on the next page. On the other hand, suppose you took the interest out each year rather than reinvesting it. That would create a different scenario, one involving *simple interest* rather than compound.

At the end of three years of simple interest, your principal and interest would amount to $1150. Compared to the compounded figure of $1157.63, the advantage of compounding seems minimal. But this is where time comes in. As money continues to compound, it increases more rapidly. If you like making spreadsheets, you could construct one to demonstrate this. If you are a visual person, the graph that follows will be helpful. As you can see, instead of increasing in a linear way, the money is growing exponentially. This exponential growth shows on the graph as a curve. After the first 20 years or so, the effect of compounding becomes dramatic. That's why the longer you can leave the investment, the better.

It follows that the sooner you start, the longer you will be able to leave it. And that is why the first twin's small amount of invested money actually amounted to as much as the other's.

Compounding Interest

	Principal @ 5%	*yields*	*$ interest*	
Year 1	$1000.00 x 5/100	=	$50.00	which is then added to P
Year 2	$1050.00 x 5/100	=	$52.50	which is then added to P
Year 3	$1102.50 x 5/100	=	$55.13	which is then added to P
Value	**$1157.63**			

Simple Interest

Year 1, 2 & 3	$1000.00 x 5/100	=	$50.00	each year
Total interest	$50.00 x 3	=	$150.00	
Value (P + I)	$1000.00 + $150.00	=	**$1150.00**	

Exponential Growth of Compounding Interest

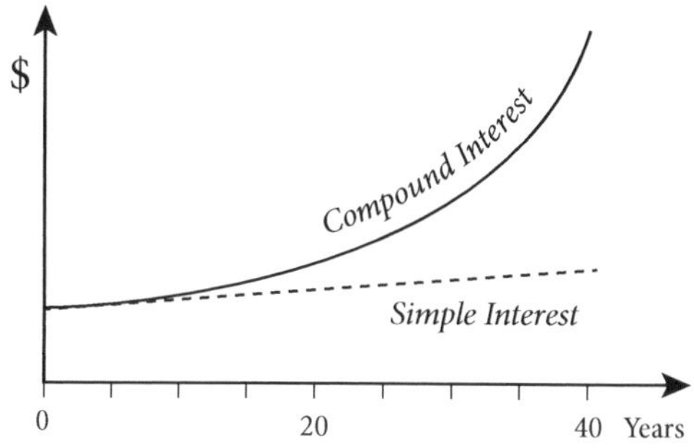

The principle here is that time is on your side. Those who start putting money away early and leave it to compound will be far ahead of those who don't. If you are young and have been wondering why you'd bother saving already when you still have so many years ahead of you, perhaps this information will give you another perspective from which to make your decision.

On the other hand, you may be older and wishing you'd started when you were young. Don't beat yourself up. Just remember that although it might have been better to start yesterday, it's better to start today than to wait until tomorrow. There are many online compounding calculators[2] for you to check this out for your own situation.

Growth factor #2: The effect of income tax on our investments...

Income tax affects the growth of your money, and that's the reason mature investors often hire advisors and accountants who are well-versed in the tax implications of investing. If you are in the early stages of adulthood, this probably is not yet a practical issue for you. However, understanding the basic territory will give you a sense of what the fuss is about. It will also help you direct your money in constructive ways as you and your investments mature.

Although most of us like to complain about income tax, it is a fact of life in developed countries. It is the way we make our contribution to keeping the country going, by funding the services, social programs, and infrastructure that we expect as citizens of an affluent country.

Nevertheless, you can legitimately reduce your taxes; this is referred to as *tax avoidance,* and includes contributing to Registered Retirement Savings Plans and claiming approved deductions when preparing your income tax. Approved deductions for post-secondary students in Canada, for example, fall into two areas. One is the education amount—an amount that may be claimed for each month of enrollment in a qualifying educational program at a designated educational institution. The other is the option to deduct specific expenses such as textbooks, bus passes, and interest on student loans. If the student has no taxable income, some of these deductions can be transferred to certain other family members. Precise details are beyond the scope of this book but can be found on the Revenue Canada website.[3]

To reiterate, the foregoing refers to avoiding taxes by means that are legally acceptable. *Tax evasion* occurs when someone does not pay the taxes they are legally obliged to pay. We sometimes hear news reports of the discovery of elaborate schemes set up by the wealthy to hide some of their money; these activities are punishable under the criminal code, and penalties vary depending on the nature of the offense. Tax evasion also occurs in smaller ways, sometimes inadvertently, even among people of modest incomes. The most common is by not claiming all of one's income, in particular income from doing work at home or from tips earned on the job. I know that many people think income only refers to money paid by an employer for which they get a T4 slip at income tax time. The tax department disagrees. It considers income to be money we are paid for providing a good or service. By that definition, tips and money earned by working at home are considered income. You may not like it, but they write the rules.

If you work as a server, I can hear you thinking, "How can they possibly know if I get tips or how much they amount to?" More than once, when this objection came up in class, a student had an experience to share. One young woman had spent the summer working as a server in a nearby mountain resort. That year, the tax department decided to audit income tax returns filed by staff in food service establishments in that town. When they discovered servers who had not declared tips, or had declared very little, they had the authority to decide what these people probably received, based on the restaurant's income and industry norms. From that, they calculated the tax that should have been paid. This amount was levied as back taxes, with interest charged if it wasn't paid in a timely manner. Reportedly, some of these servers were deemed to owe as much as $5000 in unpaid taxes. Although you might think you don't want to know this, it could save you grief later on.

Taxes paid on investment income

You may recall that investment income can be in the form of interest, dividends, or capital gains. It's useful to be aware that different types of investment income are taxed at different rates.

All interest you earn is added to your income and taxed accordingly; therefore, interest income is 100% taxable. This means if you are in a tax bracket in which you pay 30% to taxes, and if you had earned $100 in interest, then you pay $30 to the tax department and actually get to keep only $70 of your interest earnings.

Dividends come to you via certain types of shares purchased on the stock market. Through a complicated set of calculations, you get a tax credit for dividends paid by some Canadian companies. The advice of a tax accountant is useful if you intend to include dividend income in your tax-reduction strategy.

Capital gains are different again. The government has legislated the most favourable tax treatment on capital gains as a means of encouraging investment in business. When you make a capital gain, only half of it is taxed. Using our $100 example, this means that only $50 (i.e., half of the capital gain you made) is added to your taxable income. At a 30% rate of taxation, you would pay $15 tax ($50 × 30/100) and keep $85 (the exempted $50 plus the $35 not paid in tax). If you have a capital loss, it can be carried over to offset future capital gains.

Sheltering investments from taxes

People who invest commonly look for tax shelters. A *tax shelter* is a savings vehicle that is approved by the government to offer tax-saving benefits. Two Canadian examples are the Registered Retirement Savings Plan (RRSP) and the Tax Free Savings Account (TFSA), both of which are readily accessible to average income earners. If you live in another country, there may be similar programs.

Tax deferral is another tax term to be familiar with. To defer means to put off until a later time. In the case of tax deferral, income taxes are paid at the end of the process rather than at the beginning. Specifically, this pertains to RRSPs. Money put into the plan is deducted from your taxable income that year. However, when you withdraw money from your RRSP at some time in the future, the amount withdrawn is added back to your taxable income for that year and you must pay tax on it. This can be a nasty surprise if you are unaware that RRSPs are based on the principle of deferral.

Structure of the tax system

To understand the implications of tax shelters and tax deferral, it is necessary to have a basic understanding about how the Canadian tax system is structured.[4] It is a sliding marginal tax system, sometimes referred to as a progressive tax system. This system is based on the premise that people with low incomes should pay a lower percentage of income tax than do high income earners. This is accomplished through the designation of four tax brackets, which are the points at which a person moves from one taxation level to another. Visually, it would be represented as in the following diagram. This graph shows federal taxes only. In practice, the percentage paid in taxes is determined by a combined figure of provincial and federal taxes. Since provincial needs and circumstances vary, not

Canada's Sliding Marginal Tax System

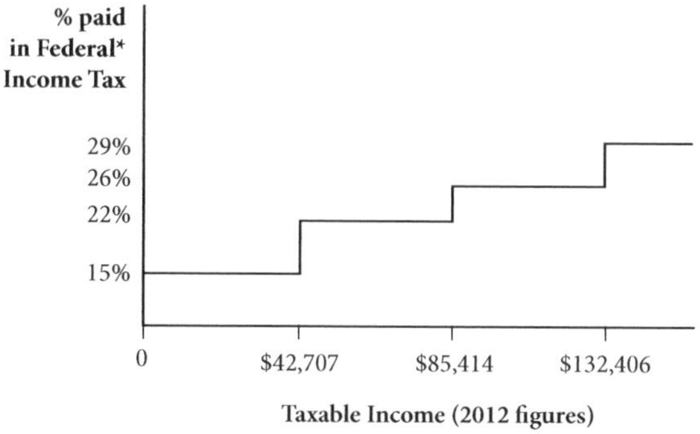

* *Provincial income taxes are in addition to this, and the calculations for each province are based on different tax rates.*

all provinces tax at the same rate. Thus the actual rate will be dependent on your province of residence.

Knowing these basics about the structure of the tax system gives you a context for understanding financial conversations. Have you perhaps heard someone say she got a raise but ended up not actually taking home any more money? That could be the effect of having moved into a higher tax bracket. Or you may have heard someone talk about putting money into an RRSP to move into a lower tax bracket.

RRSPs, a long-standing form of tax shelter

The Registered Retirement Savings Plan is a tax shelter that has been available to Canadians since 1957. "Registered" means that the investment is registered with the government and therefore qualifies for certain tax benefits. It does *not* mean that the investment is in any way approved or guaranteed by the government, although this is a common misconception. When you buy an RRSP, risk will depend on the type of investment you have chosen, since your investment is subject to the usual market factors.

What type of investment qualifies for an RRSP? The short answer is almost anything, as long as it has been registered. That's because an RRSP is not an investment per se: it's a structure to contain investments. Think of it as a shed where you can put things to shelter them. The walls and roof of the shed are analogous to the RRSP program rules that shape its structure and shelter the contents, in this case from taxation. Inside that shelter you can put any number of savings and investment vehicles, including, but not limited to, GICs, Canada Savings Bonds, cash, mutual funds, and stocks. These investments are purchased from financial institutions such as banks, investment companies, and brokerage houses. The individual investments exhibit the characteristics typical of their particular class. For example, if you have a three-year GIC sheltered in your RRSP, then you are bound by the term restrictions on a GIC with that term.

The RRSP program was set up to encourage citizens to save for their retirements, and tax benefits are the incentive to encourage us to do so. The tax benefits of an RRSP are first, the deferral of income tax in the year of your contribution, and second, tax-free growth while the money is in the plan.

RRSPs are governed by specific rules regarding yearly contribution limits, taxation when money is withdrawn, and how long the plan may be held. At some point, the accumulated money needs to be removed from your RRSP; after all, the purpose of these savings is to provide income in retirement. The *way* in which your money is removed is very important, and tax implications are the crucial factor here. Remember that an RRSP is a tax deferral program; therefore, taxes are paid when money is withdrawn. Essentially the withdrawn money is added to your taxable income for that year, and you are taxed accordingly. If you withdraw a large amount, it could put you in a higher tax bracket and you will pay more in taxes.

The RRSP program was established to encourage accumulation of retirement funds, but your access to them is not limited by age or intended purpose. You can withdraw them—paying the appropriate tax—for any purpose you choose. Do remember, though, that even if you replace the money in the following years, you will have interrupted the compounding cycle, and there is a financial cost to that.

This is enough to give you a basic understanding until you are ready to put money into RRSPs and need more information. When that time comes, check your local library and bookstores for more in-depth information.

TFSA, a newer tax shelter

In 2009, a new tax shelter was introduced. The Tax Free Savings Account (TFSA) is available to anyone 18 years of age or older, with no upper age limit. As with an RRSP, you do not pay income tax on the earnings from money in the plan.

Although the name includes the words "savings account," this tax shelter is not limited only to a bank savings account. As with RRSPs, it can shelter a wide range of investments, including cash, mutual funds, GICs, stocks, and bonds. A visual for the TFSA is an umbrella with investments hanging from the ribs.

As you would expect, the TFSA program is governed by specific rules. The contribution limit was initially set at $5000 per year and is indexed to inflation. Indexing means that the contribution limit increases over time at a rate proportional to inflation. As is the case with RRSPs, you can have more than one TFSA but your total contribution may not exceed the maximum for that year. There is an unlimited carry-forward provision for unused contributions.

Although there are many similarities between TFSAs and RRSPs, they are not identical. The main difference has to do with taxation. When you make a contribution to a TSFA, you do not get a tax deduction as you do with an RRSP. And when you remove money from your TSFA, you do not pay tax on the money withdrawn, as you would on your RRSP funds. In other words, the TFSA is not a tax-deferred program.

Rules for withdrawal allow you to remove money at any time. The money can be replaced without interfering with future contributions, but the replacement amount may not be put back until the next calendar year. This is important to know because there are stiff penalties if you put the money back in the same year you withdrew it.

How is a TFSA useful to you and me? First, it saves us paying taxes on some investment earnings. And second, given that we all need an emergency fund, a TFSA in the form of a savings account is probably as good a place as any to keep that money.

Growth factor #3: Inflation…

Another significant factor affecting the growth of our money, alluded to when I mentioned indexing of TFSA contribution limits, is inflation. Discussions and definitions of inflation can become intricate and complex, which would defeat our purpose here. So let me start by giving examples of how inflation shows up in our lives.

When I was in primary school, I received an allowance of 25¢, and with it I could buy a chocolate bar (5¢), a comic book (10¢), and still have a dime left for my piggy bank. Twenty-five years later, my children needed 25¢ to buy a chocolate bar and 50¢ for a comic book. Their allowance of $1.25 bought the same as my 25-cent allowance had. Today, my granddaughter needs $7.25 for the same "standard of living." That's inflation.

When I graduated from university in the late 1960s, my monthly salary for my first full-time professional job was $405. Sounds like very little, but then rent was about $100, and $50 could buy enough food to last me a month. Today, no one could live on that monthly income because rent for a comparable place is around $800 and monthly food cost for one person is about $400. That's inflation.

When my husband was transferred from Calgary to Ottawa in the 1970s, we sold our house in Calgary for $26,500. While we were away, there was an economic boom in Calgary. When we moved back five years later, if we'd wanted to buy that same house, it would have cost us $78,000. That's *rapid* inflation.

Inflation is most simply defined as a rise in the cost of living. It is tracked monthly by Statistics Canada, using the Consumer Price Index—a basket of about 600 commonly used consumer goods and services. Calculations using price data for these items determine if costs have gone up or down, and by how much. When we hear that the annual rate of inflation is 2.5%, this tells us that the basket of goods costs 2.5% more now than it did a year ago.

Economic theory says that some inflation is integral to a growing economy. The goal is to have a low rate of inflation—somewhere between 1 and 3%—and government policy-making is aimed at achieving that.

From the consumer perspective, inflation is an issue because it increases the cost of what we buy year after year. If our income doesn't increase proportionally, then the money we have buys less and less. Eventually, it may be impossible to make ends meet. This is the dilemma of people on fixed incomes, such as pensioners. This is also why pensions are indexed to inflation: indexing is the means of making it possible for pensioners to keep up with rising costs.

How does inflation relate to investments? The issue is whether or not the return on your investment is enough to cover rising costs due to inflation. Suppose inflation is 2.5% where you live. You have invested your money in a long-term GIC that will pay you 2.8%. What is your net (real or actual) rate of return? You are 0.3% ahead.

On the other hand, if your money is in a savings account paying 0.5% interest, you are clearly not keeping up with inflation. This is something of a catch-22 situation because you need to keep some money in a readily accessible account, which means you will be getting a low return on that money. The best you can do is to also look for higher return for some of your money, so that, on average, you come out ahead. When looking at investments promising high returns, be sure to carefully assess the risk of the investment.

Growth factor #4: Type of investment…

The last factor that impacts the growth of your money is the type of investment you have made. Broadly speaking, all investments can be divided into two types—debt investment and equity investment. Understanding the distinction will be useful when reading financial articles and talking with advisors.

The basic difference between these two types of investment is whether you gain ownership of something or are simply lending your money to someone who will pay you rent (called interest in the financial world) for the use of it.

"Equity" means ownership, and if your investment makes you the owner of something, it is called an *equity investment*. You can probably come up with examples. When thinking about it, remember that an investment is defined as something that can be expected to produce a return. This means that your furniture and car aren't investments, even though you own them, because they do not increase in value. Since they depreciate, they are defined as consumer goods rather than investments. Your house, though, would be considered an equity investment because it is an appreciating asset and can reasonably be expected to earn a return over time.

Corporate shares are also equity investments. When you buy shares—also referred to as stocks—you become an owner, small though your holding might be. Precious metals, such as gold and silver, are also equity investments, as are collectibles, such as original art, fine wine, antique cars, and even old baseball cards.

In all cases, the owners of these investments hope the value will go up over time, so they will be able to sell the items for more than they paid for them. The resulting profit is a capital gain. If there is a downturn in the market and an item is sold for less than the purchase price, the result is a capital loss.

Dividends are the other type of return in the equity category. They are regular earnings, usually quarterly or monthly, that are paid by certain types of shares. As an aside, when you have such an investment, you can set it up to compound by arranging for more of those same shares to be automatically purchased with your dividends. You would then end up earning dividends on your dividends, so to speak.

That's an overview of equity investment; the other type is *debt investment*. The name debt investment is confusing because it seems to suggest that money is being borrowed to invest in something. However, a debt investment is actually one in which *you lend your money* to a person, company, or institution, and they pay you interest in return for the use of it; so actually, *they are in debt to you*. Although we usually don't think of it that way, this is exactly what happens when you put your money into a savings account in your bank. They use your money for their purposes, such as lending to other customers, and pay you interest at a pre-determined rate. The same is true of other bank products, such as term deposits and GICs, which are also debt investments.

Canada Savings Bonds also fit in the category of debt investments. As you might have guessed, in this case you are lending your money to the government of Canada. Corporate bonds are debt investments because you are lending your money to the corporation.

"Stocks and bonds" are usually said in the same breath, and corporations do issue both and sell them on the market. However, stocks and bonds are technically different from each other. You are an owner when you buy stocks, whereas you are a lender when you buy bonds. Because of that, bonds have lower risk levels because the bondholders (lenders) are paid back before stockholders (owners), if a company goes bankrupt. There are unique aspects to buying and selling both stocks and bonds, and it would be prudent to do some reading before investing in them.

How does the type of investment relate to return? Equity investments are generally considered most risky because the return you get depends "on the market" (i.e., what people are willing to pay for the investment you own). The market for anything fluctuates over time as a result of many social and psychological factors. If you sell when the market is down, you may make little or no money on your investment. Or you may even have to sell at less than your purchase price, in which case you will lose part of the money you originally invested and end up with less than you started with. The risk occurs because price is determined by the market, and you have no control over that.

From that viewpoint, debt investment seems a better choice because the return is specified when you make the investment and is not subject to market fluctuations. However, some would argue that losses due to inflation are an equally great risk. From the viewpoint of loss due to inflation, debt investments pose a greater risk because their returns are usually lower than the rate of inflation, especially now when interest rates are extremely low.

There are no perfect solutions. Everything has some pluses and minuses, and the best we can do is work within that to optimize the results in any given circumstances. When it comes to investing, diversifying your funds so you have some in both the debt and equity categories is usually the most sensible approach to weathering fluctuations in the economy.

Think-abouts

My goal wasn't to make a ton of money. It was to build good computers.
~Steve Wozniak

A simple fact that is hard to learn is that the time to save money is when you have some. ~Joe Moore

You miss 100 percent of the shots you never take.
~Wayne Gretzky

Money is better than poverty, if only for financial reasons.
~Woody Allen

All I ask is the chance to prove that money can't make me happy.
~Spike Milligan

The Costs of Money

We all like to think about our money compounding exponentially and ensuring us of wealthy futures. Ironically, our day-to-day interaction with money is often counterproductive to that dream. So far, we've talked about relative returns for different types of investment, the benefits of tax-free saving, and the effects of compounding. Now let's look at some of the *costs* of money. Without this information, you might make decisions that end up bleeding away your funds and thwarting your intentions to save and invest. With this in mind, we'll look at the following topics:

1. Student loans
2. Personal loans and lines of credit
3. Payday loans
4. Credit cards
5. Mortgages

Student loans...

Recently I asked my class, "What is the purpose of student loans?" The immediate response was "Free money." Making their decisions from that viewpoint, students might take as much student loan money as they can get. However, in this case "free" only applies in the short term, and sooner or later they'll have to pay the piper.

Government student loans in Canada are interest-free until you graduate, and repayment can be deferred until six months after that. However, most of these loans begin accumulating interest as soon as you graduate, even though you don't have to start repaying them immediately. At the end of the six-month grace period, you can either pay the interest in a lump sum right then, or have it added to your loan principal. In the case of a $20,000 loan, the interest accrued during the grace period would be $800 at current rates. (This and all figures which follow were obtained using the CanLearn online loan repayment estimator.[1]) If you choose not to immediately repay the $800 interest from the first six months, your $20,000 loan becomes a $20,800 loan. You might recognize this as an example of compounding (i.e., interest paid on interest). However, in this case you will be *paying out* interest on interest rather than receiving it.

There was a time when, if you didn't have the money to pay for a post-secondary education, you didn't get one. The Canadian student loan program was introduced to democratize education by making it accessible to more people. That is an honourable goal. The unintended consequence has been that more people in their twenties are highly indebted than ever before. Consider these strategies to minimize your student debt:

1. Begin repaying the loan immediately after graduation rather than allowing interest to build during the grace period, if your loans start charging interest right away.
2. Pay more than the minimum payment each month, so it will be paid off in less than 10 years.
3. Reduce the amount of loan money you need by being resourceful, finding sources of income other than borrowed money, and keeping your expenses low.

Most people don't know that the default repayment period is 10 years. That is a long time to be in debt for your education, and it costs a lot in interest. On a $20,000 loan, you will pay about $9100 in interest over 10 years. If you paid the loan back in 5 years, you would save about $4800. Your monthly payment increases as the repayment period is shortened. However, it's worth it to get the loan repaid quickly. I've known recent graduates who chose to live in their parents' home for a couple of years, contributing money to food and utilities, and paying off their student loan with the money they would have paid for rent elsewhere. In this way, they were able to move out debt-free in a couple of years. When parents are willing to offer this option, it is a huge financial gift that should be considered seriously.

Another strategy for minimizing student loan interest is to take as little student loan money as possible—the smaller the loan, the less interest you will pay in total. A 10-year loan of $5000 will cost about $2200 in interest, whereas $20,000 in loans will cost $9100 interest.

If you are considering applying for student loans, it's wise to ask yourself how much you can afford. Remember that when you borrow money, you are responsible for repaying it without excuses. Even if you declare bankruptcy, your student loan is not automatically discharged. It will only be considered for discharge seven years after you've finished your studies (five years in the case of exceptional financial hardship). Even then, the government may object to the loan being discharged. If the objection is successful, you will be required to repay that loan. A rule of thumb used by Gail Vaz-Oxlade, author of *Debt-Free Forever*, is that you should only take student loans in an amount you can afford to pay off completely within five years of graduation.[2]

By being resourceful, you can minimize the amount of loan money you need. An eye-opening article on Vaz-Oxlade's website explores some of the alternatives to student loan debt.[3] She reports that there are more than 22,000 scholarships available, many from sources you wouldn't have thought of. She provides web addresses for three sites that list scholarships, and provides practical tips about applying for them.

Vaz-Oxlade also points out an interesting money-math fact: If you get a $1000 scholarship, that's the same as if you had earned $1200. Because scholarship money isn't taxable, you keep it all...unlike your paycheque. When you have earnings from a job, a percentage will be paid to income tax. If you earn $1200, you will likely keep about $1000 of it. Financial writers refer to what you get to keep as "after-tax dollars."

Scholarships rarely cover the complete cost of your education. That may leave you looking at how you can combine part-time work with some student loans to cover both your living costs and education expenses. If you can be imaginative and find part-time work that relates to your career goals, so much the better. Here are some of Vaz-Oxlade's examples:

> I know a young lass named Stephanie who worked as an assistant to a financial advisor all the way through her university years. Since she planned to go into finance as a career, this stood her in very good stead when she went job hunting. If you want to be a vet, find work in the medical arena. If you want to be a teacher, try tutoring. If you want to be an artist, hire yourself out to your professors to do their artwork for books they may be in the process of writing. My friend Ian did this and, hey, it paid some of the bills… Think outside the box. Don't get caught in the McJob simply because your lack of imagination makes you feel there's no other option. Life will be full of challenges, consider this your first biggie![4]

When you are a student, resourcefulness and thrifty practices will work to your advantage by minimizing your need for loans. For students who find that their studies require their full attention, take a year off periodically to work full-time and save as much as you can. Managing your cash flow[5] and being creatively thrifty[6] can help you save for the next year in school. The point is to keep your student loan debt to a minimum. You will undoubtedly be glad you did.

Once you have graduated, apply the same attitudes and habits toward reducing your daily expenses. This will allow you to pay off the loan quickly, leaving you debt-free and further ahead in the long run. The same principle applies to all loans—car, house, credit cards: the faster you pay them off, the less you will pay in total interest. Conversely, the longer they drag on, the more money you'll pay in interest charges.

Personal loans and lines of credit…

Personal loans allow an individual to borrow a lump sum for a specific purpose, such as furniture or a car. In such cases, the item becomes the collateral, which means it is the security for the loan and will be repossessed if the borrower doesn't make the payments. A cosigner is another kind of security that may be required. A cosigner is typically needed when the lender is unsure about the credit-worthiness of the borrower. The person who cosigns is agreeing to be responsible for payments if the borrower defaults, and the lender has a legal right to enforce that agreement. If a friend asks you to cosign a loan, consider the implications very carefully because you could be on the hook for paying off the loan, if your friend stops making the payments.

A line of credit is set up differently from a personal loan. Originally, it was designed as a tool to help businesses bridge cash flow deficits, but in recent years *personal lines of credit* have been made widely available. A line of credit is essentially pre-approval to borrow up to a specified amount of money, usually $10,000. You could think of it as a phantom bank account from which you can spend, as long as you don't exceed the limit and regularly make your payments, which will vary depending on the outstanding balance.

A personal line of credit typically has a lower interest rate than a personal loan. This could lead you to think that it makes financial sense to use a line of credit instead of personal loans. However, when it comes to money, it isn't just the math that counts, it's the psychology. Unlike with a personal loan, you don't need to ask permission or justify your expenditures to anyone except yourself when you spend from a line of credit. Thus, a person without plenty of self-discipline might over-spend because there's no external source of accountability.

There is also another type of line of credit that has come into common use in recent years—the home equity line of credit (HELOC). A *home equity line of credit* is similar to the personal line of credit in that you are pre-approved for a specified amount and may spend it at your discretion. The difference is that a personal line of credit is unsecured, whereas a HELOC is a secured loan, and the lender can take possession of the security if you default.

Your house is the security for a home equity line of credit. When you apply for a HELOC, the lender approves a certain percentage of your *equity* (the amount of the market value that is not mortgaged) as the limit on your line of credit. If you use your home equity line of credit and are unable to make the payments on it, your house will be sold so the lender could recover the outstanding amount of your loan. The interest rate on a HELOC is lower than on a personal line of credit. That's because it is secured by the property, making the loan less risky for the lender than an unsecured personal line of credit.

Home equity loans seem appealing because they provide access to large sums of money at relatively low rates. A HELOC could provide enough money to take a great vacation, to remodel the house with more luxurious finishing materials, to buy new furniture or to buy a car or recreational vehicle. But think about it; are any of these worth taking a chance on losing the roof over your head? It would be hard to make a case that they were.

It is true that a HELOC can, in certain instances, be used to your advantage in a wealth-building program. Skillful use of a HELOC can be part of an overall strategy with a long-term view toward building further equity. However, it is not a tool for financial beginners. And it should *never* ever be used to purchase consumer goods and services.

Payday loans...

The availability of payday loans has increased dramatically in Canada over the past 20 years. Sometimes called pay-advance loans, these short-term loans are used to fill an income gap. A 2010 survey in the Maritime provinces of Canada found that 71% of payday loan customers chose them over other types of credit because they are quick, easy, and convenient. This study, commissioned by the Canadian Payday Loan Association, showed that almost two-thirds of payday loans were between $100 and $399, although loan amounts can be as high as $1500. Borrowers reported they used these loans primarily to obtain emergency cash for necessities (36%) and to help out with unexpected expenses (24%).

A major criticism of payday lending is its inherently predatory nature. Practices such as rollovers and back-to-back renewals keep the borrower perpetually in debt and regularly paying high fees. These practices are termed predatory because they are so detrimental to borrowers that they are considered abusive.

Another criticism is the high cost of borrowing. When you look at the math, it is shocking that anyone takes out such a loan. But the people who use them are desperate to meet immediate needs and don't view it from the perspective I'm about to share with you. When a loan is approved, the amount is typically deposited directly into the borrower's account and a preauthorized debit is set up to withdraw the borrowed amount plus the loan fee on the next payday.

Payday loans in Canada are regulated provincially, resulting in considerable variation of legislation across the country. The following example of payday loan costs is taken directly from the website of a payday loan company and reflects Alberta legislation.

> **We charge: $23 per $100 lent**
>
> **For a $300 loan for 14 days:**
>
> **Total cost of borrowing = $69.00**
>
> **Annual Percentage Rate = 599.64%**
>
> *This information meets the requirements of the*
> *Payday Loans Regulation under the Fair Trading Act*[7]

As this example shows, it costs $69 to borrow $300. What if you wanted to borrow the maximum amount of $1500—how much would it cost you? Going back to the example, we see that each $100 will cost you $23. $1500 would cost 15 times that amount.

The cost of $1500 would be 15 × $23 = $345

The fee is typically levied as a dollar amount, and I found most websites do not state the effective annual percentage rate (APR) as in the example above. However, the APR is more useful for you to know. You can go to an online calculator to figure it out.[8] If you prefer to understand the theory, here's how to calculate interest rate as an annual percentage.

Step A: *Determine the percentage* ***for the time period of the loan****. In the above example, the time period is 2 weeks.*

Fee/Principal × 100% = \$69/\$300 × 100% = **23% for 2 weeks**

Step B: *Using that information, determine the effective* ***annual percentage****. Said another way, if the rate is 23% for 2 weeks, how much is it for 52 weeks? Use a simple ratio formula:*

If 2 weeks = 23%

Then 52 weeks = 52/2 × 23% = **598% per year**

The slight difference from their figure of 599.64% might be due to a rounding error and for our purposes is not significant. Either way, it's an outrageous amount, and not a game to be played by anyone trying to get ahead financially!

Now, what would be the interest rate if the money had only been borrowed for one week instead of two? The same process applies...

Step A: Fee/Principal × 100% = \$69/\$300 × 100 = **23% for 1 week**

Step B: If 1 week = 23%

Then 52 weeks = 52/1 × 23% = **1196% per year**

These figures are shocking, no doubt about it. They might lead you to wonder why payday loan companies are allowed to operate. It's not an easy situation to address. Some believe that payday loans should be banned to curtail unnecessary and expensive borrowing. On the other hand, there is concern that this would force people to meet emergency financial needs by dealing with pawn shops and loan sharks. It's a dilemma for governments: how much should be legislated, and to what extent should people be required to take responsibility for themselves and their choices?

Hopefully, you have not yet fallen into the pit of payday loans. But it could easily happen, as they are now readily available online and in many variations. Don't go there! If you have, do what it takes to get out; spend only the bare minimum on everything else until you get it paid off. There is no way to win in this game—unless you are the lender.

Credit cards...

When it comes to credit cards, I don't worry about the interest rate. Surprised to hear that? Why would I not be concerned about looking for a credit card with the lowest possible rate? The answer is simple, and you may have already guessed it. I make it a policy to use my card as a convenience, not as a source of borrowed money. Since I intend to never pay interest, it's a non-issue.

What is the difference between using a credit card as a convenience and as a source of borrowed money? Interest. When you borrow money, you have to pay interest. With typical credit cards, annual interest rates are close to 20%. Card issuers generally offer a grace period of about three weeks before interest is charged on purchases. When you use your card because it is convenient and pay off the balance before the grace period ends, you benefit from the convenience without ever having to pay interest. Important note: The grace period does not apply to cash advances, which are tracked separately. If you take a cash advance on your card, you will be charged interest on that amount from the first day of the advance. The same is true if you use the credit card cheques sent by your card issuer with an encouraging invitation to use them. These cheques are a cash advance on your card and are treated accordingly. Find other ways of handling your finances, and don't ever use cash advances and credit card cheques.

In addition to only using my credit card as a convenience, I make it a personal policy to avoid all the insurance and other fees they keep trying to sell me, because these are a direct cost to me. If you carry a balance on your card, any fees have to be taken into account when working out the interest rate on your purchases. This example from *Debt-Free Forever* spells it out:

While the interest rate on a credit card may be set at 19.99%, you may be paying much more than that if your card has additional fees tacked on each month. Let's look at a credit card with an insurance fee of $28.44 on a balance of $1,623, along with an over-limit fee of $35. When you add it all up:

- monthly interest = $27.03
- plus insurance fee = $28.44
- plus over-limit fee = $35
- divided by balance = $1,623
- multiplied by 100 (to get a percentage)
- and then multiplied by 12 to get the annual percentage

the effective interest rate on this card is a whopping 67%. The fees are just as important as the interest rate when it comes to determining what your credit card is really costing you.[9]

The effect of fees is one of those facts that many people prefer to ignore because the reality is shocking. It's difficult to remain complacent about the financial consequences of borrowing money using credit cards when you see that the actual interest rate is 67%.

Most people don't think about what they are really paying when they buy things on credit; they compartmentalize the price and the interest cost in two different parts of their brains and don't think of the total cost in an integrated way. That's the psychological trap of using a credit card. It's an avoidance tactic, but where is the sense in that? How can you ever get ahead if everything costs you more than you think. Being realistic is a much more powerful approach to using your credit card.

Remember that anything you buy with your credit card will cost you considerably more than the price on the tag...unless you pay off the entire balance before the grace period ends.

Another shocker

Now let's look at credit card usage from another angle—the length of time it takes to pay off a balance. Here's an example to consider:

Balance	=	$220.76
Minimum payment	=	$10/month
Annual interest rate	=	19.49%

If you do not charge anything else on this card and make the minimum monthly payment without fail, how long will it take you to pay it off completely? If the math seems daunting, take your best guess.

The correct answer is 28 months—that's over two years to pay for something worth $221. Paying $10 a month for 28 months, you will pay $280 for that $221 item. The extra $59 amounts to a 27% increase in the price of what you bought. Such a large surcharge increases your living costs substantially.

Now here's another scenario:

Balance	=	$3172
First month payment	=	$63
Annual interest rate	=	18.5%

Suppose you spent that money on a fabulous vacation to celebrate your 20th birthday. Assume you buy nothing else on this credit card and faithfully make the minimum payment each month. How old will you be when you make the last payment for that birthday trip? How much interest will you pay in total during that time?

According to information taken directly from the credit card statement used for this example, *the balance will be fully paid off in 42 years, 8 months.* Therefore, you will be four months shy of your 63rd birthday when you make that last payment on your 20th birthday celebration.

How much interest will be paid? This is not part of the required information on a credit card statement, so I found the answer by using an online calculator.[10] According to the calculator, you will pay out a total of $12,623 for that trip worth $3172. The interest is therefore $9,451. (Total paid of $12,623 – original cost of $3,172 = interest of $9,451.) The interest is three times the original cost of your celebratory trip. That's a huge surcharge, and I can't help wondering if anything is worth that much extra.

When I used the online calculator, I printed out the full repayment schedule for this loan. Looking at the printout was an eye-opener. I discovered that:

- It takes 83 payments to reduce the principal by $1000. That is 6 years, 11 months until the principal is reduced from $3172 to $2172. By then you would have paid a total of $4388 in your minimum monthly payments. Of that amount, $3388 went to interest.
- The second $1000 will be paid off after the 217th payment. That means it will take 134 more payments (11 years, 2 months more) to clear the second $1000 of the debt.
- The third $1000 is paid off after the 479th payment. That means it will take another 262 months (21 years, 10 months) after the second $1000 is paid off until the third $1000 is cleared.
- And to clear the last $173 takes 20 more months because by then minimum payments are only $10 a month.

How does this happen?

How could it take *42 years* to pay back any loan, much less one on a credit card for ordinary consumer goods, such as vacations, concert tickets, clothes, furniture, and eating out? For starters, the interest rate is high and the monthly payment is low. A rate of 18.5% per year works out to 0.05068% per day. In the first month, you will pay an average of $1.63 each day in interest.

Because your monthly payment is low, *most of your monthly payment goes to interest*, leaving very little to pay down the loan itself. In our example, only $14 of your $63 goes toward paying down the principal. To see a chart showing the complete repayment schedule, go to the previously mentioned calculator to enter the data for this example. In the box marked "Option A," the minimum monthly amount will be $10.00 and the minimum monthly percentage is 2%. You'll find that the repayment time in the resulting chart is slightly different from the 42 years, 8 months given on the credit card statement. The calculator explains that a discrepancy may occur because credit card companies are permitted to round up your balance to the next $100 when making their estimates, whereas the online calculator starts with your exact credit card balance.

Remember: *Any repayment time estimate is accurate if, and only if, nothing else is ever charged on that card while it is being paid off. If you continue to use the card while making minimum payments, you are adding to your principal each month despite paying on the loan regularly. As a result, you will be increasing the repayment time to more than 42 years.*

How can a person in this situation possibly get ahead? Certainly not by following the prescribed payments. But think about this: any extra paid each month goes directly to paying down the principal because the interest for that month has already been covered by the minimum payment.

In the previous example, when the first payment of $63 was made, only $14 went to paying down the principal. If $113 had been paid instead of $63 in the first month, the extra $50 would have gone directly on the principal, reducing it by $64 ($14 from the regular payment + $50 extra). This might seem a small difference, but the results of paying that extra $50 a month are astounding. Most online calculators have a line that allows you to explore the effect of making larger payments each month. When I did that, I discovered that *by paying $50 in addition to the minimum payment each month, the loan for that trip would be paid off in 4 years 7 months instead of about 42 years.* That is not a typographical error; it really was less than 5 years.

A monthly payment of $100 plus the minimum will see this loan paid off in 2 years 6 months. Increase the monthly payment to $150 plus the minimum payment, and it will be paid in 1 year 9 months instead of about 42 years. This is a sharp contrast to the way the debt drags on and on when you make only the minimum payments. (Remember that third $1000, which took almost 22 years to pay off according to the minimum payment schedule?)

It might take a bit of doing to find that extra $150 per month, but spending less on optional items or taking a second job for a couple years, is worth it in this situation. Getting the debt paid off fast saves you a lot in the long term, and any money you were spending on debt repayment can be put to uses that are much more satisfying than paying interest.

The benefit of paying more than the specified minimum is a crucial concept because it applies to all loans, not just credit cards. As the foregoing shows, paying more reduces the principal more rapidly. Because the principal is reduced to zero in a fewer number of months, you are borrowing the money for less time and you will be paying less in total interest. There is no fancy math in that; it is simply common sense.

Strategies to reduce credit card charges

1. Use your credit card only as a convenience, and pay the balance in full each month before the grace period is up.
2. Do not take a cash advance or use credit card cheques because there is no grace period on money you access this way.
3. Choose a card with no fees and resist their pressure to buy insurance and such extras.
4. If you do have a balance on your card, never make just the minimum payment. Pay as much extra as you can manage each month because that will be applied directly to the principal and your loan will go down much faster.
5. When paying off an outstanding balance, stop using that card for any other purchases. If you continue using the card, your extra payments will be going to new interest rather than paying down the principal on your original balance. You won't get ahead.

Mortgages...

Paying interest is more or less unavoidable when you purchase a house. Housing prices are high compared to income, so it's rare for someone to save enough to purchase a house outright with cash. However, I do have one story about that.

A few years ago, I had a student in his early thirties who had started saving from part-time jobs when he was a teenager, and continued the habit as he worked throughout his twenties. Two months before coming to college as a full-time student, he had fully paid for a condominium with his own cash. He had two roommates and used their rent payments to cover taxes, utilities, and condo fees. Since he had no mortgage payments, he was able to be a student without needing either a loan or a job.

This young man didn't need to know about the ins and out of mortgages, but most of us do. Once you understand how mortgages are structured, you'll see how to save money on your mortgage by minimizing the interest you pay.

Understanding mortgage interest so you can pay less

A mortgage is the largest loan most of us will undertake. Because of the size and length of a mortgage loan, it costs you a surprising amount in total interest. That's not all bad. Carefully chosen real estate is generally considered to be a good investment because it can reasonably be expected to increase in value. A mortgage is a means of leveraging your investment in a house when you don't have the cash to pay for it outright. As you may recall from an earlier discussion, leveraging is defined as borrowing to invest.

If you take 25 years to pay off your mortgage and the interest rate is 6.5%, you will pay as much again in interest as the amount you borrowed. So, if the mortgage was $200,000, then you will have paid the lender a total of $400,000 when the last payment is made.

When interest rates are higher, you pay more in total amount interest. For example, when rates were 11.6% in the 1970s, home buyers paid twice the amount of the loan in interest. In that case, if a mortgage was $200,000, the total paid to the lender over those 25 years was $600,000.

Clearly, anything that reduces the interest you pay is a good idea. To understand the rationale for such strategies, you need to first understand some basic mortgage terminology and how mortgages are structured.

Mortgage terminology

A *mortgage* is a loan for the purchase of real estate, with the property itself as the security. *Foreclosure* is the process of repossessing that security in the event of default (nonpayment) on the monthly mortgage payments. The *homeowner's equity* refers to the amount of the property that the borrower actually owns; it is the market value of the property minus the outstanding mortgage.

The *amortization period* of any loan, including a mortgage, is the length of time it takes until the loan is fully paid off. A unique characteristic of mortgages is that they are amortized for a significantly longer period of time than other loans—average length being 25 years.

A mortgage also has a *term,* which is shorter than the amortization period. Term is the length of time within the total amortization period for which there is an agreement at a specific interest rate. The term will normally be somewhere between one and five years, although some are as short as six months and you may see mortgage terms of seven or even ten years. At the end of the term, the lender offers you a chance to renew at whatever interest rate is then appropriate to market conditions. Also at the end of the term, you have the option to pay down the principal without any penalty.

Mortgages may be classed as either *open* or *closed.* This determines whether you can pay down the principal at times other than the end of the term without penalty. As you might guess from the name, an open mortgage gives you greater privileges for prepaying the principal. We'll discuss later why prepayment is significant in the big picture.

When applying for a mortgage, you might be asked if you're looking for a fixed or variable rate. A *fixed rate mortgage,* which is the most common, establishes the interest rate at the beginning of the term. That rate is fixed until the end of the term, then a new rate is agreed to for the next term, depending on market conditions. Your monthly payments are the same throughout the term, but may be different in the next term if interest rates have gone up or down.

A *variable rate mortgage* typically has a fixed monthly payment; however, unlike a fixed-rate mortgage, the interest rate varies as interest rates fluctuate in market. In other words, the interest rate is not locked in during the term. If interest rates go up, more of your monthly payment is used to pay off the mortgage interest. If the rate goes down, less is needed to cover the interest and therefore more can be applied to paying down the principal. Variable rate mortgages have evolved over the years and some are now structured so payments change when the interest rate does, rather than remaining the same each month. The disadvantage of a changing monthly payment is that it creates uncertainty and makes budgeting more difficult.

Mortgage structure

Here's the example we'll use to explore various aspects of mortgages, with a view to understanding how you can save on the amount of interest paid.

Amount borrowed:	$258,670
Amortization period:	25 years
Term:	5 years
Interest rate:	5.2%
Monthly payments:	$1534

Mortgages are structured with *equal blended payments.* "Equal" means that the monthly amount you pay is the same throughout the term of the mortgage. "Blended" means that each month your payment covers a combination of both principal and interest. The proportion of principal and interest varies: in early years, most of each payment goes to interest; in later years, most is applied to the principal.

In our example, $18,408 is paid each year to the mortgage lender ($1534/ month × 12 months). The monthly amounts of $1534 are used to pay the monthly interest charge and then pay back some of the principal that had been borrowed. The proportion going to interest and principal changes, while your payment is the same each month. Usually, we aren't particularly aware of the breakdown, although it is possible to find out what it is. By putting our example into an online payment schedule calculator,[11] I got the following information.

Mortgage: Equal Blended Payments in First Year

Month	Monthly payment	Amount to interest	Amount to principal
1	$1,534	$1,109	$425
2	$1,534	$1,107	$427
3	$1,534	$1,105	$429
4	$1,534	$1,103	$431
5	$1,534	$1,102	$432
6	$1,534	$1,100	$434
7	$1,534	$1,098	$436
8	$1,534	$1,096	$438
9	$1,534	$1,094	$440
10	$1,534	$1,092	$442
11	$1,534	$1,090	$444
12	$1,534	$1,088	$446
Totals for first year	**$18,408** total paid	**$13,184** to interest	**$5,224** to principal

By looking at the totals in the interest and principal columns for the first 12 months, we see that $13,184 went to interest and $5,224 was paid down on the principal in the first year.

A visual representation sometimes makes this easier to understand, so I have put the information into the following graph. Look at the horizontal axis to see how the money was distributed in the first year—$13,184 to interest and $5,224 on the principal. As you move up the vertical axis to later years, you'll notice that a bit less of the payment is taken by interest and a bit more goes to pay down the principal. In the last year, only $504 goes to interest, and the remaining $17,904 pays off the entire balance of the loan. The mortgage has been paid off or "retired."

Mortgage: Equal Blended Payments
Full Amortization

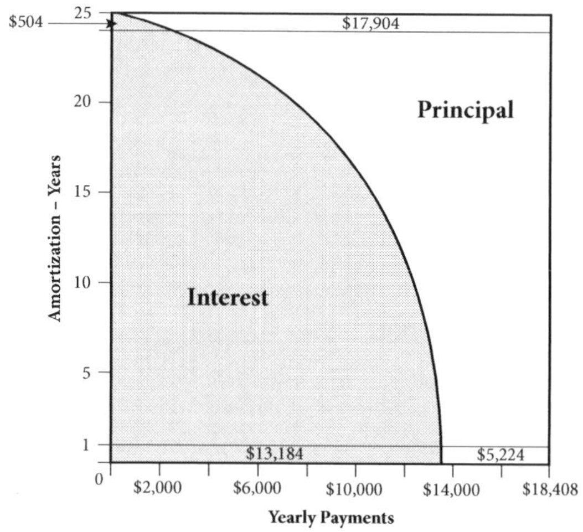

When you have a mortgage, the lender sends a statement at the end of each year to show where things stand with your loan. In our example, the first statement would say:

Principal borrowed	$258,670
Amount repaid	5,224
Loan outstanding	$253,446

As you can see, the principal did not go down very much, even though over $18,000 was paid to the lender. As the graph of the first year shows, almost three-quarters of that money went to interest. That's why it's to your advantage to use interest-reducing strategies when you have a mortgage.

Not everyone takes 25 years to pay off a mortgage

If you want to be inspired by someone who took the fast track to paying off a mortgage, search online for the article "How we paid off our house in three years."[12] Author Perry Goertzen describes the circumstances that brought him to his early thirties with $37,000 in debt, a rusty old car, few possessions, and no house. By then, he had a master's degree and a plan that changed everything. He and his wife decided to continue to live like poor students, work as much as they could, and buy a house.

> In June of 2002, we purchased our first home in a new subdivision in Milton [Ontario] for $302,000, and took on a five-year, 5.2 per cent fixed-rate mortgage for $220,000. At first, we intended to pay it off in 10 or 15 years. But then I looked at what would happen if I doubled up the payments and paid an extra 10 per cent a year. It was incredibly motivating to see how much interest you could save. So we doubled up every bi-weekly payment, from $670 to $1,340. We also made the annual 10 per cent prepayment, which was about $22,000 a year.
>
> At the end of the first year, we realized that we were saving much more than we needed, even with the doubled payments and annual prepayment, so I approached the bank and asked them if we could make an annual prepayment of 20 per cent instead. It took a little bit of coaxing and a few Tim Hortons coffees, but banks can be more flexible than you might think: don't assume the terms of your mortgage can't be changed.
>
> At that rate of payment, we managed to pay off the whole thing in exactly 952 days. By paying off the mortgage in less than three years instead of 25, we saved a total of $153,000 in interest charges, which amounts to more than half the original cost of the house. Meanwhile, the house had already increased in value to about $420,000.[13]

Key strategies to reduce the mortgage interest you pay

1. **Shorten the amortization period.** When you reduce the length of time for which you borrow money, you also reduce the total amount of interest you pay. However, this strategy will increase your monthly payments by a small amount. Play with the options, using an online calculator,[14] to find out what will work for you.

2. **Prepay the principal.** *Prepayment* means paying extra money, beyond your regular monthly payments, that goes directly to reducing the principal. Because mortgages are structured so most of your early payments go toward interest, it takes a long time to pay off the principal if you just follow the regular payment schedule. By prepaying on your mortgage, you can pay off your mortgage sooner than scheduled, while saving tens of thousands of dollars in interest. In our example of a $258,670 mortgage, prepaying $2000 a year means the mortgage will be paid off in 20 years instead of 25, and you will reduce the interest paid by $42,000. When you get a mortgage, be sure to verify that it has prepayment privileges.

3. **Pay weekly or biweekly.** Your lender may refer to this as making *accelerated payments.* If you pay every two weeks rather than once a month, you actually end up making extra payments. This extra money pays down the principal in the same way that a prepayment does. The reason you pay extra is that there are 26 two-week periods in a year, but the amount of your payment is calculated as if there were 24. Essentially, you pay 2 extra two-week periods, and this extra money goes toward the principal. In the example we've been using, making biweekly payments will get the mortgage paid off in 21 years and will save you $33,500 in interest. Think what would happen if you paid your mortgage biweekly *and* also did a prepayment each year—perhaps using the money from your income tax refund.

4. **Increase your monthly payment.** This is yet another means of applying

extra money to paying down the principal. You would, of course, need to confirm that your mortgage allows you to increase your monthly payments. Lenders vary in the options they offer and the terminology they use. Some may refer to this as the *double-up feature.*

5. **Shop for the best interest rate.** Because a mortgage is a lot of money borrowed for a long time, the effect of different rates is dramatic. Even half a percent in interest means a difference of about $22,000 in what you pay over the life of the mortgage in my example. That's enough to make it worth the time and effort of shopping around.

6. **Make the largest down payment possible.** The availability of an extra amount of $25,000 or $100,000 might sound far-fetched, but could certainly be the result of an inheritance, for example. Using it to increase your down payment and thus reduce the amount you need to borrow would be a means of investing the money for your long-term benefit.

Crunching numbers

All of this money-math may seem intimidating. However, crunching mortgage numbers is not as daunting as it first appears. And it is invaluable in helping you understand and explore your options. This comment came from one of my daughters-in-law:

> For me, using an online calculator was step one in learning about mortgages as related to buying my first place—taking theoretical numbers, crunching them, and then beginning to understand how down-payment dollars and amortization affected my payments. That is how I learned about mortgages initially. I find I still go to the mortgage calculators to figure out what we can afford for our "forever house" in the coming years. I would encourage people to "play with the numbers" to see what a difference time/payment schedule/down payment can make in their life and bottom line.

The figures in this section were generated by the Canadian mortgage payment calculator at canequity.com. I looked at several and chose this one because it allowed for flexibility in creating various scenarios, and it produced full repayment schedules that could be printed out for reference.

I have intentionally kept the figures to a minimum in this section to focus on my main point: *Mortgages are set up so that you pay mostly interest in the early years. You can substantially reduce the amount of interest you pay by using strategies to pay off your mortgage faster.* For more detailed explanations and tables supporting this point of view, refer to the resources section of my blogsite at www.TheUncommonGuides.com.

Is buying a house realistic?

Even if you use the recommended strategies to keep total interest as low as possible, there is no question that a house is an expensive purchase. It's easy to pay more than you can really afford because there are few "starter homes" on the market these days. Starter homes are smaller houses with modest finishing materials and lower price tags that used to make home ownership affordable for people starting out. Nowadays, new houses are large and filled with pricey finishing materials, such as granite countertops and wood flooring, which make them expensive to buy. Older homes have become expensive because they are located close to downtown, which increases land prices. For a while, condominiums filled the price gap. However, even they are being enlarged and upscaled, so they are no longer as affordable as they once were.

Why does it matter? If you don't keep your housing expenses reasonable, you will become *house poor.* Gail Vaz-Oxlade identifies the financial implications of being house poor:

> Folks find themselves struggling to make ends meet and keep their dream roofs over their heads. Their best intentions end up with the worst consequences. And all because they failed to add up the real costs of buying their

> home. While a mortgage is "good" debt—you're building assets, after all—too much mortgage is a fast route to bad debt. Why? Well, when it takes too much of your money to keep that "good" debt in good standing, you're more likely to turn to your credit cards and lines of credit just to make ends meet—never mind have some fun. The result: oodles of debt racked up, or a life given over to sitting in a home and staring at the bare walls.[15]

The idea that we should all aspire to a "dream home" is embedded in the cultural meta-narrative—that over-arching story that usually goes unquestioned. A conscious spender would not blindly accept it as a given. The conscious approach is to think about what is important to you in a house—and what you are willing to give up to get it. Vacations? Post-secondary education for your children? Financial freedom? Peace of mind? Examining the concept of a dream home can be a good focal point for thinking about what is essential to you, and why. It is particularly valuable for couples to have this conversation, since they frequently come together with different backgrounds and expectations.

What can be done to make your housing purchase manageable and avoid becoming house poor? Start by looking at your expectations. Until now, young people have expected that their first home would match the standard of the home where they grew up. It was a reasonable expectation until recently. The economic realities of this time no longer make that possible. Today's young adults are the first generation that will find its housing standard *below* that of its parents. This may not seem fair, but it is the reality.

Changed expectations may relate to the size of the house, whether it's single and detached, and how many people live in it. A large, detached house with one or two occupants in an expensive suburb is now a luxury. A more affordable option is a small condominium in a modest neighbourhood. To further reduce your costs, you could consider taking a roommate or two, as my student did. Their rent money will help pay your mortgage. Or, for your first house, you might buy one with a basement suite so you can live on one level and have a renter on the other. You can charge more for a main-floor suite than one in a basement, so you may decide to live in the lower suite to generate the most income to apply toward the mortgage. Note that there are regulations prohibiting suites in some areas. If you buy a house without a suite and plan to turn the basement into one, be sure to check that this is allowed, before you make the purchase.

Another sound strategy is to acquire the largest down payment you can. The more you put down, the less you need to borrow and the lower your payments will be. Often older family members, appreciating the challenges of starting out today, are willing to lend you some money, perhaps even at a favourable interest rate. A strong note of caution, though: Be absolutely scrupulous with the initial arrangements and the repayments when dealing with family and friends. It's tempting to delay or skip payments on the assumption that they'll cut you some slack. Don't. These are people who will be in your life for a long time, and it's not worth jeopardizing your relationship with them.

Think-abouts

Many people take no care of their money until they come nearly to the end of it, and others do just the same with their time.
~Goethe

If money was my only motivation, I would organize myself differently.
~Placido Domingo
Spanish tenor and conductor

In the end, how we value money says something about how we value ourselves, our labor, our time.
~Fred Brock

Investing Your Money

Your money can grow in many ways—when you put it into a savings account or certificate in a bank, when you buy a house and get the mortgage paid off, and when you invest it in the stock market. Technically, a savings account, investment certificate, and house are investments because you expect to get a financial return when you put your money there. However, when people speak about their investments, they are usually referring to mutual funds and the stock market. Mutual funds bear a relationship to the stock market but are more accessible to novice and small investors, so we'll start there.

Mutual funds are accessible to small investors...

Mutual funds are sold through many financial institutions, including your bank, and can be purchased with relatively small sums of money. Both of these factors make mutual funds readily accessible.

A mutual fund has a manager and team of financial professionals who build and maintain a group of shares and/or bonds that are purchased with a pool of money from small investors. No investor owns a particular share; each owns a small portion of all of them. A mutual fund is like a cake: it's made up of separate ingredients, and each slice contains a bit of all of them combined into something with its own unique character.

A significant benefit of mutual funds is that diversity is built into the system. Why does that matter? Think about it this way: If you have all your money in shares of one kind, such as the energy sector, and the price of oil takes a nosedive, the value of your investment will do the same. If it's the only investment you have, this would result in financial disaster.

Diversification of your holdings means dividing your money between shares in several sectors of the market. By doing this, you are better able to preserve your capital, that is, not lose the amount you originally invested. In a diversified stock portfolio, you might have some of your money invested in financial institutions such as banks, some in oil, some in transportation, and some in agriculture. Although shares go up and down over time, it is unlikely that several industries will experience a drop at the same time. The theory is that diversification helps you maintain the overall value of your portfolio: if one type of stock goes down, hopefully another one of your stocks goes up to offset the loss.

Diversification is a challenge for small investors who do not have enough money to invest in several different companies at the same time. There is actually no minimum investment required, but it wouldn't make sense to buy only $100 or even $500 worth of shares. There is a commission, also referred to as the brokerage fee, that must be paid when you buy and again when you sell your shares in any company. People who engage in frequent buying and selling get reduced transaction fees, but a small investor does not. Even with an online account, which has the lowest fees because of the minimal advisory services offered to investors, the fee is typically around $20 at each end of the process. That means $40 in expenses must come out of your earnings before you make any profit. It is unlikely that a $500 investment in stocks would make enough profit to cover commissions and leave you some profit. This is why you need to have thousands of dollars in order to be able to diversify in the market. Mutual funds address the challenge of diversification for small investors by using their pooled money to buy a diversified portfolio of stocks and/or bonds.

Considerations when buying mutual funds

When buying mutual funds, you have the choice of three general types—debt funds, equity funds, and balanced funds. These designations are based on the types of investments that have been purchased by the fund managers. As you may recall, investments in general can be categorized as debt investments (in which you are lending money—bonds and GICs, for example) and equity investments (in which you become an owner—stocks, for example).

Debt funds are generally recommended for older investors because these funds are not subject to the ups and downs of the market. Practically speaking, a person nearing retirement needs to know that the money will be there when it is required. If the retirement fund is in equities and the market goes down, there may suddenly be much less money for retirement. This happened to many people during the financial collapse of 2008.

Equity funds are usually more suitable for young people, who can weather those ups and downs because they have more time to keep the money in the investment. In the last 10 years before retirement, equity funds should be monitored and switched into debt funds when the value is up. This will lock in the profits that were made by the equity fund. The long-term return of equity funds tends to be higher than debt funds, although this generalization does not apply in all cases.

Balanced funds have some of each. These were developed to combine the strengths of both—the stability of debt investments and the higher return of equity investments. However, as with any investment, profitability is not guaranteed. It depends on the individual fund and how it is managed.

When making a decision about which fund to buy, it's prudent to compare past records to see how they've done over time. You can consult any number of books and charts, or you can do an online search of Globefund or Morningstar to generate a list of high income earners over a five-year period. This can be a useful strategy for narrowing down your choices.

In addition to determining which type of fund suits you best and generating a list of funds with good past performance records, you need information about the fee structure of the mutual funds under consideration. There is both a one-time purchase fee and an ongoing management fee. The purchase fee is referred to as the *load*. A no-load fund is one with no purchase fee; this is typical of mutual funds bought at your bank. Funds with fees can either be front-end or back-end loaded. With a front-end load you pay the fee up front, at the time of purchase. Back-end loading means you pay the fee when you sell your fund units. These are commission fees, and tend to range from 5% to 9%. On a $1000 investment, you would pay $50 to $90 in fees. Fees can seriously cut into the profit you realize from your investment, so it is worth finding out what they are before you decide to buy.

The second fee associated with mutual funds is the *management expense ratio* (MER). This reflects the cost of managing and administering the fund and is expressed as a percentage, usually between 0.2% and 2%.When you are evaluating the historical earnings of a fund, it's important to know whether earnings have been reported before or after subtracting the MER. A return of 7% looks attractive; but if the MER was 2% and has not been taken into account, the real return of that investment would be only 5%.

The funds with the lowest MER are *index funds*, which have low management costs due to their unique structure. Index funds consist of the same stocks that make up a particular market index, such as the TSX or the Dow Jones Industrial Average. Because this predetermines the composition of the fund, the need for management decisions is reduced, which keeps the management expense ratio low. As for performance, an index fund goes up and down in tandem with the particular market on which it is based. *Exchange-traded funds* (ETFs) are another variation of this concept.

When making your purchase arrangements, you might want to think about incorporating *dollar cost averaging* into your strategy. Dollar cost averaging is a means of countering the problem of market timing. What's that? Well, as you know, the stock market goes up and down. Ideally, you want to buy mutual fund units and stocks at their lowest price. Of course, when they are at their lowest price is impossible to know until after the fact. You might never buy any shares at all because you can't be sure when they are at their lowest price.

Dollar cost averaging is based on a different philosophy. Instead of making a lump sum investment at the perfect time, you invest the same specified dollar amount on a regular basis, usually monthly. When the unit price of your mutual fund is high, you buy fewer units with that fixed amount of money. When the price is low, your fixed amount of money buys more units. Over time, it averages out—hence the name, dollar cost averaging. To make sure the purchase is made monthly, set it up as an automatic withdrawal from your bank account.

To summarize, mutual funds were developed to meet the needs of small and novice investors. Remember, though, they are not risk free. Different types of funds suit people at different stages of life. Some funds are better-managed and perform better than others. Returns will vary, especially when you consider the fees you are required to pay, so comparison shopping is necessary.

What about the stock market?

At some point, you might want to invest in the stock market directly, rather than via mutual funds. If stock market investing is part of your family culture, then you will have access to a range of resources and expertise. If not, begin by reading some of the many books available. For beginning investors, a good place to start is *The Motley Fool Investment Guide for Teens: 8 Steps to Having More Money Than Your Parents Ever Dreamed Of*. Even if you are no longer a teenager, it's worth reading.

You might also find it helpful to consult daily or weekly financial papers and magazines, such as *Businessweek*, the *Financial Post*, *The Globe and Mail*, and *The Wall Street Journal*. These are available online and in libraries, so you don't have to take expensive subscriptions when starting out.

The first thing to learn is the language. This will make it easier to follow what you're reading and allow you to formulate intelligent questions. Look for people with whom you can have relevant discussions, as this will help you clarify your understanding of what you've read and see how it might apply in your life.

A basic understanding

The *stock market* is a particular market where shares are bought and sold. A *stock exchange* does not itself own any shares; you might think of it as a flea market for stocks, except that the individual owners do not show up to sell their wares. In order to buy or sell your shares in the stock market, you must go through a *brokerage firm*. You can have an online account or one at a full-service brokerage house where you meet with a stockbroker in person.

Online accounts are not difficult to get or to use. The disadvantage is that you have no one to talk to or to guide you. Buying and selling happen with just a few mouse clicks, so a beginner could make serious mistakes. According to Jason Anthony, author of *Financially Fearless by 40*, there are two very serious pitfalls of online trading. One is investing too much before you are experienced. He recommends no more than $3000 to start. The other is *buying on margin*, which allows almost anyone to borrow cash to get started in the stock market. He advises, "It's a bad idea and you shouldn't do it."[1] He describes the risk:

> When you open an account … you will be asked if you want to "margin-enable" your account. Margin trading allows you to borrow a percentage of the amount of your original investment (up to 50 percent), so you can invest more than you have. So if you have $10,000 to invest you could buy up to $15,000 in stocks. Of course, you don't actually own the entire $15,000 investment. You only have $10,000. The $5,000 must be repaid. You are wagering that your stock will rise so you can cover the $5000 and pocket the difference.… If a stock bought on margin falls too low, the lender has the right to make a margin call. This means you must come up with the cash to cover the loan.… Margin trading violates one of the most sacred tenets of investing: Don't invest more than you are prepared to lose.[2]

The major Canadian stock exchange is the TSX Group, of which the Toronto Stock Exchange (TSE) is the original member. There used to be exchanges in Vancouver, Calgary, and Winnipeg; all are now amalgamated into the TSX Group. The U.S. exchanges you most frequently hear of are the New York Stock Exchange (NYSE)—which recently integrated the American Stock Exchange—and the NASDAQ. The top three exchanges in the world, according to World-Stock-Exchanges.net are the NYSE, Tokyo Stock Exchange, and the London

Stock Exchange.

The terms *stocks* and *shares* are used interchangeably; they are the units of ownership that we buy in a company. The value of these units fluctuates depending on a variety of factors, including consumer confidence, corporate management, and world events. A striking example of the latter, illustrated in the following graph, is the plunge that the stock market took just after September 11, 2001, following the attack on the twin towers of the World Trade Center in New York City. That shocking event caused people to pause and rethink, resulting in a dramatic drop in the market, as shown at the far right of the following graph.

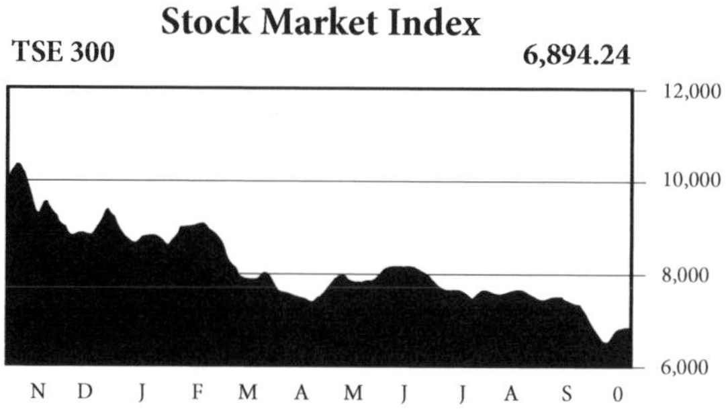

Close on Friday, October 5, 2001

There are other examples of the effect of world events on the stock market. In 1973–74, conflict in the Middle East caused an oil shortage in North America. As a result, oil prices shot up, as prices do in times of short supply. We have also seen gold prices go up when there is increased unrest in the world. Many investors perceive gold to be more tangible and useable than stocks in the event that economic and political systems were to collapse. This increases demand, which pushes the price of gold higher.

The ups and downs of the market are measured by indices. A *stock market index* is a measuring tool that tracks the value of a representative group of shares on a particular stock exchange. It is reported in "points," as in "The S&P/TSX has dropped 18 points today."

The S&P/TSX Composite Index is the general index for the Canadian stock market. When reading older Canadian investment books, you will find reference to the TSE 300 or the TSX, which were the previous indices of the Toronto Stock Exchange.

The Dow Jones Industrial Average (DJIA), Standard & Poors 100 (S&P 100), and NASDAQ-100 are the most commonly quoted U.S. indices. In each case, the index is made up of a specific range of shares. For example, the S&P 100 consists of 100 major, blue chip companies across multiple industry groups.[3]

The change in value of an index from day to day is related only to itself; it is not a means of comparing one index to another. The previous graph of the TSE 300 shows that it stood at more than 10,000 points in October 2000 and dropped to less than 7,000 points a year later. On any particular day, the other exchanges would have been reporting different numbers. For example, on the day I wrote this, *The Globe and Mail* reported that the S&P/TSX was at 12,354, whereas the Dow was at 13,056. S&P 500 was at 1393, and the NASDAQ was at 3064.

The fact they are all radically different is not significant. The difference occurs because they use different measuring scales. You could compare it to measuring the distance you travel in your car. You might drive for an hour on the highway at a fixed speed and cover 100 kilometres or 62 miles. The numbers are different but the distance is the same.

That being said, there may be parallels between the movements of various indices. The following illustration repeats the previous TSE graph and shows the Dow Jones index from the New York Stock Exchange for the same time period. Note that the numbers along the side are different, but the pattern of significant drops is generally similar.

Similar Effect on Two Indices

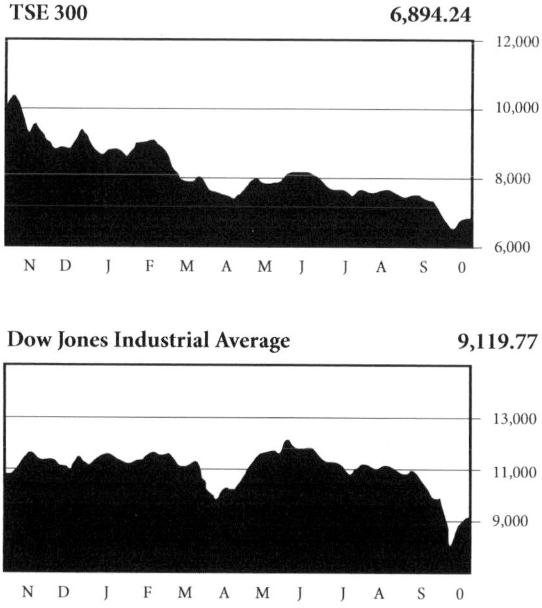

Close on Friday, October 5, 2001

When you hear people talking about a *bull market*, or saying that the market is bullish, they are referring to the market when it is on an upward trend. A *bear market* is the opposite—a market that is trending down. If you have trouble remembering which is which, think about a bull charging the matador in a bull-fight, and a bear retreating to its cave to hibernate.

Thinking about investing in the market?

Stocks are divided into three general types depending on certain characteristics that have implications for their level of risk as an investment. From low to high risk, they are blue chip, growth, and speculative shares. *Blue chips* are stocks in solid, established companies that have a proven track record and can generally be counted on to yield good returns. These shares often pay dividends. *Growth stocks* are those in newer companies that are in the development stage, doing well, and putting profits back into the company rather than paying dividends to shareholders. Their profitability to the investor comes through the capital gains resulting from their growth. *Speculative shares* are risky. That's what the word "speculation" means: maybe they will take off, or maybe they won't. Gold mining is a classic example, but there have been many other, long-forgotten ones along the way.

When you invest, you'll want to think about strategies to minimize your risk. The first risk management strategy is to become knowledgeable, so you can make informed decisions. The second is to diversify your investments—between debt and equity, and between different industries. There is much written about these various aspects of diversification, usually under the heading of asset allocation. *Asset allocation* is a strategy to balance your risk and reward when investing. Taking into account your risk tolerance, financial goals, and age, it apportions your investments appropriately over the three asset classes (debt, equity, and cash) to achieve that balance.

The third thing to think about before investing is an *exit strategy*. In other words, once you are in, when will you sell those shares? Will you hold them no matter how low they go? This is referred to as the buy-and-hold method. It is based on the philosophy that the market goes up and down over the long term, so if you wait long enough, your shares will eventually be worth more than what they cost you, even if they went down for a while. A very different exit strategy is to know at what point you will cut your losses and move on. In this case, you pick a percentage drop—say 25% below its highest price—and sell if your shares drop below that. People in favour of using this exit strategy believe it is the best way to avoid the pitfalls of what is commonly referred to as investor psychology.

Investor psychology

Investor psychology is a frame of mind that causes people to make counterproductive investment decisions. The intention for investing is to buy stocks at a low price and sell them for more in order to make a profit. An understanding of investor psychology helps you see why it is not uncommon for people to do the reverse—buying shares at a high price and selling them at a lower one. Buying high and selling low won't earn you capital gains. In fact, you will accrue a capital loss. It makes no financial sense, so how does it happen?

It is a question of poor timing, and it often has to do with following the crowd. An investor may not think of buying a particular stock or commodity until it has started a run up and is making news headlines. Typically, experts predict it will go higher yet. Convinced, the investor buys, even though the price is already quite high.

The price may go up some more but then heads down. Certain that this is a simple case of market fluctuation, the investor holds on; after all, the experts are predicting a significant increase. Even when it's clear the stock is on a firm downtrend, investor psychology keeps the buyer hoping it will turn around. This hope becomes ever-stronger, as the stock approaches the price for which it was purchased. The buyer holds onto the hope and the stock, as the price continues its downward slide. Eventually, the buyer admits it isn't going back up and sells at a loss. Visually, the process looks like the following graph:

The Effect of Investor Psychology

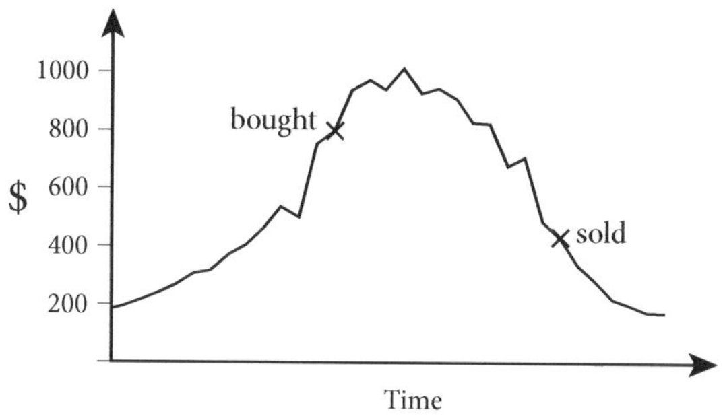

The graph shows that each share was bought at $820 and sold at $400. Profit (or loss, if it is a negative amount) is calculated by subtracting the purchase price from the selling price. In this example, the result is a loss of $420 per share:.

amount for which it was sold-		*purchase price*	=	*profit or loss*
$400	-	$820	=	– $420

In retrospect, it seems obvious that buying at such a high price was a bad idea; however, in the midst of it all, nobody knows what will happen. The stock *could* have gone way up, even though that didn't actually happen. We just can't know.

This is what happened with gold in 1979–80. The price spiked and went back down in a short period of time. There were people who made a lot of money from gold in 1980—buying when it was just starting its run up, and selling very near the peak. No doubt some will do so again in the current explosion of gold prices. Some people have a sixth sense when it comes to the market, and they don't get tripped up by investor psychology. For the rest of us, dollar cost averaging and a firm exit strategy help prevent large losses due to investor psychology.

Think-abouts

You get recessions, you have stock market declines. If you don't understand that's going to happen, then you're not ready, you won't do well in the markets.
~Peter Lynch

Investing should be more like watching paint dry or watching grass grow. If you want excitement, take $800 and go to Las Vegas. ~Paul Samuelson
economist

The four most dangerous words in investing are: "This time it's different."
~Sir John Templeton
investor and philanthropist

Big-Picture Planning

So far, we've been talking about managing yourself and your finances to accumulate funds so you can live the life you want. However, there is a bigger picture. Life is not certain, and none of us can predict how long ours will continue. Therefore, responsible financial planning also takes that fact into account.

Looking at your financial affairs with a view to the big picture is referred to as *estate planning*. Your estate is the property and money you leave behind, including personal belongings (clothes, jewellery, furnishings, car) as well as your house, bank accounts, and investments. Estate planning challenges you to think ahead to when you're gone, arranging things to minimize difficulties for your survivors. Estate planning typically involves life insurance, your will, living will, power of attorney, and sometimes income tax, depending on the size and complexity of your estate.

Life insurance...

Life insurance is an important aspect of big-picture planning, especially when you have people depending on your income for their well-being. You might be supporting aging parents or a disabled sibling, but for most people, their dependents are their children.

You need the most life insurance when your last child is born. This is when you have the greatest number of dependents, and they will need financial support for the longest period of time. In contrast, by the time your children have left home and you've paid off the house, you may actually need very little life insurance.

The purpose of insuring your life, after all, is to replace your income so that your family has continued financial support when you aren't there to provide it. For most families, the absence of one income would make life very difficult. It could mean the surviving spouse has to sell the family home and move the children to smaller, unfamiliar surroundings in order to make ends meet. It could mean a stay-at-home parent suddenly has to find work and put the children in daycare. This is stressful and disruptive to your survivors. Making sure there is enough insurance to cover living costs is the kind and responsible thing to do.

Life insurance fills the income gap by replacing missing income. It takes a sizeable policy to do that. Yet the unfortunate truth is that many people are greatly underinsured, for one of two reasons: Either they have no idea how much life insurance they reasonably need, or they know how much they should have but were talked into purchasing the wrong type of insurance—one that is so expensive they cannot afford the amount they need.

How much life insurance?

How much life insurance do you need? It helps to think in terms of the following four areas, estimating your needs for each and then totalling them. The result is the amount of the policy that you need.

1. **Immediate cash** needs should be covered, so your family will not have to take out a loan (and pay interest) to cover immediate personal costs, such as your funeral, income taxes, and fees associated with processing your will.

2. **Loan repayment** ensures that large debts are paid off, so they do not drain the family's resources. Your mortgage is the largest and most obvious one. Arrange for enough insurance to pay off the outstanding mortgage; this will permit your family to continue living in the house without having to make monthly mortgage payments. The same is true for other secured loans, such as the family car, recreational vehicle, or cottage. If your family is unable to make payments on these items, the lender will repossess them. Your life insurance should also cover your outstanding credit card balances and lines of credit, as outstanding unsecured debts such as these must be repaid from the estate and will reduce the amount of money left for your family.

3. **Replacement income** is intended to provide ongoing support for dependents until they leave home. Therefore, the younger your children are, the more money you will need in this category. Calculate this amount by counting the number of years until your last child reaches independence and multiply that by a yearly amount for support. A common figure for this yearly amount is 70% to 80% of current combined family income, based on the premise that the family will not need the full amount when there is one less person making up the household.

4. **Children's education** can include whatever you want it to. As a general guideline, if you were intending to provide a four-year post-secondary degree, you'd likely need to allow at least $60,000 per child—more if the child will be living away from home. Education costs have been going up recently, so you'd be wise to periodically revisit your calculations.

We buy insurance to reduce our financial risk.

Insurance of all kinds is based on the principle of *spreading the risk.* To do this, the insurance company collects money from a large number of people who wish to protect themselves from financial risk if a particular event occurs. From the pool of money collected each year, the company pays out to those participants who experience the insured event. The yearly rates paid by the participants are determined according to the probability of the insured event occurring.

Car insurance is a familiar example for most of us. We pay for insurance each year and hope that we never have an accident. But if we do, we're grateful the costs of repairing both vehicular damage and personal injury are covered by our insurance; these could range from a few thousand dollars to a million or more, if there is a liability lawsuit. By paying a relatively small amount that is predetermined each year, we do not have to cover catastrophic costs.

If you have a poor driving record (such as several accidents and a conviction for dangerous driving) your insurance rate will be higher than someone with a clear record because you present a much greater risk of having an accident. Since there is a strong chance that a large sum of the money pool will have to be spent due to your actions, you are required to put in more to compensate. In other words, your insurance rate will be higher than average.

When it comes to life insurance, our activities and choices—smoking, engaging in risky hobbies such as parasailing, or working in an occupation such as law enforcement, for example—also affect risk and therefore our life insurance rates. The other factor, which affects us all, is how old we are. Statistically, our chances of dying are greater as we age, so life insurance costs more as we get older. The good news is that we need the most when we have a young family, and that's when our rates are lower—*if* we buy the right type of insurance.

Unfortunately, many people are convinced by life insurance sellers to buy very expensive insurance that does not adequately cover their needs. The following is an overview intended to help you avoid a costly mistake. It is based on the premise that term insurance is the best choice for most people.

If you'd like an audio-visual explanation, I suggest Suze Orman on YouTube. She's a well-known and outspoken U.S. financial expert who has dedicated her career to helping people get on track with their finances. She calls it as she sees it, and she has a strong knowledge base to back up her position. Among other things, she is licensed to sell life insurance in all of the continental United States. Suze Orman is a strong proponent of term insurance. To hear what she has to say, check out her YouTube segments on life insurance.[1]

A few life insurance basics

To intelligently interpret what you read and hear about life insurance, you need to understand some basic terminology and principles. Life insurance can be divided into two fundamental types: term and cash value (also called whole life, universal, or permanent) insurance. *Term insurance* provides protection against the insured event (your death) and is as straightforward as car insurance. *Cash value insurance,* on the other hand, has a "savings" component in addition to protection against your death. This additional component is referred to as the *cash surrender value.*

Face value is the amount of money that will be paid to the beneficiaries when the insured person dies. A *beneficiary* is someone who receives all or part of the face value of the policy. The *premium* is the amount paid regularly, either yearly or monthly, to keep the policy in effect.

You can check and compare premiums online before deciding on an insurance company. My research was done on www.life-insurance-quotes.ca.[2] I looked at several sites and found this one the best for information-gathering. I discovered that most online calculators are being used as sales prospecting tools and required me to give my name and telephone number before I could access the information. This one did not, so you can use it to research your own life insurance costs without receiving sales calls afterward.

Things to know about cash value insurance

1. Cash value insurance is much more expensive than a term policy because you pay extra for the cash surrender value. I did an online comparison of premiums, based on a face value of $450,000 for a male, age 30, non-smoker, and in excellent health. A cash value policy cost $3072 per year, whereas a term policy with the same company was only $333. The cash value policy was nine times as much, making it unaffordable for many young families; yet that is when they need the largest amount of life insurance.
2. When the holder of a cash value policy dies, the beneficiary gets only the face value of the life insurance. Although your insurance agent may speak about the death benefit and savings, they are mutually exclusive. You get one or the other, but not both. Here's how it is explained on one industry website:

> Cash value is what the policy is actually worth to the policy holder at any given time.... When the insured person dies, the cash value of

a life insurance policy ceases to exist.... The reason that cash value disappears when the insured dies is that you may receive either a death benefit or a cash value from a whole or universal life policy, but not both.[3]

3. If you have a cash value policy, you may borrow from that cash value. You will be required to pay interest, as you would with any other loan. If you take a loan against your cash value and die before it is repaid, the outstanding balance is deducted from the face value of your insurance policy before the beneficiaries are paid. Suppose the loan was for $10,000 and face value of the policy was $450,000. If the full loan was still outstanding, the beneficiaries would receive $440,000.
4. If you decide to remove the cash value from your policy instead of just borrowing it, your policy is cancelled. You have the cash value but are no longer insured.

Why term insurance is a better choice

1. Term insurance is more straightforward. You pay only for insurance and are not adding a layer of investment, so your yearly insurance cost for a term policy is much lower.

2. Buying term insurance makes it possible to afford the full face value that you need. Suppose you looked at your budget and found that you could afford only $333 a year for life insurance. If you buy term, you will get a face value of $450,000 with that amount of money. If you were to choose a cash value policy instead, your $333 a year would buy only $50,000 of face value. If you needed $450,000 of insurance, you would be grossly underinsured with the cash value policy.

3. If your budget is not so tight and you have $3072 to spend each year, it

makes more sense to *buy term insurance and invest the extra money yourself.* It's a much better option than putting your money into a cash value policy, which is structured to provide *either* the face value *or* the cash value, but not both. With term insurance, your beneficiaries will get *both* the face value *and* whatever you have put into your own investments. Furthermore, you will most likely get better returns on investments that you make for yourself.

Buy renewable term

When buying term insurance, be sure it is *renewable term.* If your policy is renewable, it means the company agrees to renew your insurance without requiring a medical. This is important because as you age, your health may deteriorate. If you have a non-renewable policy and don't pass the medical exam, the company may refuse to insure you for a new term. A renewable policy will cost a bit more than one you can't renew, but this is one place you do not want to save money. *Always* buy the renewable one.

Don't argue with the seller

I've always thought it odd that we would give our insurance company extra money to invest for us. If your car insurance company asked you to do that, you'd wonder what on earth they were thinking. But somehow, we've accepted it as reasonable when buying life insurance. I suspect this is due to a lack of information combined with lots of sales pressure. It's often said that life insurance is sold, not bought. This statement highlights the reality that it's the seller who is in charge in the transaction, not the buyer.

My eyes were opened on this point during the second year I taught consumer economics. I had an evening class in which there were several mature students with full-time day jobs. One worked in general insurance at a company that also had a life insurance division. He told us that one of the life insurance salesmen regularly received monthly commission cheques of $9000. That was an enormous monthly income at the time, and one of the other employees asked him how he did it. He reportedly said, "It's easy. I just don't leave until they sign what I want." What he wanted was for them to buy cash value insurance, which has much higher premiums and paid him that large commission.

The industry has set up the system to suit its revenue-generating needs, and the salesman who wants to earn good income knows what he has to sell. I don't mean to suggest that all insurance sales representatives are deliberately selling products they think are bad for you. In fact, their employers provide them with plenty of training to convince them that the expensive product is also the best for the customer. However, as I've pointed out, cash value insurance is not in your best interests.

Even if you have listened to Suze Orman and taken to heart what I have said, I wouldn't recommend engaging in a debate with an insurance seller. They are highly trained in selling techniques and have access to enough information to confuse and confound all your newly gained perspective. You can be sure they will quickly have you doubting your decision to buy term, and you won't have enough information to develop counter-arguments.

Before making an appointment with a seller, do your homework. First figure out how much life insurance you need.[4] Then decide on the type—term or cash value. Finally, do an online rate comparison to get an idea about what you might expect to pay.[5]

With this information, you are ready to go shopping. And where might that be? Life insurance is sold in four different ways. *Brokers* represent several different companies and will look for what suits you best among the products of those companies. *Agents* are representatives of one particular insurance company and sell their employer's products exclusively. Products of *direct sellers* are sold via telephone from a call centre rather than from a local agent. *Group plans* provide life insurance to members of particular groups—a workplace or university alumni, for example—and you must be a member of that group to participate.

Pick what you think will work best for you, bearing in mind that brokers have access to a wider range of choices. Then prepare yourself to meet or speak with the seller. I have two recommendations—one is about *where* you meet and the other is about your *approach.*

Location: This applies to those instances where there will be a face-to-face meeting. It has been traditional, particularly for company agents, to meet with potential clients in their own homes. They say it's so people can feel comfortable.

I think they have two more-compelling reasons. First, coming into your home gives agents many clues about who you are and what you value. They use this information to tailor their approach and manoeuver you into buying what suits them; that's how insurance is sold, not bought. Second, you have invited them into your home, and it isn't always easy to get them to leave. Think back to the story of the salesman who made huge commissions. Enough said. Given all this, I recommend declining their requests to meet with you at home. Arrange to meet in their office or a coffee shop, where you can leave when you've heard enough.

Approach: As with consumer complaints, negotiating contracts and agreements is most successful when you use an assertive approach. An assertive approach combines confident statements with respectful listening. It is neither passive nor aggressive.

A *passive* approach is one in which you don't take an active role, going along with whatever the seller suggests and not asking questions or otherwise engaging in the process. There is nothing reciprocal in such a meeting. On the other hand, an *aggressive* approach creates an adversarial situation that also interferes with mutual exchange and usually doesn't do you much good. Aggressive and passive approaches are opposite ends of a continuum, both with limited effectiveness.

Taking Another Way

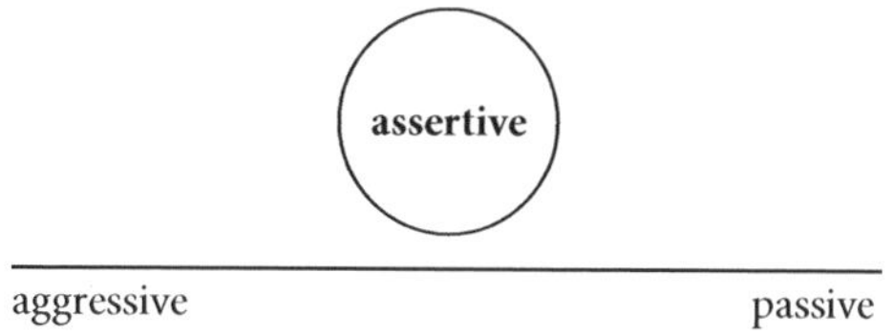

As shown in the foregoing diagram, an *assertive approach* is a third option. It affirms the speaker's right to a particular point of view without either giving in to or denying the other person's viewpoint. An assertive approach is a constructive alternative to debating the merits of term versus cash value. Such a debate would most likely result in your being backed into a corner and not getting what meets your needs.

To use an assertive approach, you would simply state what you need. For example, you might say, "I require $300,000 of term insurance. Could you please tell me how much that will cost?" The seller may respond by trying to convince you that a whole life policy would be better. If that happens, simply restate what you need, without arguing: "That may be true, but I've looked at my situation, and what I need is $300,000 of term insurance. Could you please tell me how much that will cost?"

There may be another round of the seller giving you the reasons why term is a bad thing for you. Once again, restate what you need. By then, the seller should realize that you will be buying term or nothing. Or you will realize that this seller is someone you're not interested in dealing with. In that case, if you are meeting in a location outside your home, you can politely excuse yourself and leave. Your next step, of course, would be to look for another salesperson who *will* help you get the term insurance you need.

This is enough to give you a basic understanding until you are ready to buy life insurance. When that time comes, refer to the resources section of my blog-site at www.TheUncommonGuides.com.

Wills…

At time of death, most people leave assets in their name. What happens to the cash, the stocks, other investments, and personal belongings that a person has accumulated over a lifetime? It depends on whether or not the person had a will. A *will* is a legal document that directs what happens to a person's assets upon his or her death. It also specifies guardianship of any minor children, which is around the age of 18 in most places.

Many people die without having made a will. Some never get around to it because they are intimidated by the cost of hiring a lawyer. Yet, for straightforward situations, lawyers often quote a flat fee that is usually quite reasonable. Couples should make their wills together, so the provisions dovetail. In this case, the lawyer will usually quote a combined fee, which is less than the cost of two individual wills. When looking for a lawyer to make your will, don't be embarrassed about asking up front what the fee will be. It is your right as a consumer purchasing a service, and it is always a good practice for you to look after how you spend your money.

If you've never hired a lawyer before, ask for recommendations from people you know. Failing that, look for a lawyer referral service to provide names of lawyers in your locale. A lawyer referral service is offered by the law society in many places. Referrals will help you narrow down your search, although you still need to interview potential lawyers and select one you feel you can work with.

Free and low-cost services are frequently available for those who are unable to afford a lawyer. Legal Aid is a community service available to those who meet the eligibility criteria. Student Legal Services, typically found at universities with a law school, are staffed by volunteer law students under supervision of their instructors.

Apart from concern about cost, there are other reasons why people don't make their wills. Some do not want to admit their mortality. They feel that making a will means they are expecting to die soon, even though logic tells us that a will is not meant to be made at the moment of impending death. Some aren't even aware of the reason they are avoiding making a will; it is an unconscious belief that drives their behaviour. However, unconscious and illogical beliefs are still very powerful. As I've said before, the way past them is to recognize what is stopping you from doing what you need to do, and then consciously dissolve these counterproductive beliefs and move on.

Another reason for not making a will is thinking you don't have anything to leave. That may be true of a student living at home. However, once you set up your own household, you might be surprised at what you have. Listing your assets and their value can be a revealing exercise. Remember to include cash and investments as well as your belongings. Then subtract your outstanding debts. The resulting picture of what you actually have is referred to as a *net worth statement* in financial planning.

If you die without a will

If you're wondering if you need to make a will, it's helpful to know what happens if you die *without* one. Someone who dies without a valid will is said to have died *intestate.* When that happens, the *Wills and Succession Act* describes how the distribution of your belongings is determined. Essentially, it sets out an order of distribution based on the family tree, starting with the closest relatives—spouse or partner, then children. If there are none, it goes to parents, siblings, grandparents, aunts/uncles and so on, in a prescribed order. If no relatives are found within two years, the estate is turned over to the Alberta government and held under the *Unclaimed Personal Property and Vested Property Act.* Should no valid heir come forward within 10 years, the property belongs to the government.

If there is no will, and minor children are left without parents, the court appoints a guardian for them. The court's main concern is the welfare of the children, and it will choose from among suitable family members, unless there are none. In this case, the children would be placed in a foster home.

Since this is all looked after under the legislation, you might think there's no need to make a will. On the surface, that would appear to be true. However, it is usually more complicated and expensive to process an estate when there isn't a will. In addition, the succession pattern established under the law may not suit your particular situation, and laws do not generally have flexibility to adjust to individual circumstances. For example, what would happen in the case where a person is separated from a spouse (although not divorced) and living with another partner (referred to as an adult independent partner in Alberta law)?

In addressing this question, the Centre for Public Legal Education Alberta says:

> In such a situation (i.e.: where there is both a spouse and an adult interdependent partner), if you die without a Will, either all or some of your estate will be divided between the two (depending on whether there are also children and/or grandchildren involved). This may not be as you wish. For this reason you should consider writing a Will that sets out your wishes (bearing in mind any legal obligations you may have to either or both your spouse and your adult interdependent partner). Also, given the general complexities of the situation, you may wish to consider consulting a lawyer.[6]

If it were possible to imagine all the scenarios that might arise after your death, you might be able to know if the legislation would work in your favour or not. However, it's probably easier to just bite the bullet and make your will.

Terminology for wills

You—the person making the will—are known as the *testator*. Your *estate* consists of the assets you have acquired. A *beneficiary* is someone who inherits something from your estate. A *bequest* is what you leave to your beneficiaries via the terms of your will.

In your will, you designate an *executor* (*executrix* is sometimes still used as the feminine form of the word) to look after administering the will following your death. You can think of this person as a business manager who ensures your affairs are properly wrapped up and the estate is dispersed to the beneficiaries.

Once the executor has completed the necessary steps, an application for grant of probate will be submitted to the government. *Probate* means proving the will. It is a legal procedure for verifying that the person named in the will has died, that the will is valid, and that the executor is confirmed. This is required before property may be sold or transferred, and before a financial institution may release funds that belonged to the deceased.

If there are minor children, *guardians* should be named to designate substitute parents until the children are of legal age and able to live independently.

Ways to make a will

There are different ways you can make a will. We've already mentioned consulting a lawyer. You can, in most places, also make your will yourself. If you do it correctly, it will be considered valid by the court.

When making your will without legal assistance, it is crucial that you obtain current information about the legal requirements where you live. These have to do with dating, signing, and witnessing, among other things. If you don't follow the requirements, your will is invalid. For example, the law will only consider the will with the most recent date. If you revise your will and neglect to date the new one, it will be invalid: your previous will with a date on it would be the one used. You would not want this to happen, so be certain to date any will you write.

There are intricacies about the witnessing of wills that you also need to be aware of when you do it yourself. If you do not follow correct procedures, you could end up inadvertently disinheriting someone you have mentioned as a beneficiary. Be sure to research this before signing your self-made will.

The guidance of a lawyer helps ensure that mechanics such as witnessing are correctly implemented. Another advantage of hiring a lawyer is that you'll be asked questions and given advice about things you haven't thought of. For example, suppose you are leaving your car to your brother. If your brother dies before you, what would you want to happen then? You could specify that if your brother dies first, your bequest will go to his heirs. *Or* you can name someone else entirely—perhaps your sister or a friend—to be the alternate beneficiary in that case.

What if you described the car by stating make, model, and colour, and then no longer had the specified vehicle when you died? In that case, your brother would not get any vehicle, even if you had really meant for him to inherit whichever vehicle you owned at the time. Your lawyer would help you clarify your intention and would word the will to achieve the result you want. The lawyer isn't going to tell you what to do. That is up to you. The lawyer's role is to make sure you don't leave any loose ends or unclear directions.

In some places, a *holograph will* is accepted by the courts. This is a will you make yourself, completely in your own handwriting, dated and signed by you. A holograph will does not require witnesses. In Canada, holograph wills date back to pioneer times, when life was dangerous and there were few lawyers, particularly as the West was being settled. Allowing people to write their own wills made sense at the time. In Alberta, Saskatchewan, and Manitoba, this type of will is still on the books. If you make a holograph will where it is legally accepted and then move somewhere else, be sure to check if it still applies. You may have to make a will in a different form to avoid dying intestate.

You might wonder about making an audiovisual will. These days that is easily done, but the law still requires a written copy. That being said, there's no reason you can't leave a DVD, CD, or MP3 with your will if you fancy doing that. Just make sure it is a supplement to the written will, not the only way you leave your instructions.

Decisions, decisions

Whether you hire a lawyer or write your own will, your first step is to gather information and make some fundamental decisions. These are:

1. Decide on an **executor** to look after settling your estate. You'll want to choose someone who is reliable and trustworthy as well as capable. Since the executor will be looking after your business affairs, it helps to select someone who is comfortable with paperwork and dealing with professionals. Your executor may hire an accountant and a lawyer to do most of the work but would need to liaise effectively with them. When you decide on an executor, make sure that person agrees, before naming him or her in the will. This is important because someone named as an executor may decline if unable or unwilling to accept the role. If that were to happen, the court

would appoint an administrator. The work would be done, but at greater expense to the estate, so avoid this complication. A beneficiary may be an executor. In fact, spouses and partners frequently make each other their executors, with an alternate in case they both die at the same time. The executor may live outside the province, but this makes things more complicated in settling the estate.

2. If you have minor children, decide on **guardians,** and get their agreement. Guardians are substitute parents, and there are many factors to think about, from shared values to geographical location. Appointing guardians is generally the most difficult decision because often there is no easy and clear-cut choice. The most constructive thing you can do is sort through all the factors to make the best decision you can. If you leave it unmade, the courts will do it. You have no guarantee their decision would be what you'd want, and at that point you won't be able to do anything about it. Do not default on the decision of guardianship because you believe that your children's godparents will automatically become their guardians. This is not the case. Godparents are appointed under the authority of the church for the purpose of ensuring the child gets a proper religious upbringing in that particular faith. The court is a separate system and requires you to specify your choice for guardians in your will. However, there is nothing to stop you from naming the people who are the godparents to also be your child's legal guardians, if that would best suit your situation.
3. Prepare a **net worth statement,** so you are clear about what you will be passing along to those you leave behind. A net worth statement is a snapshot of your financial worth at the time. Your net worth is calculated using the following simple formula:

   assets – liabilities = net worth

   Assets are what you *own.* They can include personal belongings, car, house, cash, and investments of all types. Make a list of your assets, assign each a dollar value according to how much you could sell it for today, and add them to find the total value of your assets. *Liabilities* are what you *owe.* They include all your debts—the outstanding balance on your credit cards and outstanding loans of all types (student, personal, car, home equity, mortgage, line of credit, consolidation, and loans from family members or friends). Calculate the total amount that you owe. It is important to understand that debts must be paid from the estate before the beneficiaries get anything. You might say in your will that you leave $100,000 to someone, but if you don't have it, they won't get it.

4. Decide on your **beneficiaries** and what they will inherit. By and large, if you have it, you can leave what you want to whomever you want. The most notable exception is that you cannot legally disinherit dependents. This is for good reason; they are your responsibility. If you could disinherit dependents, the welfare system would have to care for them, which is an unfair burden on society. Generally speaking, lawyers will advise you to word your bequests broadly to avoid the need for frequent revision of your will. An example of a broad statement is the stipulation that "…my estate be divided equally among my three children, as named below…" If there are sentimental items you have promised to specific people, you can handle this informally by putting a name label on the bottom or creating a list of such items and advising those involved, including the executor. The value of such bequests would be counted as part of the person's share of the estate.

Changing circumstances

Your will should be reviewed whenever you encounter a major life event—marriage, separation, divorce, birth or adoption of a child, purchase of a house. **Marriage, separation, and divorce** change your responsibilities and dependents. The same is true of beginning or ending a relationship with an adult independent partner. In some jurisdictions, the ex-spouse or ex-partner is disqualified as a beneficiary of your will. However, it is far better to be certain your will reflects what you want rather than leaving it to chance.

Your RRSPs and life insurance policies are not processed through your will unless your estate is designated as the beneficiary. More likely, you named someone to receive it directly, usually your spouse or partner. Those beneficiaries will not change with separation and divorce, so you must contact the issuer and take steps to change your beneficiary.

Birth or adoption of a child, unquestionably a major life event, requires you to decide on guardians and rethink what you are leaving to whom. Since you now have greater long-term financial responsibilities, you'll also find yourself considering buying more life insurance in addition to revising your will.

In the case of **buying a house,** the issue is to make sure you have arranged things so it is properly passed along. If you are a single owner of the property, your will should state who is to inherit it. When two people are buying real estate together, there are two different ways it may be registered and these have implications for how it is processed after your death. When you buy property with another person, there are instances when it is desirable for it to be transferred directly to the survivor without going through the probate process. This is usually the preferred arrangement for couples, who typically hold property as *joint tenants.* In other cases, it is preferable to name a beneficiary and have the real estate processed through the will. This type of ownership is known as *tenants in common,* and is usually used when the property is part of a business arrangement. By being aware of these options and their application, you'll be able to ensure your property is registered in the best way for you.

When you need to change something in your will, handwritten changes on your original document are not sufficient. There are two accepted practices. One is to make an entirely new will, which is the best method when making extensive changes. The other is to prepare an amending document, known as a codicil, and attach it to your will. A codicil must meet certain format requirements, including being signed and witnessed.

Other practicalities

The will needs to be **stored safely** and at the same time must be accessible to the executor to give immediate direction on your death. A will made by a lawyer may be stored in that office for you, if you wish. Another possibility is your safety deposit box in the bank. If this is your choice, check with the bank regarding the conditions under which they can release the will. The law generally requires that a safety deposit box be sealed until probate is granted, yet the executor needs the original will to submit with the application to obtain probate. The usual bank policy is to allow supervised removal of the will immediately. However, the executor may be required to produce a photocopy of the will and photo identification, proving he or she is the person named as the executor. Therefore, it is crucial to make sure that each of your executors has a copy of the will with a notation at the top indicating where the original is stored. If that is a safety deposit box, also note where the key is kept. If the executor does not have the key, there is a substantial charge to drill open the box.

Your survivors need to know your **funeral wishes.** However, this is more useful if written in a document separate from your will, since funeral decisions need to be made immediately after your death. If you do put them in your will, then this is another very important reason for your executor to have a copy of the will.

This brief overview gives you a sense of what's involved in making a will. For more information, refer to *Making a Will,*[7] one of an excellent series of booklets developed by the Centre for Public Legal Education Alberta. Although based on Alberta law, it alerts you to the kind of information to look for, and questions to ask, about making a will wherever you live.

When you are alive but incapable of making decisions…

A will can only come into effect after you have died, and applies to your assets but not your self; it has no authority over the care of your person when you are alive but mentally incapable. For that purpose you need a living will, which may also be referred to as a personal directive.

A living will or personal directive is a legal document that comes into effect when you are alive but unable to make your own personal decisions. A living will does not apply to your financial decisions. For that purpose you require yet another document, generally known as a power of attorney.

This visual summary shows what comes into effect when you are alive (top two squares) and when you have died (lower two squares). The two squares on the left relate to your person and living conditions. The two squares on the right pertain to your finances.

Documents to Deal with Illness and Death

	Your Person	Your Finances
Alive but Incompetent	Personal Directive (Living Will)	Enduring Power of Attorney
Deceased	No legal document; make funeral wishes known to family	Will

Living will (personal directive)

Laws vary considerably, but the following description based on Alberta legislation will give you an idea of the scope of a personal directive and some of the issues. Making a living will challenges you to think seriously about your values, beliefs, and wishes related to medical treatment and living arrangements. A fundamental decision is whether or not you want to be kept alive on life support or let nature take its course—in other words, do you want heroic measures or simply care and comfort? Also consider the following questions. Who do you want to act on your behalf (known as your agent)? How much authority do you want your agent to have? Do you want this agent's actions to be periodically reviewed? If so, by whom? Who will determine if you are capable of acting for yourself or not?

That's a lot of soul-searching and tough decision-making. Why should you bother? Probably the most compelling reason is that it helps those close to you in difficult times. Legally, there is very little they can do without your written instructions. They may know you would not want to be kept alive for years on life support, but they will be powerless if you have not written a living will. Powerlessness is one of the most stressful states we can experience. Making a living will is a kindness to your family.

In the absence of clear instruction from you, serious family disputes may occur. We saw that in the high-profile case of Terri Schiavo, a young U.S. woman who was kept alive for many years, while her husband and parents battled in court to do what each thought was best. Having suffered severe brain injury due to lack of oxygen when her heart stopped, she was in a largely vegetative state, able to breathe but requiring a feeding tube to stay alive. Her husband, appointed her legal guardian, applied to the court to have the tube removed on the basis that his wife had told him she would never want to be kept alive in such circumstances. After two years, the court ruled the feeding tube could be removed. Her parents challenged that decision by suing her husband, and court battles continued for seven years, until she died 13 days after the final court order to remove the tube. Not a pretty picture—yet those on either side strongly believed they were doing the very best for her. The problem was that there was no way to prove what she wanted.

Apart from being a kindness to your family, your personal directive is also for your own assurance that your living conditions will line up with your beliefs and preferences. For example, someone who eats a vegetarian or vegan diet for ethical reasons may want to be reassured that their dietary preferences will be honoured in the nursing home where they ultimately live. A couple may feel strongly that they want to be housed in the same facility in order to maintain contact. Your living will is your chance to make these preferences known.

When making your personal directive, be sure to check the legal requirements where you live. In Alberta, a personal directive is optional and voluntary. However, when one is made, it must meet certain prescribed conditions to be legally valid. For one thing, it cannot request assisted suicide, euthanasia, or anything else that is illegal.

Although advancing age commonly prompts an individual to make a living will, incapacity can occur at any time as a result of illness or injury. In Alberta, a personal directive may be made by anyone 18 years of age or older; you do not have to wait until you are a senior citizen to make one.

To be legally binding, a living will must be signed, dated, and witnessed. A lawyer may do it for you, but that is not necessary as long as you research the legal requirements and follow them carefully. More detailed information about making a personal directive can be found in *Making a Personal Directive*,[8] another of the booklets available from the Centre for Public Legal Education Alberta. It is based on Alberta law but makes you think about the general kinds of issues and considerations that come to the fore when making a living will. Since legal requirements vary from place to place, you can research location-specific requirements when you're ready to make yours.

As with your will, you need to let your family know you have prepared this document and where to find it. Usually it's best to inform them about your wishes and who has agreed to be your agent. Give them a copy of your personal directive for their future reference. If for some reason you wish to keep the contents confidential, tell them where the document is kept and also put a card in your wallet with this information. That way, they'll be able to find the document when it's needed. You may also want to leave copies with your doctor, lawyer, and/or clergyman. In Alberta, you may also register a copy with the Alberta Personal Directives Registry to make it readily available to health professionals in an emergency.

Power of attorney

A living will gives your family instructions about your wishes for care of your person but does not give them authority over your financial matters. Here is a very real example. If I were alive but incapable of living on my own and directing my affairs, my condominium would have to be sold to generate funds for placing me in a more suitable environment. The hassle-free way of ensuring this is for me to assign power of attorney to my adult children while I am still competent. They would then be able to sell my condo and relocate me.

An *Enduring Power of Attorney* is set up in advance to take effect if you become mentally incapable. My power of attorney specifies that it only comes into effect when it has been determined that I am mentally incompetent, and it identifies the means for making that determination. As with wills and living wills, you should provide copies of your power of attorney to those involved.

There are times other than incapacity that may warrant giving someone power of attorney over your financial affairs. One of my sons, for example, took some of his post-secondary education overseas. The first year we hadn't thought about how he would deal with matters such as student loans, certain educational applications, and other matters requiring his signature. It was much easier the next year when I had power of attorney. However, I was keenly aware of the high degree of trust that had been placed in me and my responsibility to carry out my assignments with great care. As the lawyer pointed out when we signed the document, my son was legally bound by my signature, as if it were his own for the period of time the arrangement was in place. This power of attorney—for a specific purpose or time period—is called an *Immediate Power of Attorney*.

As with the other documents we've been discussing, these are meant to make life easier for the people you care about. Think about it now...while you can.

Think-abouts

I think that I shall
never see
A billboard lovely
as a tree.
Perhaps, unless the
billboards fall,
I'll never see a tree at all.
~Ogden Nash

The essence … is to travel gracefully rather than arrive. ~Enos A. Mills

It's not how much money you make, but how much money you keep, how hard it works for you, and how many generations you keep it for.
~Robert Kiyosaki

The price of anything is the amount of life you exchange for it.
~Henry David Thoreau

We cannot direct the wind, but we can adjust our sails.

4

Health, Safety & Integrity of the Future

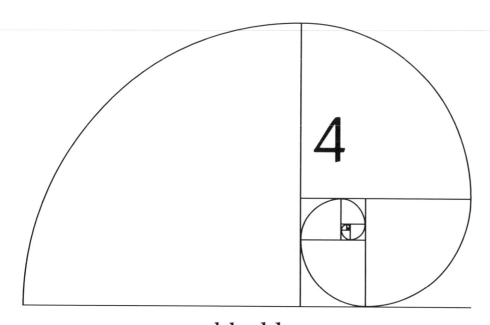

Integrity of the Future

Important as it is to make good financial choices and get our financial systems in order, life is about more than that. We must consider the bigger picture and make decisions from a broader perspective. The ideas you encounter in this section will give you perspectives that will contribute to your quality of life rather than simply your financial well-being.

To preserve the integrity of our future, we are being challenged to change because what we're doing cannot be sustained. *Sustainability* has become a catchword of the environmental movement, and we probably all have a general concept of what it means. I particularly like how Paul Hawken describes it in his book *Blessed Unrest: How the Largest Social Movement in History Is Restoring Grace, Justice, and Beauty to the World*:

> Sustainability is about stabilizing the currently disruptive relationship between earth's two most complex systems—human culture and the living world. The interrelation between these two systems marks every person's existence and is responsible for the rise and fall of every civilization. Although the concept of sustainability is relatively new, every culture has confronted this relationship, for better or ill.... Today, for the first time in history, an entire civilization—its people, companies, and governments—is trying to arrest the downspin and understand how to live on earth, an effort that represents a watershed in human existence.... At this point in our environmental freefall, we need to preserve what remains and dedicate ourselves to restoring what we have lost.[1]

What will happen?

No one knows for sure what will happen in the world. We are currently experiencing the results of many years of what Hawken refers to as "frenzied self-destructive behaviour"—not just individually, but collectively. We have developed an economic system and consumer culture that creates insatiable wants. The materials to satisfy these wants are pulled from the earth and taken, by and large, on a one-way trip. We have disregarded the inescapable fact that we live in a world where everything is interconnected—what we do in our part of it has implications in many other places. David Suzuki is a well-known Canadian scientist, writer, and broadcaster. Since the late 1980s, he has warned us about the dangers inherent in this attitude:

> Human use of fossil fuels is altering the chemistry of the atmosphere; oceans are polluted and depleted of fish; 80 per cent of Earth's forests are heavily impacted or gone yet their destruction continues. An estimated 50,000 species are driven to extinction each year. We dump millions of tonnes of chemicals, most untested for their biological effects, and many highly toxic, into air, water and soil. We have created an ecological holocaust. Our very health and survival are at stake, yet we act as if we have plenty of time to respond.[2]

Are we in a hopeless situation? No. The game isn't over until it's over. As long as people continue to believe there is another way and take steps in that direction, there is hope for regaining the integrity of our world. In *Blessed Unrest*, which is about the civil society movement, Paul Hawken elaborates on what is happening to move us in a positive direction:

> While so much is going wrong, so much is going right. Over the years the ingenuity of organizations, engineers, designers, social entrepreneurs, and individuals has created a powerful arsenal of alternatives. The financial and technical means are in place to address and restore the needs of the biosphere and society. Poverty, hunger, and preventable childhood diseases can be eliminated in a single generation. Energy use can be reduced 80 percent in developed countries within thirty years with an improvement in the quality of life, and the remaining 20 percent can be replaced by renewable sources. Living-wage jobs can be created for every man and woman

who wants one. The toxins and poisons that permeate our daily lives can be completely eliminated through green chemistry. Biological agriculture can increase yields and reduce petroleum-based pollution into soil and water. Green, safe, livable cities are at the fingertips of architects and designers. Inexpensive technologies can decrease usage and improve purity so that every person on earth has clean drinking water.[3]

A civil society?

Hawken goes on to highlight the principles of the civil society movement. They are: growth without inequality, wealth without plunder, work without exploitation, and a future without fear. Imagine what it would feel like to live in a world where those ideas prevailed—and remember the power of thought. If enough people believe such a world is desirable and possible, it will be.

Marketers know this as the *theory of critical mass*. They recognize that in the early stages of introducing a product, there is little consumer interest. However, as the marketing campaign continues and more people become aware of the product, sales gradually increase. Then something almost inexplicable happens: there's a tipping point after which sales increase dramatically. This point is known as critical mass. Represented on a graph, it would look like this:

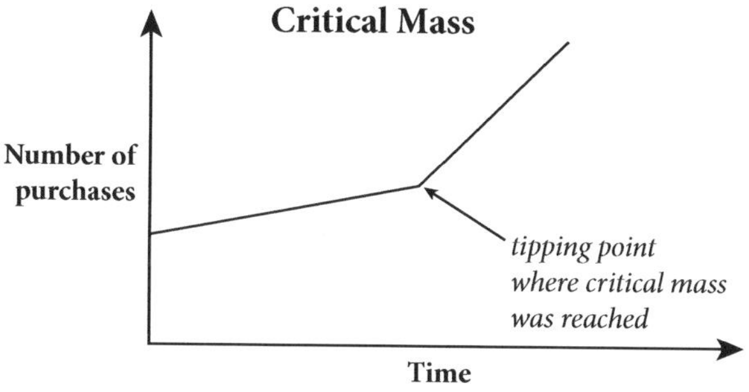

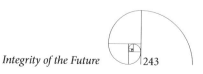

The same phenomenon can occur with thoughts as well as products. Once enough people envision a world in which there is growth without inequality, wealth without plunder, work without exploitation, and a future without fear, we will reach critical mass, and it will be so.

Visionaries set the stage…

Visionaries are the people who can see another way of doing things. At the beginning of this book we talked about economic visionaries. The founders of organizations that make up the civil society movement are also visionaries.

Not all of us are visionaries, but most of us can see the potential in an idea if it's presented to us—although that's not always true either, as the following example reveals. I recall a dinner-table conversation with a man who had worked in the computer industry since the very early days. He recounted a conversation he had with a friend around 1982. At that time, computers were generally used only in large companies, and all the processing was done by a "mainframe" that took up an entire room and stored data on large reels of one-inch–wide magnetic tape.

His friend, whose field of expertise was something other than computers, speculated that it wouldn't be long before people had computers in their homes. The computer specialist replied that the idea of home computers was preposterous. This is indeed a curious response, considering it came from a highly qualified expert in the field of computing. But perhaps it isn't surprising, when you think about it. The truth is that people immersed in a field don't always see what *could be* because they are highly focused on what *is*. Visionaries are not necessarily experts, but rather people who explore possibility and come up with other ways of doing things.

Change can be frightening…

Other ways of doing things implies change, and the prospect of change evokes mixed response in most of us. If the change simply involves a manufacturer tweaking the design so its cell phone can do more, that doesn't seem too threatening. But if the change requires us to think or act completely differently, if it demands a different viewpoint or mindset, we tend to become protective of our present position, holding onto the thought that how things are is how they should be.

It seems a natural human reaction to hold onto the status quo. There is comfort in familiarity. That's what traditions are about—the same foods and the same activities at religious celebrations and holidays, such as Thanksgiving. The known gives us a sense of security.

This phenomenon also explains to some degree why a person stays in a "dead-end" job. Despite being mundane and unsatisfying, it nonetheless provides the security of predictability. It takes an enormous amount of confidence and courage to break away and step into the unknown.

Interestingly, it is the *anticipation* of change that is most frightening. Because we don't know what to expect, our minds tend to run away with us and imagine all the daunting and terrible things we might encounter. We have no proof they will happen, but they could. We just don't know for sure. This uncertainty makes life challenging for those of us who are wrestling with the tremendous need for change in our economic and environmental practices. We know things need to change but are also afraid.

Often we stay where we are because we're afraid of losing something—material goods, money, status, our job...life as we know it. What if we looked at the unknown from a different viewpoint? Deepak Chopra, in *The Spontaneous Fulfillment of Desire*, takes this view: "The known is the prison of past conditioning. The unknown is always fresh, which is a quality of the field of infinite possibilities.... Change is the dance and rhythm of the universe."[4]

There's no doubt about it, change can require us to take a risk. But perhaps the reward will be even greater than what we experience now. We won't know if we never try another way. This applies both in our individual and collective lives.

Seeing change as opportunity...

What if we could change our viewpoint? What if we could see that change might represent opportunity instead of loss? Think about it for a moment, rather than immediately dismissing the possibility. If we keep ourselves open to possibility and change, despite the discomfort we feel, who knows what we might discover? Revisioning our world could result in a better life for everyone.

Jacque Fresco has a vision for organizing society into a *resource-based economy.* The following description of his vision, named The Venus Project, is taken from the FAQ page of his website:

> ...The Venus Project presents an alternative vision for a sustainable world civilization unlike any political, economic or social system that has gone before. It envisions a time in the near future when money, politics, self- and national-interest have been phased out.... Earth is abundant and has plentiful resources. Our practice of rationing resources through monetary control is no longer relevant and is counter-productive to our survival.... We could easily create a world of abundance for all, free of servitude and debt based on the carrying capacity of Earth resources. With the intelligent and humane application of science and technology, the people of the earth can guide and shape the future together while protecting the environment. We don't have enough money to accomplish these ends but we do have more than enough resources. This is why we advocate a Resource-Based Economy.[5]

The photo gallery in the technology section of his website[6] shows an amazing array of ideas that are well beyond what we currently see. You may think they look like science fiction, but who's to say Fresco's designs couldn't work? We may be approaching a time when, as our existing systems become ever more cumbersome and fragile, we will be glad there are alternatives ready for the trying. Fresco's ideas are not the only ones. All around the world, people are implementing forward-thinking ideas.

Hopeful developments...

Forward-thinking ideas are the subject of *The Geography of Hope* by Chris Turner, a Canadian writer who spent a year traveling the world to talk with people who have undertaken specific projects based on the mindset of sustainability. He saw the results, listened to the project originators, and took note of the thinking behind what they were doing.

For example, he visited Jørgen Tranberg and his off-shore wind farm on the tiny Danish island of Samsø. Turner describes this as a particularly ambitious experiment in renewable energy. To explore sustainable housing, he visited *Heliotrope* in southwestern Germany. This structure, designed and built by architect Rolf Disch as his family's home, produces more energy than it uses. The house rotates on a stilt-like structure to orient itself toward or away from the sun, depending on the season and whether Disch wants to warm the house or keep it cool. A geothermal heat exchanger brings in heat from the ground underneath when needed. Solar vacuum tubing heats water. Rainwater is captured for washing dishes and clothes. These are just a few of the features that allow the house to create more energy than the family uses. Disch has also created a neighbourhood of 59 townhouses, each of which produces more energy than it uses.

Doing things differently requires thinking differently—and the thinking has to go beyond innovative ways to use the technology. Doing things differently starts with a sense of the bigger picture and our place in it. According to Disch, "When you build a house ... you have a responsibility for the whole society."[7] Echoing Jacque Fresco's observation, Disch says that we already have the technology to build socially responsible housing. What we lack is the will to do it.

Sometimes a high-tech solution isn't what is needed. Turner suggests we look for the "rightest" solution. "There might be more than one answer to a given problem, a number of technically satisfactory *right* ways to do the job, but the *rightest* thing is the one that does it most elegantly and it might not be the most scientifically advanced."[8]

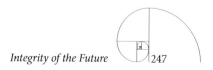

Turner's quest for elegant solutions took him to Bangkok, Thailand, where he met architect Soontorn Boonyatikarn. Dr. Soontorn built a pioneering super-efficient green home, one that used only 15% of the amount of energy typically required by similar Thai houses. Following completion of that house, he had an "aha moment" inspired by eating a mango. As he tossed away the seed, he thought, "I am so stupid! Look at the mango. It doesn't consume energy. It uses nothing. However, it produces fruit for me to eat. And the next generation home should be like the mango."[9]

His next design was based on the simple but revolutionary premise that the house should give rather than consume. Someone living in one of Dr. Soontorn's Bio-Solar homes might never again have to pay an electricity or water bill, yet will be able to live comfortably in Thailand's hot, humid climate. Some of the features that work together to make this possible:

- large roof overhang to create a buffer of shade
- photo-voltaic cells on steep south-facing roof slopes, which generate more power than the house uses (excess is sold to the state power company)
- heat-blocking glass and insulated walls to keep heat *out*, making air conditioning requirements of this house only 10% of a comparable Thai home
- water harvesting and storage for a closed-loop water system that makes the house independent of the municipal water supply
- a roof coating that keeps the roof temperature a couple of degrees below air temperature, thus causing dew to form, which can be collected from the roof and stored in a water storage tank buried in the yard

Turner also introduces us to Mark Falcone, a very different sort of property developer who turned a dying U.S. shopping mall into a vibrant multi-use area with pedestrian-friendly streets connecting commercial and residential spaces. Falcone expresses his philosophy this way: "There's lots of choices and decisions we make every day here that don't necessarily translate into higher revenue or more profitability. And, in fact, it might be the other way around. But we know that they are all in pursuit of this bigger purpose, this bigger mission that we're trying to fulfill."[10]

The Geography of Hope goes on to describe many elegant solutions: the Grameen Bank, the microlender that is tackling poverty by making business loans to the poorest of the poor; Interface, Ray Anderson's flooring company that is waging a successful war on waste; Mike Reynolds's *Earthships*, unique human dwellings in Taos, New Mexico, that are entirely self-sustaining; and the "Ecological City of Tomorrow" created when Malmö, Sweden, converted a derelict industrial site into highly livable space in less than a decade. Turner introduces many significant concepts, including the recycling trap,[11] the wisdom of small,[12] and the importance of projects being replicable rather than scalable.[13] *The Geography of Hope* is recommended reading for anyone wanting an expanded sense of what's possible.

Why shouldn't things change?

Even in the face of possibility, there are strong forces keeping things the way they are. One is our desire for familiarity—that comforting feeling of knowing what to expect. Another is the desire to protect our investment of energy in a particular point of view. David Suzuki, who has spent many years making the case for changing our attitudes and behaviours, puts it well: "People … especially people in positions of power … have invested a tremendous amount of effort and time to get where they are. They really don't want to hear that we're on the wrong path, that we've got to shift gears and start thinking differently."[14]

Nevertheless, life is about learning and growing. Most of us can recognize this pattern in our own lives. We try something, consider whether it's working for us or not, and make an appropriate adjustment when needed. Sometimes the adjustment is a minor tweaking of what we were doing. Sometimes it means abandoning the course of action completely and embarking on another that might be more constructive.

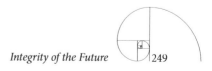

Why would it be any different at a societal level? Why shouldn't things change if they aren't working? And aren't we glad there are people who have been thinking about it? The challenge of possibility is that it demands change. When we see that there are ways to do things differently, how can we not respond?

Think-abouts

By accepting responsibility, we take effective steps toward our goal: an inclusive human society on a habitable planet, a society that works for all humans and for all nonhumans. By accepting responsibility, we move closer to creating a world that works for all.
~Sharif M. Abdullah

Helen Keller said, "I rejoice to live in such a splendidly disturbing time." What do you find splendidly disturbing about this time we are living in?

A man is usually more careful of his money than of his principles.
~Oliver Wendell Holmes Jr

When the grasp of inertia is broken, life is quite thrilling.

The Complexities of Health and Safety

People generally value good health and personal safety. On the surface, this would seem a straightforward goal to achieve. However, in a consumer culture, there are many factors that make it challenging for us to maintain our health and safety. For one thing, life in a consumer culture requires that we earn an income. We can sometimes become so busy earning a living that we eat fast food and find little time to exercise, thus jeopardizing our health.

A double-edged sword…

Technology is another of our consumer challenges. There is no question that much good has come from technology, and the medical field is full of examples. But these advances in technology also present us with a variety of consumer dilemmas. Infertile couples can now have children, using a variety of technologically assisted methods that are very expensive. Should the general public bear this cost? Are we penalizing infertile couples if they are required to pay for treatments themselves? It seems cold-hearted to talk about health in terms of public cost, but it is a real issue. If we don't manage the decisions well, the system could break down and become one in which there is great disparity, depending on your income. Should we put a pacemaker in the heart of an 80-year-old? Should we give a lung transplant to a smoker? What lines do we draw—and where?

Apart from the issues of affordability, there are important questions about what is humane in such situations. Does it improve the quality of life to keep an 80-year-old heart going for another 10 years by artificial means? Should we engage in painful and psychologically difficult fertility treatments just because we can?

We should also think about what happens to the gene pool when babies are produced by anonymous donors through a sperm bank. A donor's sperm will be available to participate in more than one pregnancy. In a single instance, that is not problematic. However, as more and more of the population is fathered this way, do we not run the risk of birth defects that can occur from inbreeding? The traditional means of reproduction keeps this in check, but a system of anonymous donors changes it all. Are there checks and balances in place to prevent this? Who is in charge of the big picture? Are we thinking about the unintended consequences?

Four years after the first "test tube baby" was born in Britain in 1978, philosopher Mary Warnock prepared a report on issues surrounding reproductive health. An article in *The New York Times* quoted an e-mail from Baroness Warnock: "It is quite unpredictable what the ultimate effect on the gene pool of a society might be if donors were permitted to donate as many times as they chose."[1] According to this article, there are now groups of donor half-siblings in the United States that number 50 or more, and at least one group of 150. Frequently, siblings live close to each other, and often there is secrecy about the child being conceived with donor sperm. Under these conditions, accidental incest becomes a very real possibility. Although some countries limit the number of children that can be fathered by one donor, the United States has no such regulation. Nor does Canada. A 2011 article in the *National Post* reports that Canada's only sperm bank has a policy that limits donors to "three live births per 100,000 population in a given geographic area, though that could mean as many as 75 offspring in a city the size of Toronto."[2]

Reproductive technology raises many thorny ethical questions. *The Globe and Mail* recently published a thought-provoking article about embryo testing—a practice that began in London in 1989. It was hailed as a means of improving the success of in vitro fertilization for infertile couples. However, according to author Carolyn Abraham, preimplantation genetic diagnosis (PGD) "is now morphing into a whole new approach to baby-making, one that gives people an unprecedented power to preview, and pick, the genetic traits of their prospective children."[3] This technology is opening the door for parents to create saviour siblings (those who have compatible genetics to provide donor tissue for a child who is in need of it) and designer babies (who have been selected for what are generally considered cosmetic factors, such as intelligence, height, and eye colour). Is this setting us on the slippery slope of viewing our children as commodities? It raises many social questions that transcend our technological ability to do the procedure. Will we become cold and uncaring as we breed out the traits we don't like? At what point does this become eugenics? Will parents of engineered "super babies" have undue expectations of them? Does it reinforce inequities between people who can afford this testing and those who cannot? These are important questions.

The technical ability to transplant organs has also created consumer dilemmas. Transplants have allowed many people to survive when their own organs fail. However, we have a shortage of organs because demand now exceeds supply from our own citizens. As a result, North Americans are going to the developing world to buy organs—some legally, some obtained through the black market—from countries such as India, China, Brazil, and the Philippines. However, according to a recent article in *The New York Times*, this practice has now spread to poor parts of Europe, such as Spain, Italy, Greece, Serbia, and Russia. EU special prosecutor Jonathan Ratel is quoted as saying, "Organ trafficking is a growth industry. Organized criminal groups are preying on the vulnerable on both sides of the supply chain: people suffering from chronic poverty, and desperate and wealthy patients who will do anything to survive."[4] Kidneys, lungs, livers, and corneas are up for sale, facilitated by the Internet. Although most donors provide organs willingly for the payment they will receive, this is apparently not always the case. Canadian human rights activists David Kilgour and David Matas have documented allegations that Falun Gong practitioners are being taken as political prisoners and executed so their organs can be "harvested" and sold for profit to transplant tourists.[5]

As these issues have emerged, it becomes clear that the possibilities offered by technology must be balanced with strong ethics and intentions for good. Conscious spending is based on the intention to meet our needs without causing harm to other people or to the environment. Intention is what keeps us on track; it is the aim that guides our actions. Being aware of our intention is a strong step toward preserving the integrity of our future.

Unintended consequences...

Yet for all our good intentions, our actions sometimes have unintended negative consequences. We have discovered over time that many products appear harmless until in widespread use; then we discover results that weren't intended. Such was the case with the depletion of the protective ozone layer above Earth due to the use of chlorofluorocarbons (CFCs) as a refrigerant and as a propellant in aerosol spray cans. More localized and highly baffling was a rash of water main breaks in Los Angeles in the summer of 2009. In the end, it was determined that the cause was the city's water conservation policy, which limited watering to Mondays and Thursdays. The sharp changes in pressure on watering-only days caused stress that the aging pipes were unable to withstand.

A recent, unintended consequence that is affecting people worldwide is the U.S. policy that requires all gasoline since 2007 contain 10% ethanol. Ethanol for this purpose is primarily made from corn. Five years later, we see that this policy has had a severe effect on food prices, although that was not intended. The requirement to include ethanol in gasoline was meant to ease dependency on foreign oil and to cut greenhouse gas emissions. The intended outcomes appear to be small but positive. However, the effect on food prices is devastating in poor countries.[6] The price of corn has tripled in those five years, due to increased demand. The price of other crops—wheat, soybeans, and rice—has doubled[7] due to a shortage of supply as acreage is shifted to corn. The cost of producing animal foods that are fed on corn has also increased.

Although increased food prices are difficult for everyone, North Americans can shift their expenditures to buy other, cheaper foods. That is not the case in poor countries. "When cereal grain prices jump by 67.4% as they did over the last year, the poor must simply consume less; there are no cheaper foods to substitute towards."[8]

Reducing unintended consequences...

Unintended consequences often occur when we approach a problem from a single-minded viewpoint, without taking the bigger picture into account. Sometimes, instead of erring on the side of caution, we embrace an action or a product because we don't have definitive proof of harm. Two things can help us avoid unintended consequences—holistic thinking and the precautionary principle. Both are commonsense approaches that we can adopt to some degree in our own decision-making.

Holistic thinking is related to the word "whole." Holistic thinking requires us to see connections and interconnections. It means looking at the bigger picture, not just a limited aspect. This is challenging for science, which is designed to study things in isolation. However, in our lives and in the world, nothing occurs in isolation. As we have seen, when we use corn for vehicle fuel, some people go hungry because food becomes more expensive.

There is much in the world that cannot be proven by science. We would like to think scientists can give us definitive answers about what is good for us and what is not, but this is not the case. Science can often show that things are related but cannot prove whether it is a cause-and-effect relationship. This leaves us in a state of scientific uncertainty.

Scientific uncertainty is an uncomfortable fact of life. Years ago, when I was investigating the relationship between food additives and children's behaviour, I watched a film in which a highly placed Canadian health official talked about food additives and safety. He said, "We can never definitely prove safety. At the most, we can say that, in the quantities given and under the conditions of the test, a particular additive is *probably not unsafe*." I remember this so vividly because it was one of those moments when a bubble burst. Before then, I had lived under the happy illusion that if something had been tested and approved, then it was clearly safe for consumption. In that moment, I realized that this is not true. Stating that something is "probably not unsafe" is quite different from providing an assurance that it is safe.

Decisions about products that affect our health and safety are usually based on risk assessment. Officials weigh the risk versus benefit, and the fundamental question becomes: How much harm is allowable? For example, it is generally acknowledged that nitrates, put into most processed meats such as sausage and bacon, form a cancer-causing substance called nitrosamine. However, without nitrates there is potential for serious food poisoning if processed meats are carelessly handled during processing and retailing. Government officials base their decision to allow nitrates in food on the relative balance of long-term cancer risk against the possible short-term threat of a lethal form of food poisoning. When they decide in favour of allowing nitrates because of the potential risk, they are not saying they are safe. They are saying that it is safer than not allowing them.

The risk/benefit approach has resulted in many new products appearing on the market and used widely until unintended consequences begin to show up, at which time regulations change or products are banned. Trans fats and artificial sweeteners are two examples that come to mind.

However, we could turn our thinking around. Rather than allowing new products to be widely used until proven harmful, we could create a culture of preventing harm. Instead of asking how much harm we are willing to permit, we could ask how little harm is possible.

The *precautionary principle* is based on this important distinction. Originating in Germany in the 1970s, the precautionary principle has now become part of international law. The most widely quoted definition was developed at the 1998 Wingspread Conference held in Wisconsin in January of that year. In a concluding statement from the conference, 32 individuals with wide-ranging backgrounds expressed their concerns:

- We believe existing environmental regulations and other decisions, particularly those based on risk assessment, have failed to adequately protect human health and the environment, as well as the larger system of which humans are but a part.

- We believe there is compelling evidence that damage to humans and the worldwide environment is of such magnitude and seriousness that new principles for conducting human activities are necessary.
- While we realize that human activities may involve hazards, people must proceed more carefully than has been the case in recent history. Corporations, government entities, organizations, communities, scientists and other individuals must adopt a precautionary approach to all human endeavors.
- Therefore it is necessary to implement the *Precautionary Principle*: *Where an activity raises threats of harm to the environment or human health, precautionary measures should be taken even if some cause and effect relationships are not fully established scientifically.*[9]

Why is it important that we proceed with caution? "The precautionary principle...gives us a way to change our behaviour, personally and collectively. It reminds us to acknowledge our mistakes, admit our ignorance, and act with foresight and caution to prevent damage."[10] Your grandmother probably said the same thing, but more succinctly, if she ever advised you to look before you leap.

The same philosophy of caution is shared by Physicians and Scientists for Responsible Application of Science and Technology (PSRAST). This global network of professionals is concerned about the widespread adoption of technologies without sufficient evaluation of safety:

> We find that there is an urgent need for evaluation of applications of science and technology from a comprehensive long term global perspective including systemic/holistic considerations. It must be truly impartial and independent of industrial and political interests. Our ambition has been to contribute to such evaluation. In addition, in cases where we find that applications are potentially hazardous or have already been approved in spite

of incomplete knowledge, we will campaign and lobby at a global scale for disallowing their release until impartial and thoroughly interdisciplinary safety evaluations are made.[11]

Genetic modification of food...

Genetic modification of food is a major concern of PSRAST, whose members see it as a technology that has been approved and adopted without sufficient caution:

> In spite of considerable deficiencies in the knowledge of the health and environmental consequences of genetically altered food organisms, scientific advisors of national and international regulatory organs have approved their release into the environment and their use as food. This is especially remarkable as potentially serious hazards have been warned for, and present GE foods are of little or no value to mankind.[12]

Genetic modification (GM), also referred to as genetic engineering (GE), involves manipulation of the fundamental material of living cells to create results that can't occur naturally. This process permits crossing the species barrier, something that could never happen in nature under normal conditions. The resulting plants and animals are referred to as genetically modified organisms (GMOs).

The splicing of a fish gene into a tomato is a memorable example of crossing the species barrier. The "problem" with tomatoes is their sensitivity to cold, a characteristic that limits where they can be grown because of the length of the growing season. That's their natural state, but these limitations are inconvenient in commercial production. The solution was taken from a fish that lives in very cold water. Scientists identified the gene associated with cold adaptation and spliced it into the genetic material of a tomato.

Splicing involves snipping the DNA strand and inserting a piece of foreign

DNA into the genetic structure of an organism. This is quite different from the traditional approach of selective breeding, which is used to concentrate desired traits in plants or animals. Selective breeding allows breeders to create larger plants or more productive milk cows, for example, by eliminating the smaller plants or less-productive cows from the gene pool. Desired characteristics can be brought to the fore within a plant or animal, but it is not possible to get qualities of a plant in an animal through natural reproduction. However, this *is* possible by splicing in genes or using other methods such as viral vectors to introduce foreign genetic material.

Although the product of the fish/tomato experiment never made it to market, many GM foods have. Soy, canola, and corn are the most common GM crops. Over half of Canadian-grown corn and soy are genetically modified, as is almost all of our canola.[13] Not only do we eat these crops directly, but we also eat products from animals that are fed on them.[14] Canada also imports genetically modified cottonseed oil, papaya, squash, and milk products from the United States.

Why are foods genetically modified?

A primary purpose of genetic modification is to create "super-foods" which are hardier, more resistant to disease and insects, faster growing, and/or undamaged by pesticides. These measures are financially attractive because they increase productivity and profitability of the crops. Other reasons for genetic modification centre around "feeding the world." From this perspective, genetic modification is seen as the solution to many problems. A "Declaration in Support of Agricultural Biotechnology," signed by over 3000 scientists, including 25 Nobel Laureates, affirms their belief that "recombinant DNA techniques constitute powerful and safe means for the modification of organisms and can contribute substantially in enhancing quality of life by improving agriculture, health care, and the environment."[15]

From another perspective, genetic modification is seen to be the cause of more problems than it solves. According to Greenpeace—a high-profile environmental activist organization—there are plenty of reasons to be concerned about GMOs:

> The planting of GE crops on millions of hectares of land and their introduction into our food supply is a giant genetic experiment. As living, reproducing organisms, GMOs form a type of living pollution that can spread across vast areas creating environmental risks that are unprecedented and possibly irreversible. Some of the dangers include the loss of biodiversity, the development of superweeds and superpests leading to increased use of toxic pesticides; contamination of organic and conventional crops; and harm to beneficial organisms. Health risks associated with GE food include the development of antibiotic resistance, allergic reactions, nutritional changes and the creation of toxins.... As the [Canadian] government requires NO long term testing of GE foods, it's impossible to determine what effects they are having.[16]

Environmental effects, human health risks, and no long-term monitoring—all of these are significant issues. There are also important issues concerning our loss of freedom when biological organisms are modified and owned by corporations. No one knows this better than Canadian farmer Percy Schmeiser, who was sued by Monsanto when genetically modified plants were found in his canola field.

Because Monsanto holds the patent, it is the owner of genetically modified plants grown from its seed. Therefore, no one has the right to use those seeds without paying the required fees to Monsanto. Farmers using Monsanto seed must sign a contract agreeing to buy new seed each year rather than saving and reusing seed from one year to the next. Monsanto says this is necessary to recover the costs of development of its seed. To make sure there are no infractions, the contract gives Monsanto the right to inspect fields. In addition, Monsanto operates an anonymous phone line to encourage farmers to report neighbours they suspect of using Monsanto seed without having paid licensing fees.[17]

Although some Monsanto plants were found in Schmeiser's field, he maintained he had not planted the GM seeds and indeed did not want them contaminating the crop he had spent 50 years developing and refining through selective breeding. His position is that saving and using seed from year to year should be a farmer's right. The case went through the Canadian court system right to the Supreme Court, which found in favour of Monsanto by a narrow margin.

Percy Schmeiser's battle with a corporate giant reminds us that patenting life can lead to loss of freedoms that we take for granted. Schmeiser lost the freedom to practise farming in traditional ways. Organic farmers whose crops are contaminated with GM seed may lose their certification. Both organic and conventional producers could lose their markets and livelihood, if their crops become contaminated with GM plants—something that happens readily and is a major worry for producers choosing *not* to grow GM crops.

What to do?

The American Academy of Environmental Medicine issued a press advisory in 2009 calling for a suspension of activity on genetically modified foods because they pose a serious health risk. According to this organization of health professionals, "Multiple animal studies have shown that GM foods cause damage to various organ systems in the body. With this mounting evidence, it is imperative to have a moratorium on GM foods for the safety of our patients' and the public's health."[18] They urge immediate long-term safety testing, labelling of GM food, and educating their patients and the community to avoid GM foods.

Labelling genetically engineered foods is required in Europe, Australia, New Zealand, China, and Japan.[19] Canada has taken a different position, making labelling voluntary rather than mandatory. Practically speaking, this means Canadians won't be able to tell which foods have been genetically altered because manufacturers are unlikely to voluntarily proclaim the presence of GM ingredients in their products.

Avoiding GM foods

Since you can't count on GM foods being identified on the label, you may decide to avoid eating at least the major GM crops—corn, canola, and soy. This is easier said than done, since all of these crops appear in many forms in our diet. Consider corn, for example. While you would naturally be suspicious of popcorn, corn oil, and corn on the cob, the following list of ingredients and additives may also be derived from corn. Yet few of them have corn in the name, so how would you know?

corn syrup	sucrose
cornstarch	gluten
citric acid	maltodextrin
benzoates	malt syrup
sorbates	diglycerides
dextrose	MSG
dextrin	sorbitol
fructose	vegetable gum
glucose	

This list contains 17 different ingredients that are commonly used in packaged foods for various purposes, such as sweetening, thickening, preserving, and intensifying flavour. If these ingredients were manufactured from genetically modified corn, then they will carry the altered DNA. Since few of us routinely read package labels, you may not even be aware of these substances. Have a look in your cupboard to find examples of products made with them. It's a good way to increase your awareness and make this more real.

Start by looking at packaged foods, such as cereals, cookies, canned and dried soups, seasoning mixes, and frozen pizza. Also look at pasta, sweetened apple sauce, enriched baby formula, and vanilla extract. Then there are the non-food items that make their way into our bodies—cough drops, vitamins, nutrition supplements, toothpaste, mouthwash, and glue on stamps and envelopes. Remember that any of the items from the ingredients list could have started out as corn, and there's statistically a very good chance it was GM corn.

Genetically modified foods and ingredients are becoming increasingly prevalent. With so much debate about their safety, and convincing arguments on both sides, it's difficult to know what to do. This is where the precautionary principle is helpful. Until the controversy is resolved and we actually *know* that GM foods are not causing harm, it makes sense to make other choices:

- Buy organic. This is the surest way to avoid GM foods.
- Refer to the Greenpeace shopper's guide, "How to Avoid Genetically Engineered Food," found on their website.[20] It gives a comprehensive listing in multiple food categories to help you identify which brands are made without GMOs and which are. This booklet was produced on the premise that citizens have a right to know and is an excellent resource if you are eliminating GMOs from what you eat.

Toxic pollution is not just outside...

Like genetically modified foods, toxic chemicals surround us in everyday life. That may not seem worrisome because we tend to think of chemical pollution as something that is "out there." While it is true that manufacturing puts toxins into the environment, a larger proportion of our toxic exposure is the result of daily choices—food we eat, personal care products we put on our bodies, chemicals we use to clean our homes, and products and furnishings in those homes. All of these pollutants are in our "near environment," not the one "out there" that is controlled by other people's decisions. Choices about your near environment are the ones *you* make. Fortunately, that means you are in charge.

The magnitude and risks of toxic exposure are documented in *Slow Death by Rubber Duck: How the Toxic Chemistry of Everyday Life Affects Our Health.* Written by Canadian environmental activists Rick Smith and Bruce Lourie, this book is the result of both their passion and experience. It's not an arms-length theoretical book: they investigated by experimenting on themselves. For two days, they lived in an apartment where they exposed themselves to seven major toxins in foods, personal care products, and household items. All were consumer products that are readily available and widely used. Smith and Lourie had their blood levels monitored before and after, and it was shocking to see the increase in levels of these chemicals in their bodies after only two days' exposure. You can see them describing the process and some of the results on slowdeathbyrubberduck.com.[21]

What motivated them to do this experiment? According to their website, they wanted to concretely demonstrate the impact of our daily toxic load. In their book, they describe the magnitude of the situation we are in:

> Pollution is now so pervasive that it's become a marinade in which we all bathe every day. Pollution is actually inside us all. It's seeped into our bodies. And in many cases, once in, it's impossible to get out.... Deodorants—and nearly every other common product in the bathroom—can contain phthalates (pronounced "tha-lates"), which have been linked to a number of serious reproductive problems. Phthalates are also a common ingredient of vinyl children's toys.... The truth of the matter is that toxic chemicals are now found at low levels in countless applications, in everything from personal-care products and cooking pots and pans to electronics, furniture, clothing, building materials and children's toys. They make their way into our bodies through our food, air, and water.... it's been estimated that by the time the average woman grabs her morning coffee, she has applied 126 different chemicals in 12 different products to her face, body and hair.[22]

Technology has allowed us to produce a multitude of "new and improved" products over the past 50 years, and we have accepted them into common use without much question until recently. In this way, we've become test subjects in an uncontrolled experiment that is having many unintended consequences:

> Not surprisingly, a large and growing body of scientific research links exposure to toxic chemicals to many ailments that plague people, including several forms of cancer, reproductive problems and birth defects, respiratory illnesses such as asthma and neurodevelopment disorders such as attention deficit hyperactivity disorder (ADHD). We have all become guinea pigs in a vast and uncontrolled experiment.[23]

Because so many of these chemicals have made their way into our water and air, we can't avoid everything harmful. But it makes sense to do what we can: reduce our toxic load as much as possible by making the best choices in the circumstances.

The big issue is not industrial pollution and toxic waste dumps, significant as those are. It is our private spaces—our homes. The good news is that we can make choices about what we buy and bring home. Ultimately, government regulation is needed to remove these harmful substances from the marketplace. In the meantime, we can educate ourselves and carefully choose the products we buy and use.

Steps toward lightening the toxic load

Slow Death by Rubber Duck identifies seven common toxins: phthalates (associated with fragrances), PFCs (the non-stick products), PBDEs (flame retardants), mercury, triclosan (antibacterial), pesticides (to kill plant and animal pests), and Bisphenol A (a plasticizer). *Slow Death by Rubber Duck* is a book you should have in your bathroom. In the meantime, here is some key information about these chemicals of particular concern, including sensible steps you can take to avoid them.

Fragrance (phthalates)

- Phthalates are used to give fragrance a lasting quality, and also to make vinyl products soft and flexible.

- In our bodies, phthalates may "adversely affect reproduction and development," according to a fact sheet by Health Canada.[24]
- Watch for phthalates in body products, air fresheners, and soft plastics often used in shower curtains and toys.
- Canada's *Cosmetic Regulation* does not require phthalates to be identified on the label. Manufacturers are allowed to keep their fragrance blends as trade secrets, and may use the generic term "parfum" rather than listing ingredients individually.
- In January 2011, Canada announced new regulations to limit the quantity of phthalates in toys and child care articles that might be placed in the mouths of children under four years of age.
- Sensible Steps

    1. Buy fragrance-free products.
    2. Open windows to freshen your house instead of using chemical "air fresheners."
    3. Replace your plastic shower curtain with one made of polyester or natural fibres, such as cotton, linen, or hemp.
    4. Check on safety before buying plastic toys—go to healthystuff.org and type "toys" in their site search engine.

Non-stick products (PFCs - perfluorochemicals)

- Non-stick products make our lives easier by shedding food and dirt from items to which they've been applied—pots and pans, some food packaging, clothing, and upholstered furniture.
- According to the U.S. organization, Environmental Working Group, PFCs affect numerous body systems by causing biochemical or cellular changes.

These changes result in brain and nervous system damage, birth or developmental effects, organ system toxicity, and cancer. PFCs also affect the immune system (including sensitization and allergies), and reproduction and fertility. PFCs accumulate in the body rather than being excreted, and so build up over time.[25]

- You'll find PFCs applied to frypans, carpets, and upholstered furniture, as well as in windshield washer fluid and lipstick. You might recognize them by the brand names Teflon, Gore-Tex, and Scotchgard.
- You will also find PFCs in fast food wrappers, pizza boxes, and microwaveable popcorn bags.
- Sensible Steps

    1. Replace old non-stick pans; there are new ones with a non-toxic ceramic coating if you really want the non-stick quality. Or use well-seasoned cast iron instead; it will give the same effect.
    2. Avoid fast food except when there is no other alternative. This strategy limits your exposure to PFCs in packaging.
    3. Make popcorn in an air popper rather than from a micro-pop bag in your microwave.
    4. Be alert to the term "stain-resistant" when buying furniture and clothing. That's a clue that a PFC may have been applied.

Flame retardants (PBDEs - polybrominated diphenyl ethers)

- Flame retardants are used in highly flammable synthetic materials. PBDEs are typically found in electronics, and in foam used in furniture and carpet underlay.
- In our bodies, PBDEs have been linked to cancer, adverse effects on the developing brain, and immune and reproductive problems.[26] PBDEs are

persistent, meaning that they accumulate in our bodies over time. A Health Canada fact sheet explains that PBDEs can be slowly and continuously released from the products both in use and after disposal, and states that they have been found "in the environment and in humans, including in human breast milk in Canada, the United States and Europe."[27]

- Sensible Steps
    1. Avoid PBDEs as much as you can. Government action is proceeding slowly, so be proactive in your own choices.
    2. Ask what options are available when shopping for furniture, carpets, and electronics. PBDE-free options are now being offered by some manufacturers—and the more you ask, the more will be produced.

Mercury

- Mercury is found in some fish (especially tuna), certain dental fillings (amalgams), and products such as batteries, thermometers, compact fluorescent lights, and fluorescent tubes.
- In our bodies, mercury is a "potent neurotoxin that can affect the brain, liver and kidneys, and cause developmental disorders in children.[28] Health Canada advises, "You should try to reduce your exposure to all forms of mercury whenever possible."[29]
- Sensible Steps
    1. Buy canned light tuna (skipjack) rather than white albacore, which has higher mercury levels. If you are pregnant or have children, you might choose to eat little or no canned tuna. Fish accumulate mercury from the environment they live in. Larger fish, especially those that feed on smaller fish, accumulate the most. Tuna is the most common of these, although this is also an issue with other deep-sea fish, including swordfish, sea bass, and halibut.

2. Reconsider amalgam fillings when having dental work done because they contain mercury. Controversy arises over whether harmful effects occur as mercury leaches from these fillings over time. Health Canada does not recommend replacing all existing amalgam fillings but does suggest that "when the fillings need to be repaired, you may want to consider using a product that does not contain mercury."[30] It also advises that pregnant women, people allergic to mercury, and those with impaired kidney function should avoid mercury fillings, and that children's teeth should be filled with non-mercury fillings.
3. Dispose of mercury-containing products mindfully. It is generally accepted that anything containing mercury should not be put in your garbage to go to the landfill because that will allow mercury to seep into soil, groundwater, and the air. However, some municipalities will not accept them at hazardous waste depots. Nevertheless, you can dispose of batteries and fluorescents by returning them to stores, such as major hardware chains, which have recycling programs.

Antibacterial/antimicrobial products (Triclosan)

- Triclosan may be found in hand sanitizers, body products of many kinds, toothpaste, household cleaning supplies, and some clothing (socks, sandals, and underwear). According to *Slow Death by Rubber Duck*, triclosan may be found "under the brand name Microban. Watch for this on products like cutting boards, J Cloths, knives and even aprons."[31] Other brand names they identify are Biofresh, Irgasan DP 300, Lexol 300, Ster-Zac and Cloxifermolum, as well as its chemical name 5-chloro-2-(2.4-dichlorophenoxy) phenol.
- According to the U.S. Food and Drug Administration (FDA), recent studies raise questions about the safety of triclosan. In particular, they identify the ability to disrupt the delicate endocrine system, which regulates growth and development. Another concern is whether triclosan helps to create bacteria that are resistant to antibiotics.[32]

- Some products containing triclosan may identify their product as antimicrobial or antibacterial, but many do not. However, if triclosan is present, you will be able to find it identified in the ingredients list.
- Sensible Steps
    1. Look for a hand sanitizer with ingredients such as alcohol or peroxide rather than triclosan if you feel that thorough washing with soap and water is not enough.
    2. Check the labels of the personal care and cleaning products you currently use to see if they contain triclosan.
    3. Substitute less toxic alternatives. The Guide to Less Toxic Products at lesstoxicguide.ca is a valuable resource. A few of my favourites are described later in this section under "Non-toxic alternatives."

Pesticides

- "Pesticide" is a general term for chemical preparations that destroy plant, fungal, or animal pests. You may also encounter the more-specific terms herbicide (for plants), fungicide (for fungi), and insecticide (for insects).
- Pesticides get into our lawns and gardens when we use pesticide-containing products. They are on food we buy if it has been grown with pesticides.
- In our bodies, pesticides cause a variety of health issues in the reproductive system, as well as the brain and nervous system. Pesticides have also been shown to cause a variety of cancers.[33]
- Sensible Steps
    1. Buy food that is pesticide-free or organic. Shop for locally produced food at the farmer's market. If you shop at the supermarket, look for the organic section.

2. Washing fruits and vegetables is a good general practice, but be aware that it does not remove all pesticides because some are absorbed internally as the plant grows.
3. Grow a chemical-free lawn and garden. If you have to use a chemical for a specific reason, choose the least toxic one possible.

Bisphenol A (BPA)

- Bisphenol A is a plasticizer widely used in the production of consumer goods, particularly food containers.
- In our bodies, BPA is an endocrine disrupter, which means it interferes with the natural production and function of the body's hormones. Babies and young children are especially sensitive to the effects of BPA.
- BPA may be found in plastic containers and bottles, as well as the lining of food cans, including some baby food cans.
- Sensible Steps

    1. Never microwave foods in plastic. Although Health Canada issued this warning years ago, many people still don't know about it. Hot foods can leach plasticizers from the plastic and you end up eating them. This goes for plastic wrap as well. Instead, microwave foods in glass or china containers. If they need to be covered, place a plate on top to act as a lid. It does the job, keeps you from eating plastic chemicals, and is much better for the environment because the plate is reusable.
    2. Store foods in glass rather than plastic. Wide-mouth jars work very well for most things. The bonus is that you can see what's there and use it up before it spoils.
    3. Don't wash plastic containers in the dishwasher. The heat and deter-

gent break down the surface, and plasticizers can leach out.

4. Buy food in glass jars rather than cans and plastic, or use frozen products instead.
5. Look for canned goods that are BPA-free. Eden Organics stopped using BPA in can liners in 1999. Now, because of consumer concern, some of the major manufacturers are making changes to can linings despite the higher cost per can. An online check will tell you which ones are BPA free.
6. Check online for up-to-date guides. Good sites are zrecsguide.com and toxicnation.ca.
7. Use only those plastics that aren't bad for you. Remember this rhyme, courtesy of *Slow Death by Rubber Duck.*

   4, 5, 1 and 2; all the rest are bad for you.

   The numbers refer to numbers printed on the bottom of plastic items to denote the type of plastic. They are there to help recyclers know how to handle them; they also provide useful information for consumers.

Non-toxic alternatives

You do not need to use toxic products to have a clean house. There are plenty of effective non-toxic alternatives for cleaning and disinfecting. Most manufacturers now have eco-friendly versions of the products, although it is much cheaper to make your own using basic household ingredients.

Vinegar removes dirt and calcification from hard water. Use a vinegar solution to wash windows and mirrors without leaving streaks, and to clean floors without leaving a soap residue. Pour vinegar into the water in your electric kettle and let it stand to dissolve the calcium build-up. Spray a vinegar solution onto sinks and showers to remove soap scum.

Baking soda deodorizes, so put some in the water when you wash out the fridge, and leave some in an open dish at the back of a shelf to absorb odours.

(There's no need to buy a special deodorizer package of baking soda to do this. It's just the same product in a fancier package.) Baking soda can also be used to scour your sink and pots. To clean a burnt pot, pour in some water and add about a quarter cup of baking soda. Bring to a boil, turn off the heat, and let stand until cool. The baking soda will lift the burnt material. Repeat the process, if needed. For burned-on spills on stove-top and oven, dampen with water and sprinkle generously with baking soda. Place a wet cloth on top; let stand for an hour or two, and then scrub off. Repeat, if necessary.

White vinegar and hydrogen peroxide are the simple, inexpensive, and readily available ingredients in my favourite sanitizer. The method was developed by Susan Sumner, a U.S. food scientist looking for a way to disinfect fruits and vegetables. Her method was found highly effective in killing bacteria, and can be used on other surfaces, such as countertops, sinks, and cutting boards.[34]

The vinegar and hydrogen peroxide are the usual strengths that you buy in the grocery store or pharmacy. Vinegar goes into one spray bottle and hydrogen peroxide into another. They are sprayed onto the item to be cleaned, first one liquid and then the other. It doesn't matter which one you spray first. Let stand one minute and rinse off.

Vinegar and hydrogen peroxide have a synergistic effect when used in this way, together killing far more bacteria than either one alone. You might wonder if it would be more efficient to mix them together in one bottle, but this is not a good idea because it would have to be used immediately. Storing in separate bottles means you can keep the solutions longer and will have an effective combination each time they are sprayed one after another on a surface. Light decomposes hydrogen peroxide into water and oxygen, so it should be stored in a dark bottle. You can screw a spray nozzle onto the bottle in which you bought it, and use it that way.

You can find many recipes for home-made cleaners on the Internet. Choose some that appeal to you and give them a try. And remember what your grandmother knew—hot water and "elbow grease" are indispensable for keeping a house clean.

Think-abouts

Our current approaches to health care have done much to extend our life span, but our health span may not be so impressive.
~Ilchi Lee

Live bravely in an unreliable world. ~Rabbi Harold Kushner

All great changes are preceded by chaos. ~Deepak Chopra

We have the power to make this the best generation of mankind in the history of the world, or to make it the last. ~John F. Kennedy

Looking After Yourself

We can hope that our governments will use the precautionary principle to guide their decisions and avoid unintended negative consequences. At the same time, it's important that we all take individual action to look after ourselves because many things allowed in the marketplace are detrimental to our health and well-being. Just as there are no credit police, neither are there any health police. As long as you aren't breaking any laws, what you do is up to you. And some choices are definitely more health-affirming than others.

We must realize that choices are important. Choice and consequences are two sides of the same coin. When we make a choice, there is a consequence of some sort. That is unavoidable. *Not* making a choice, when you are at a decision point, doesn't give you a free pass to avoid consequences. It simply means that you will be dealing with consequences that are not of your choosing. As my friend Carol says, not choosing is, in itself, a choice. Some people refer to this as *choosing by default*—letting the choice be made by someone else because you didn't. If you don't keep your wits about you, that someone else could be a corporation with a vested interest in your reacting a certain way, usually by buying into their advertising campaigns and purchasing their products.

Self-responsibility...why bother?

One of the opportunities and challenges of adulthood is taking over the responsibility for your well-being. When you were young, your parents directed what you ate and the activities you engaged in. When you're an adult, it's up to you.

It takes effort to live in a self-responsible manner, so why would we bother taking responsibility for our own health? The obvious reason is to live a good quality of life right into old age, rather than being hampered and slowed down by aches, pains, and illness. If you are a relatively young person, this possibility will seem a long way off. I encourage you to ask relatives or friends over 60 whether they think you should be thinking about your future health now. It's always helpful to get the perspective of someone with experience, and they'll appreciate being asked.

In addition to quality of life, there is another reason to stay healthy—the cost. You may be thinking that cost isn't an issue because there is no charge when you go to the doctor. However, remember that it just doesn't cost you *directly*. Canadians all pay for health care indirectly through taxes, since we have a publicly funded health care system. And we pay a lot. According to a recent fact sheet published by Alberta Health and Wellness,[1] 39% of the provincial budget will go to health care in 2012–2013. Every *hour,* we spend $1.8 million to maintain and improve Alberta's system. That amounts to $16 billion over the course of the year. And that is only one province. Imagine the yearly cost for the entire country.

If you take the trouble to keep yourself healthy and out of the system, everyone benefits. Not only are you doing your part to keep health care costs down, you will also feel better and enjoy life more. For all of those reasons, it is worth taking responsibility for your health.

Health care in Canada...

Universal health care is not very old in terms of Canada's history. It was the vision of a politician who would not be deterred from his belief that all citizens deserved health care, independent of their ability to pay for it. That visionary was the late T. C. (Tommy) Douglas, who is generally recognized as the father of Canadian Medicare. In 1962, in the face of a doctors' strike to prevent it, a health act was passed in the province of Saskatchewan, thus bringing his vision to reality. The strike was short-lived, and public health care was a success. In 1967, the Canadian government passed the Canada Health Act to bring the system to the entire country. The five principles of the legislation are universality, accessibility, comprehensiveness, portability, and public administration. The resulting system—of which Canadians are justifiably proud—was ranked 30th of 190 countries by the World Health Organization in its 2000 report.[2]

Philosophically, few Canadians would argue against public health care. The problem with such a system is the cost of operating it. There are concerns about whether it is sustainable, and to what extent services can be privatized without losing the spirit of the Canada Health Act. The system was founded on the principle of public administration, which means being funded though taxes and run by the government. In recent years, high demand for health care, compounded by limited resources to meet that demand, have resulted in overcrowded facilities and long wait-times to see a specialist or have elective surgery. The privatization viewpoint holds that the system would operate with greater efficiency if it were turned over to for-profit companies instead of being publically operated.

Privatization has occurred in a few provinces. The Council of Canadians, Canada's largest citizens' organization dealing with issues of social and economic concern, identifies the following issues with a for-profit system:

> Private clinics typically charge 10 to 15 per cent more than the public sector for procedures, to cover administration costs and shareholder profit. At the same time, these clinics draw doctors and other health care professionals away from the public system, which already faces shortages. The result? There are longer wait times in the public system for people who can't afford to pay high enrollment fees and annual fees [characteristic of for-profit clinics] or inflated surgical costs.[3]

Their estimate of a 10–15% cost increase in the private system is conservative compared to the results of a study conducted at McMaster University and published in the *Canadian Medical Association Journal*.[4] Analyzing data spanning a 15-year period in several thousand American hospitals, this research found the cost of operating for-profit hospitals to be 19% higher than not-for-profit institutions. This study confirms what seems common sense to me: if profit needs to be included in the cost of a service, then how can it *not* cost more?

Private medical clinics are not the only form of privatization in the health care system. Public-private partnerships (P3s) have recently been introduced for the building of health care facilities, such as hospitals. The Council of Canadians assesses P3s this way:

> P3s are attractive to governments because they are seen as a way to invest in infrastructure without the full cost of the project appearing all at once. These deals allow governments to make announcements about new facilities, without showing the financial consequences for several years. But when private companies take over a public project, the focus shifts away from the public interest and meeting community needs to ensuring a profit for the companies' shareholders. The tried and true public funding model is less expensive, more accountable and more transparent than the P3 model.[5]

Health care delivery and infrastructure represent large costs, as do new technologies and treatments. But an underlying aspect of the high cost of health care is our "fix it" mentality: I'll do as I please and you can fix me when my body stops working properly. This is the downside of a publicly funded system—a sense of entitlement that says it is my right to be fixed at public expense, even if I have acted irresponsibly.

The dilemmas of this situation are well addressed in an excellent article entitled "Overeaters, smokers and drinkers: the doctor won't see you now."[6] Published in *Macleans*, it addresses issues that arise when we provide health care at public expense to people who engage in self-destructive behaviours, such as smoking, drinking, and overeating. The reality is that waiting lists are long. Resources are stretched thin. Should time and energy be directed toward people who refuse to change their behaviour when their ongoing care prevents others from being diagnosed and treated?

If a doctor refuses to treat a patient who continues to smoke, is that discrimination, or is it a means of making the patient accountable for his or her lifestyle? The article states the question bluntly: "If people won't stop hurting themselves, can they really expect the same medical treatment as everyone else?"[7]

The health conditions at issue here are mainly those that result from detrimental lifestyle choices. The good news is that those are the things we can do something about. If we are to keep the system going, we must each take responsibility for doing everything we can to stay healthy. Then, when health problems arise despite our best efforts, we will have the comfort of knowing that there is still a publicly funded, readily accessible health care system available to support us.

Informed choice...

To make informed choices, one of the first things you need is good background information. It's tempting to assume that if something is available to buy, then it is good (or at least not bad) for your health. But think about cigarettes, which are sold throughout the world. The negative health effects of smoking are well documented. So much so, that in 2011, the Canadian government revised its health labelling regulations to require that a full 75% of the front and back of a cigarette package be covered with health warnings. These 16 different warnings pertain to the multiple health effects of smoking, including throat cancer, heart disease, mouth cancer, addiction, lung cancer, second-hand smoke, bladder cancer, and sudden infant death syndrome.

The inside of each package is required to carry health information messages with graphics and colour to make them attractive and readable. These messages are meant to encourage smokers to quit, by pointing out why that is a beneficial choice. "Thinking of having a baby?" advises:

> Quitting smoking before pregnancy will increase your chances of having a healthy baby. You'll lower your risk of
>
> - miscarriage
> - stillbirth
> - having a baby with serious health problems.

> Although quitting is most beneficial before conception, there are some benefits to quitting at any time during your pregnancy. Talk to a health care provider.[8]

My point is that we cannot assume safety just because something is available for purchase. Clearly, cigarettes are an acknowledged health hazard. Yet they are still on the market. It is the same with food. There are many unhealthful things sold for us to eat, such as fast food.

I am aware that one point of view says fast food is not a problem when eaten as part of a balanced diet. That's probably true if a person eats a fast food meal once a month or less. However, people who eat fast food usually eat it much more often than once a month.

A classic experiment to observe the effects of fast food was undertaken by Morgan Spurlock and reported in his award-winning documentary *Super Size Me.*[9] Spurlock set out to do a simple experiment: he would eat all his meals at McDonald's for 30 days, and super size his order when they asked him if he wanted to. (This happened nine times during the experiment.)

He undertook this experiment under the supervision of doctors, a dietitian, and a fitness expert. After initial tests and blood work, they declared him to be in excellent health and exhibiting above-average fitness. When he asked what they thought might happen during his 30 days of fast food, they did not anticipate much change, except for some increase in triglycerides, a type of fat found in the blood.

However, by Day 12 on his fast food diet, Spurlock had gained 17 pounds. By Day 18, he had developed a noticeable "pot belly." His blood pressure had increased significantly, his cholesterol was up, and his liver was thickening. The doctors expressed concern about the risks to his health if he continued. On Day 21, the doctor described the results as "outrageous" and way beyond what was originally anticipated. He recommended that the experiment be stopped. After serious consideration, Spurlock decided to see it through.

Day 30 results showed a total weight gain of 24½ pounds. He reported feeling depressed and exhausted, and was experiencing mood swings and food cravings. The cravings occurred about an hour after a meal, and he got headaches when he didn't eat again right away. All of these were conditions he had not experienced prior to the experiment.

Clearly, his intensive 30 days of fast food had done him harm. What did it take to return his body to his normal healthy state? He went on a vegan diet to help his body detoxify. A vegan diet consists only of plant foods and is rich in enzymes and nutrients when carefully designed. Because it has no animal products, a vegan diet is easier to digest and allows the body to clear out accumulated toxins. After two months on the vegan diet, his liver and cholesterol returned to normal, and he resumed his regular diet. Losing the accumulated weight took much longer—five months for the first 20 pounds, and another nine months for the remaining 4½ pounds. It took 14 months to lose what he had gained in one.

Clearly, fast food is not benign. Yet it is cheap and accessible. No one polices your food choices: What you eat is up to you. This is one of the major challenges of staying healthy in a consumer culture.

Food additives…

I became interested in food additives in the early 1980s when one of my children began exhibiting inexplicable and perplexing behaviours related to hyperactivity. As I searched for a solution, I was intrigued by some diet-and-behaviour research being conducted at the Alberta Children's Hospital. Psychologist Bonnie Kaplan and dietitian Jane McNicol were studying the effect of food additives on hyperactive preschool boys. Their experimental diet was free of colours, flavours, and stimulants (caffeine and chocolate). It was also low in sugar. About half of the children showed behaviour improvements on this diet.[10]

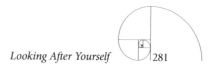

I undertook a two-stage experiment, modeled after their study, to see if food was affecting my son's behaviour. The first stage involved eliminating all additives from our diet. During that stage, I read a lot of labels and learned to skip certain aisles of the supermarket. I also found additive-free replacements for foods I typically used. Because my son was eight years old and not always in my sight, I needed to enlist his cooperation in only eating foods that came from home. The purpose of this first phase was to clear additive residues out of his body in preparation for the next step. I also made notes about his behaviour, so I would have a basis for comparison when we got to the next stage.

That phase was the "junk load," when we would give him a high dose of additives and observe whether his behaviour changed as a result. I bought enough additive-laden foods for three days. It was an odd shopping experience for me, reading labels and deliberately looking for the ones with most additives. A few of the things I remember purchasing were breakfast cereal flavoured and coloured like blueberries, frozen pizza, packaged chocolate pudding, cake mix, a can of icing and coloured sprinkles for the top, flavoured potato chips, and a huge bottle of cola. We started on Friday night. By Saturday supper, the child couldn't sit still and his mouth was going a mile a minute. He wasn't quite swinging from the chandelier, but the difference in his behaviour was obvious. Although we had intended to carry on for a couple more days, I halted the experiment then and there. We had sufficient evidence that food additives were affecting him.

At the time of this experiment, it was controversial to suggest that behaviour could be influenced by what we ate. However, seeing it first-hand was a catalyst for me. I began thinking about the stress caused when our bodies have to deal with foreign materials that they were not made to handle. I wondered how food additives might be affecting me. It could be argued that hyperactive children are overly sensitive to additives, and maybe they are. If that is the case, then I think of them as canaries in the coal mine[11] and take it as a warning that these additives could also be affecting me even though I'm not aware of it yet.

Because I am a researcher and problem-solver by nature, I read a lot and developed recipes for additive-free versions of favourite foods. With this experience behind me, I taught an adult education class on additive-free foods for several years. I learned several things that made me realize that I shouldn't be complacent about the additives in our food.

For one thing, the government doesn't directly test the food additives it approves. Instead, it reviews the results of safety tests provided by the manufacturer with the application for a new food additive.[12] These tests are conducted by a third party, an independent lab hired by the manufacturer. Theoretically, this should mean the results are unbiased because testing is done at arm's length. However, the sad truth is that research fraud happens.[13] In January 2012, the *British Medical Journal* reported results of a survey that found that 13% of UK scientists and doctors had seen colleagues falsifying or fabricating data, and 6% admitted misconduct themselves.[14] In practice, scientists are under a lot of pressure, usually related to either career advancement or funding. Sometimes their response is to falsify or fabricate data. This breach of professional ethics has serious ramifications when public health decisions are based on their false information.

It's also a disturbing fact that experts reviewing the same studies sometimes come to different conclusions. For example, Allura red—a food dye used in candy and soft drinks, among other things—is permitted in Canada and banned in Denmark, Belgium, France, Germany, Switzerland, Sweden, Austria, and Norway.[15]

Furthermore, scientific testing is limited in what it can prove. The testing of food additives doesn't duplicate conditions of actual use because additives are tested individually. Yet our consumption pattern is different: products typically contain several additives, and we eat a number of such products during a day. Research has barely begun to study the synergistic effect of multiple additives together in the body. Synergy is a state in which the total result is greater than the sum of the individual effects. One of the few investigations into the synergistic effect of additives is a British study published in *Toxicological Sciences* in 2005. Researchers looked at the effects of two pairs of additives on developing nervous tissue. They reported that "both combinations are potentially more toxic than might be predicted from the sum of their individual compounds."[16] That is, there is a synergistic effect.

Truth is, there isn't definitive proof that food additives are harmless. In fact, although they are approved for consumption, less is known that we would like to think. According to the British researchers who confirmed the synergistic effect, "very little information about the neurotoxicity of food colors is available, and the mechanism by which they exert their toxic effect on nerve cells is not clear."[17] Given this reality, it becomes crucial that we make conscious choices when we buy food.

Avoid additives

Start by eliminating artificial colours, artificial flavours, nitrates and nitrites, BHT (butylated hydroxytoluene), BHA (butylated hydroxyanisole), and MSG (monosodium glutamate). They are found in a wide range of packaged foods, and the only way to know whether they are in something is to read labels. To simplify shopping when you are going additive-free, eliminate packaged goods from your diet or switch to organic foods. If you are a parent wondering if elimination of additives would help your child's behaviour, you'll find some useful information in "Dietary Sensitivities and ADHD Symptoms: Thirty-five Years of Research" in *Clinical Pediatrics.*[18]

Imitation foods...

Technology has given us the ability to produce imitation foods—imitation butter for our toast and sandwiches, imitation cream for our coffee, imitation sugar for our sweet foods, imitation puddings for dessert, and imitation fruit juice for breakfast. These replacements for real food have been widely embraced and used for many years. The irony is that people use products such as artificial butter, imitation coffee cream, and synthetic whipped cream thinking they are doing the right thing, in the same way they give their children an artificial sweetener because they think it is better for them than sugar.

Yet imitation foods are *not* good for our health: imitation butter and cream contain trans fats, which are now known to increase our risk of heart attack and stroke. Imitation sugars, such as sucralose and aspartame, may actually cause us to overeat and *gain* weight rather than lose it. Imitation fruit juice, which is little more than additives dissolved in water, is nutrient-deficient and provides little of the nourishment you would get from a glass of real juice. The same is true of powdered soups and packaged puddings.

Margarine was one of the first imitation foods to become widely available. It was introduced in Canada around the middle of the 20th century as a cheap replacement for butter. This was just the beginning of our honeymoon with the wonders of technology. If we could make a cheaper food that tasted and performed almost like the original, what *couldn't* we do?

The people who weren't happy were dairy farmers. Fearing loss of sales, they successfully lobbied governments for restrictions on this new product that pretended to be the same as theirs. During my childhood, the sale of coloured margarine was illegal in Alberta, on the premise that buying white margarine made it clear to consumers that they were not buying real butter. Margarine was sold in white blocks with little packets of colouring that could be mixed in to make coloured margarine. As you can imagine, both the mixing and cleanup were messy jobs. We were thrilled when one brand became available in sealed plastic bags with colouring contained in a small plastic bubble inside. To colour the margarine, you squeezed the bubble to release the liquid, then kneaded the bag for several minutes to distribute the colour evenly. Compared to the other method, that was a breeze. Even when it was coloured, the product did not look much like butter because Alberta law specified it had to be dark, almost orange. A neighbouring province had much less severe regulations about the colour of margarine, and I recall my mother-in-law coming back from family visits with pounds and pounds of creamy yellow margarine that really did look like butter.

Somewhere along the line, these restrictive regulations disappeared, and consumers came to think of margarine and butter as interchangeable. You will certainly notice this in recipes, which almost always specify "or margarine" when they call for butter. However, butter and margarine only *seem* the same. As far as your body is concerned, they are not. When liquid oil is turned into a solid fat such as margarine, the configuration of the fat molecules changes. Molecules are transformed from their original state (known as the *cis* form of the molecule) to the *trans* form. Recently, trans fat has come under scrutiny because of its negative health effects.

What's all the fuss about trans fat?

For many years, the transformation of liquid oil to solid fat was accomplished by *hydrogenation*, a chemical process in which liquid oil is processed under high temperature and pressure with a metal catalyst and hydrogen. The oil becomes saturated with hydrogen, and its molecular shape changes slightly. This is known as the *trans* fat. Your body isn't equipped to handle this new structure very well. Trans fat increases risk of heart disease because your body is unable to break it down in the normal way. This causes clogging of the arteries leading to the heart and brain. According to the Center for Science in the Public Interest, trans fat is the most harmful fat of all.[19]

Trans fat is found wherever you see "hydrogenated" or "partially hydrogenated" on the label. This may include dairy replacements, such as solid margarine, non-dairy coffee creamers, and artificial whipped cream. Foods that are deep-fried in fat (doughnuts and French fries, for example) are also potential sources. Products using fat as an ingredient are often made with trans fat—cake and pancake mixes, ready-to-use frostings, instant soup and noodle kits, salad dressings, frozen pizzas, packaged cakes, crackers, microwave popcorn, and, surprisingly, energy bars.

Until recently, health experts weren't concerned. In fact, in the early 1980s when I first learned about trans fat and the issues of using margarine, anyone expressing concern about the effects of trans fat was dismissed as a "health food nut." The tide turned in recent years when the role of trans fat in heart disease was confirmed. Some countries have now banned or restricted trans fat, while others—including Canada—require that the trans fat content be specified on nutrition labels so consumers can make informed choices.

The requirement for labelling has prompted manufacturers to begin reducing and eliminating trans fat. This is accomplished in various ways, such as switching the main ingredient from partially hydrogenated vegetable oil to either water or liquid vegetable oil, adding modified palm or palm kernel oil, or using a process known as *interesterification.*

Interesterification is a chemical process in which liquid oil is combined with a small amount of saturated fat and heated with enzymes or chemicals to move fatty acids around in the molecules. This solidifies oils without creating trans fats. The resulting product performs well in commercial applications because it is stable for frying and keeps for a long time without becoming rancid.

Although interesterification doesn't create trans fat, it results in molecules that do not exist in nature and are foreign to the human body. This raises questions about whether or not interesterification of fat is preferable to hydrogenation. A 2007 human study published in *Nutrition and Metabolism* suggests it is not. The research compared the effects of saturated fatty acids with two modified replacements fats—a partially hydrogenated oil containing trans fat and an interesterified fat mixture. After studying the effect on blood fats and sugars, the researchers reported the following:

> Both modified fats [trans fat and interesterified fat] adversely altered metabolism of plasma lipoproteins [fats] and blood glucose [sugar] in humans. Further investigation is warranted before interesterification is disseminated as the process of choice for replacing partial hydrogenation as a primary means for hardening vegetable oils for use in foods.[20]

The practical question is: Should we eat butter or margarine? As is the case with many health issues, you will find professional opinions on both sides of the debate. The position in favour of margarine advises you to eat only margarine that specifies "no trans fat" on the label. This approach does not take into account the likelihood that such products are made with interesterified fat, which has also been altered and is an unfamiliar molecule for your body to deal with. As the previously quoted researchers stated, more research is needed before we can use this replacement fat with confidence. The pro-margarine view also does not consider the other ways in which such a highly processed product is inherently harmful. Before the solidified oil is palatable enough to sell, it must be neutralized to remove as much of the catalyst as possible, then bleached, deodorized, coloured, and flavoured to bear a resemblance to butter. These processes introduce potentially undesirable chemicals into the product.

Those in favour of butter point out that it is much less processed. Butter is made by churning cream that has been separated from milk. The mechanical agitation of churning causes butterfat molecules to clump together, resulting in lumps of butter in a watery liquid. The liquid, known as buttermilk, is drained off, and the butter is kneaded into a coherent mass. Salt is usually added at this time, and colour may be added to commercially produced butter. It is a much gentler process than the making of margarine, and results in a product that is not denatured, has fewer additives, and no chemical residues. Purists choose organic butter because then they are assured that the cream was free of contaminants and provides maximum nutrients.

Healthy practices

Trans fats make it possible for manufacturers to use cheaper fats and increase the shelf life of packaged goods. They do not offer health advantages. If you use any of the products previously identified as potential sources of trans fats, check the labels to find the brands that are free of trans fats. However, remember that they could very well contain interesterified fat instead. Our bodies require fat to function properly. Here's how to make sure you are eating good fats:

- Use extra virgin olive oil on salads. If the label says it is "cold pressed," it will have been processed without heat; this preserves maximum nutrients.
- Use coconut oil in cooking. It has many healthful properties, and its high

smoke point means it does not break down into harmful components when heated.

- Use butter on your toast, not margarine. Butter gives you fat that your body can assimilate and does not contain chemical additives or modified fats.
- Reduce your intake of processed foods. The fewer packaged things you eat, the less chance you'll encounter trans fats, and the simpler your life will be because you just don't have to think about it.

Artificial sweeteners…

Artificial sweeteners are another widely used food substitute. In the last half of the 20th century, artificial sweeteners were promoted as a solution for two problems, both related to unhealthful effects of sugar overconsumption. The first is diabetes, a condition in which the body's insulin system is not working as it should and sugar cannot be properly processed. The other problem is obesity. An artificial sweetener that doesn't add calories to the diet seemed the ideal solution to dealing with sweet cravings.

Artificial sweeteners have been around longer than you might think. The first, *saccharin*, was produced in the late 1800s and became popular as an alternative when sugar was rationed during the two World Wars. In the early 1970s, widespread use of saccharin came into question when research showed that it caused cancer in laboratory rats. On this basis, saccharin was banned as an ingredient in packaged foods, although Canada continued to allow its sale as a table-top sweetener. The saccharin ban is being reconsidered, since further research showed that saccharin does not have the same effect on humans as on the experimental rats.

Cyclamates were introduced in the 1950s in the form of powder and pills for sweetening coffee and tea. Cyclamates were also permitted in some prepared foods, most notably diet soft drinks. They were highly successful because cyclamates do not have the unpleasant metallic aftertaste that saccharin has. Sales of diet drinks exploded in the 1960s along with public aspirations for attaining model-thin figures. Then a cancer connection was discovered, and cyclamates were banned. The soft drink industry was left scrambling, as described in the lead paragraph from a 1969 article in *Time* magazine:

> After the Government banned cyclamates, the diet-food industry last week began one of the fastest turnarounds in U.S. industrial history. Officers of firms in the $1 billion-a-year diet market hustled to cut their ties with cyclamates, to find an acceptable substitute, and to redirect marketing efforts to preserve demand for their heavily promoted brands. From now on, many of the diet drinks will be sweetened by a sugar-saccharin compound that may contain 30 calories in eight ounces, compared with only one or two calories in a cyclamate drink and 105 in a cola sweetened with straight sugar. The revised drinks will, of course, be labeled "new," and printing on the package will note prominently that they contain no cyclamates.[21]

The diet food industry coped by using saccharin, even though its strong aftertaste made a less-desirable product, but within a short time the safety of saccharin came into question. Fortunately for manufacturers of diets foods, another sweetener was in view. A few years earlier, a scientist developing a treatment for ulcers had accidentally stumbled on what came to be called *aspartame.* He was working with a combination of two proteins that are not usually found together in nature. During his investigations, he discovered that the resulting product was intensely sweet.

Aspartame was approved within a few years of the saccharin ban amidst criticism that there were serious irregularities in the FDA approval process, that the evidence of safety was unclear, and that the original lab work of the manufacturer was seriously flawed.[22] To some observers, it seems that the approval was being pushed through:

In October 1980 after great controversy and corporate pressure to re-approve aspartame, a Public Board of Inquiry (PBOI) was impaneled by the FDA to evaluate aspartame safety. The Board found that aspartame caused an unacceptable level of brain tumors in animals tested. Based on this fact, the PBOI ruled that aspartame should not be added to the food supply. One year later, aspartame was shockingly granted approval.[23]

Seizing the opportunity offered by this approval, industry introduced a number of aspartame-sweetened products—jelly powders, flavoured drink powders, breakfast cereals, and diet soft drinks.

Aspartame is the generic name of a sweetener that until recently has been known by the brand names NutraSweet and Equal. In 2010, a major manufacturer rebranded aspartame as AminoSweet and began promoting the "naturalness" of it.[24] Their use of this strategy illustrates why it's good consumer practice to know and look for *generic* names of ingredients. The generic name is a product's chemical name; brand names may change, but the generic name stays the same. When you know the generic name, you know what you are really consuming.

Aspartame solved an immediate problem, but even it was not a perfect solution. The main practical problem with aspartame, from a manufacturing perspective, is that it isn't stable when heated. This means it can't be used in baked goods. When sucralose was invented, that problem was solved because sucralose is heat stable. *Sucralose* is chlorinated sugar. The chlorination process makes it 600 times as sweet as regular sugar. This means that only a very small amount is needed, and therefore it contributes virtually no calories to the food. The generic name is sucralose, but it is most widely known by its brand name, Splenda. When sucralose is mixed with a carrier such as maltodextrin, it becomes a granular product that can be substituted for sugar in most home cooking recipes, although adjustments may need to be made in preparation methods and baking times.

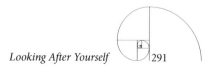

Both aspartame and sucralose are widely used in our food supply, and both are subjects of controversy regarding their safety. For example, a 2008 study found evidence that aspartame has numerous effects on the brain and concluded, "From all the adverse effects caused by this product, it is suggested that serious further testing and research be undertaken to eliminate any and all controversies surrounding this product."[25] On the other hand, the industry maintains that aspartame has been thoroughly tested, and there is no cause for concern.

As for sucralose, a study of the effect on rats found that "a 12-wk administration of Splenda exerted numerous adverse effects."[26] These effects included a significant increase in body weight when compared with control animals, a large reduction in beneficial bacteria in the intestine, and interference with the body's ability to absorb therapeutic drugs and nutrients. One of the main criticisms of sucralose is the lack of long-term human studies. Since approvals were granted on the basis of short-term tests on animals, it is quite possible that sucralose will have unexpected effects on people over time. Maybe not, but the point is that we just don't know.

Setting aside the safety issues, do these sweeteners have the desired effect when used as a substitute for sugar? When it comes to weight loss, research suggests that artificial sweeteners can cause a person to eat more and actually *gain* weight.[27] According to one theory, non-caloric sweeteners confuse the normal connection between sweet taste and caloric content, causing increased food intake and/or diminished energy expenditure.[28] Ironically, then, these products appear to be counterproductive to their intended purpose.

How to cope?

An Internet search reveals contradictory positions on the use of artificial sweeteners, most of them quite convincing on both sides of the matter. Trying to decide who's right and whose research is most valid becomes a daunting undertaking. Here is a common sense view about dealing with this lack of definitive answers.

- **Maintain healthy skepticism.** Remember that the availability of artificial sweeteners on the market is no guarantee that they are safe. Remember that the research is far from conclusive, and you will find scientists with equally strong views on both sides of the issue. Remember that all commercial products have financial vested interests at play, and these interests may influence approval decisions.

- **Apply the precautionary principle.** Where an activity raises threats of harm to the environment or human health, precautionary measures should be taken, even if cause-and-effect relationships are not fully established scientifically. Remember that you don't have to wait for the government to change its mind and ban artificial sweeteners; you can take a precautionary approach in *your decisions* about what to buy and consume.
- **Take the simplest approach.** Avoid artificial sweeteners until the risks are clarified by both research and the experience of many years of widespread use. If you just don't bother with artificial sweeteners, all this controversy becomes a non-issue and doesn't absorb your time and energy. Be wary of labels that say "sugar-free." On any product that is usually sweet, such as a drink or baked product, this usually means it is artificially sweetened in some way.
- **Use a natural alternative sweetener such as stevia.** Stevia is a natural, non-caloric sweetener that is suitable for diabetics because it does not cause spikes in blood sugar levels.[29] Extracted from the leaves of a South American plant, stevia has been used by natives for centuries. Despite that, some researchers suggest testing should be more rigorous before approvals are granted for widespread use of stevia. Check into it and see what you think.
- **Use traditional sweeteners, such as sugar, molasses, honey, agave syrup, and maple syrup—with restraint.** Traditional sweeteners are real food, not manufactured chemicals. The less-processed version of any of them has more nutrients than the highly refined form. For example, molasses

has more minerals than white granulated sugar, which is its highly refined form. However, even less-refined sweeteners should be consumed in moderation, especially by people with diabetes.[30]

Think-abouts

You only need one thing in the world.
It is not money.
It is not fame.
It is not even food.

All you need in the world is hope. As long as you have that, you have everything.... If you keep hope, all your other necessities will come soon enough. ~Ilchi Lee

In the long run, we shape our lives, and we shape ourselves. The process never ends until we die. And the choices we make are ultimately our own responsibility.
~Eleanor Roosevelt

Parents can only give good advice or put their children on the right paths, but the final forming of a person's character lies in their own hands. ~Anne Frank

This is your life. You are responsible for it. You will not live forever. Don't wait.
~Natalie Goldberg

Spending Consciously

When we spend consciously, we are able to navigate the consumer culture in a manner that preserves our health and safety as well as the integrity of our future. Without those, money doesn't matter. With them, money becomes a vehicle for creating quality of life, a means of using resources—yours or society's—in a sustainable manner.

We've covered a lot of ground in this book. As a result, conscious spending may seem a daunting prospect. It's important to remember that you don't need to do everything at once. Think in terms of *taking steps*. Pick something that seems both significant and doable—whether it's an attitude adjustment or a plan for changing a spending habit—and take steps to do it. Once you've got that in place, move to another issue. Bit by bit, things will change and, when you look back a year from now, you may well be surprised at how far you've come.

Conscious spending is about engaging mindfully with the consumer culture, rather than reacting in a knee-jerk fashion. It comes from a viewpoint of win-win rather than one of succeeding to the detriment of others. And it is based on the concept of enough. Conscious spending requires us to think for ourselves. It is a simple concept, although not always easy to put into practice when we live in a culture where strong external forces exert an influence on our decisions. Nevertheless, spending consciously gives us the satisfaction of knowing that we are financially responsible.

Conscious spending requires us to have an open mind and to look for other ways of thinking and acting. It requires us to take responsibility for ourselves. And it challenges us to remember that we are all connected...to each other...and to everything on the planet.

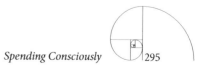

When we act consciously, we are aware and mindful of what we are doing. When we are mindful, we see more than just the mechanical and routine workings of the systems that surround us. Mindfulness implies attention of a particular kind—seeing both the deeper significance and the broader context. In this way, mindfulness gives us an advantage over simple and superficial awareness.

I hope this book will have increased your awareness in many areas of life in a consumer culture. Perhaps you didn't know how mortgages are structured and how much interest you pay when following the typical 25-year repayment schedule. Perhaps you didn't know that credit card interest is compounded daily and therefore increases exponentially over time if you don't pay the balance in full when it's due. Perhaps you were unaware that food additives and substitutes are not guaranteed safe; they are just "probably not unsafe." When you apply mindfulness to your new awareness, you consider that information in the bigger picture: How does it fit into the context of life on this planet? Who and what are affected by your choices? Do they lose if you win?

When you apply mindfulness, you also look more deeply into yourself: In what ways does the information and new awareness fit with your values? How does it help you create the kind of life that is meaningful to you? You could say that you bring *your self* to bear on the situation. So your awareness spirals both *outward* into the world where you live and *inward* to your core. By bringing the two together, you are making decisions and choices in a conscious way. The Fibonacci spiral on the cover of this book is a reminder of that spiraling inward and outward.

In mindfulness, there is a sense of purposefulness. Your new awareness has not landed in a void. You are synthesizing it as part of your growth as a person. You are making conscious choices rather than reacting in mindless ways to the demands of the culture.

Conscious spending is based on the intention of meeting our needs without causing harm to other people and the environment. Conscious choices are not always easy or popular, but they are ultimately the most satisfying. When your decisions and actions are based on conscious choice, you've done everything you could.

Conscious choices in everyday life…

Food is a good place to start practicing conscious choice. We make food choices daily, and what we choose affects workers and the environment, in addition to our own well-being. In order to make conscious choices, we need to be aware of more than the nutritional value or the possible presence of food additives.

Food production is no longer something done by people on their own patch of land to feed themselves. In many underdeveloped countries, families have lost the land on which they grew their own food. Their land, crucial for subsistence agriculture, has been taken over by large operations growing food for export, so the country can meet its balance of trade obligations.

In developed countries, most of us choose the greater convenience of buying our food rather than growing it in our back yards. With the ready availability of supermarkets and the vast array of products they carry, it is so much easier that way. Thus, the production and selling of food have become big business. Even organic products sold in a supermarket are grown on huge farms, albeit ones meeting the requirements for organic production.

Cheap food is a good thing, isn't it?

Mass production and distribution allow supermarkets to provide us with relatively inexpensive food. This is a good thing, isn't it? Maybe. Maybe not. It depends on *why* the food is cheap and what we do with it.

Any food is cheapest when it is in season, which means there is an abundance of it because it is the local season for growing the item. For that reason, prices are low. Conversely, prices will be high when an item is out of season and must be transported by truck or airplane over great distances. Buying in season makes a lot of sense. Not only is the produce less expensive, it is better for the environment because less fuel is used to transport it. Besides, it tastes better because it comes from a short distance and can be left to ripen longer before picking, allowing the flavour to mature and develop.

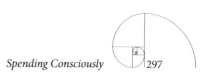

Much that passes as food is cheap because it isn't really food—powdered juice imitations, jelly dessert powders, and margarine come to mind. Sometimes, real food is cheaper than you would expect because retailers have squeezed producers to sell their goods at ever-lower prices. Because retailers are now mainly huge chain stores, they hold the power, and producers have little choice or leverage in the bargaining process.

Back to the question, then: Is cheap food a good thing? It could be, if it *actually* saves you money. However, it is a fact of human nature that people overbuy when price is low. It could make sense to buy good quality bread when you see it at a very low price and then put it in your freezer. On the other hand, if you buy a large quantity of discounted yogurt on the day it expires, and most of it spoils because you couldn't eat it fast enough, you've wasted money rather than saved it.

I learned from my own experience that it costs me money to buy food I like on sale because I overeat. I'm much better off to only buy one package on occasion, whether it's on sale or not, and eat it until it's done. Then I don't buy another for a few months. I spend less in the long run and am not continually overindulging in treats.

Overconsumption is not an accident…

Being aware of our tendencies and habits is useful in helping us manage ourselves and our money. It's not an easy job because the system is set up to encourage overconsumption and overspending.

In the world of business, making a profit is the point of being in business, and everything is geared toward generating that profit. This means inducing consumers to buy—preferably more than they planned to. That's the basis of the super-sizing concept. And it's why retailers offer "two-for" or "three-for" deals: they want you to buy two or three of an item rather than just one. Most of us do, in an automatic psychological response to the thought of getting a deal. However, most often you can still get the sale price if you buy only one. So beat them at their game and buy only what you need.

Supermarkets are arranged to encourage impulse buys. Music is upbeat to put you in a good mood, but slow enough so you'll have time to see the items you pass. None of this happens by accident. According to Marion Nestle, author of *What to Eat:*

> ...breathtaking amounts of research have gone into designing these places. There are precise reasons why milk is at the back of the store and the center aisles are so long. You are forced to go past thousands of other products on your way to get what you need.... The stores *create* demand by putting some products where you cannot miss them. These are often "junk" foods full of cheap, shelf-stable ingredients like hydrogenated oils and corn sweeteners, made and promoted by giant food companies that can afford slotting fees [money paid by the manufacturer to "rent" prime shelf space in the store]... and advertising. This is why entire aisles of prime supermarket real estate are devoted to soft drinks, salty snacks, and sweetened breakfast cereals, and why you can always find candy near the cash registers. Any new product that comes into a store must come with guaranteed advertising, coupons, discounts, slotting fees, and other such incentives.[1]

These strategies expose us to a large proportion of the 30,000 to 40,000 items supermarkets carry. How does this affect us when we shop? As Barry Schwartz found when he studied the paradox of choice,[2] sometimes our eyes glaze over, we cave in, and buy whatever. Other times we become paralyzed with indecision in the face of too much choice. Neither caving in nor becoming paralyzed is a constructive response.

Strategies to simplify and civilize food shopping...

- **Shop the perimeter at the supermarket.** That's where the basics are, so this strategy allows you to deliberately skip the middle aisles, where impulse items are shelved.

- **Buy as much local produce as you can at the farmers' market** and go to a small supermarket for the remainder of your grocery list. You don't need anywhere near 30,000 grocery items, and it is tiring to sort through the clutter to find what you want.
- **Decide on brands you like and stick with them** until they no longer work for you (as I found recently when my brand of dishwasher detergent changed its formula) or until they disappear from the market (a frustration I've experienced many times because I seem to like less-popular items). Browsing and "trying new things" is an expensive proposition and usually results in half-used packages cluttering up shelves because you can't bear to waste money by throwing them out. (This is fallacious thinking because the money was wasted when you bought the item in the first place, and keeping it in the cupboard will not recover the money.)
- **Buy basic ingredients that can be made into many things**, instead of purchasing specialty items. If you have flour, sugar, baking powder, milk and eggs, you can make pancakes. No need for a special bag of pancake mix. (Look at the label sometime; there's not much in a bag of pancake mix besides flour.) If you add butter to the five basic ingredients, you can bake cakes, cookies, breads, and scones. This makes shopping so much less complicated...and less expensive.

One of my favourite books about food choices is Michael Pollan's *Food Rules: An Eater's Manual.* A small book with a commonsense perspective, it is the best way I know to achieve uncomplicated eating. Although the title refers to rules, he clarifies his viewpoint in the introduction:

> While I call them rules, I think of them less as hard-and-fast rules than as personal policies. Policies are useful tools. Instead of prescribing highly specific behaviours, they supply us with broad guidelines that should make everyday decision-making easier and swifter. Armed with a general policy such as rule number 39 ("Don't eat breakfast cereals that change the color

of the milk."), you'll find you won't have to waste as much time reading ingredient labels and making decisions standing in the cereal aisle. Think of these food policies as little algorithms designed to simplify your eating life. Adopt whichever ones stick and work best for you.[3]

I like his description about establishing personal policies to simplify decision-making. Although I had never defined my own approach that way, I realize that is what I do. I just looked again at my strategies for simplifying and civilizing food shopping and realize they could be described as personal policies. Like Michael Pollan, I recommend you establish some personal policies with a view to streamlining your food shopping. Pollan divides his 83 "rules" into three categories. Here are just a few of my favourites:

What should I eat? *(Eat Food)*

- Avoid food products containing ingredients that no ordinary human would keep in the pantry.
- Avoid food products with the word "lite" or the terms "low-fat" or "no-fat" in their names.
- Eat only food that will eventually rot.
- It's not food if it arrived through the window of your car.

What kind of food should I eat? *(Mostly Plants)*

- Eat well-grown food from healthy soil.
- Eat more like the French. Or the Japanese. Or the Italians. Or the Greeks.

How should I eat? *(Not Too Much)*

- Consult your gut.
- Eat slowly.
- Do all your eating at a table.
- Cook.

These "rules" are followed by one-page explanations that are a combination of information and common sense, which I find refreshing. Rather than trying to paraphrase them or add my own comments, I recommend you read *Food Rules: An Eater's Manual*. It is well worth having in your kitchen.

What about organic food?

Michael Pollan's recommendations may leave you wondering if organic food is better for us. The short answer is yes. Foods grown with pesticides and herbicides absorb them as the plant grows, and they cannot be removed simply by washing. Organic foods are grown without pesticides, so you don't consume chemical residues when you eat organics.

The conventional practice of regularly feeding antibiotics to healthy animals is resulting in drug-resistant strains of bacteria, which means that commonly used antibiotics will no longer be effective in treating human illnesses.[4] Organically raised animals are fed plants grown without pesticides, and their feed does not contain low levels of antibiotics to promote growth.

It is not only animal health or your health that is of concern in nonorganic (conventional) food production. Pesticides and herbicides used in conventional production pose dangers to the workers, especially in Third World countries, where there are few safety regulations to protect them. Pesticides also pollute the air and ground water in any area where they are used. Once in the air and water, they affect all citizens. It is often argued that these pollutants become dispersed and therefore aren't that much of a problem. Yet shouldn't this make us even more concerned? These chemicals are persistent: they do not degrade and disappear quickly. And they accumulate over time. If they disperse in the environment, that means they are accumulating everywhere.

Apart from their health benefits, organics usually taste better. There is some evidence that organic foods are more nutritious, but this may not be significant in the bigger picture. I'm inclined to agree with biologist and food writer Marion Nestle, who says, "My guess is that researchers will eventually be able to prove organic foods marginally more nutritious than those grown conventionally, and that such findings will make it easier to sell organic foods to a much larger number of people. In the meantime, there are loads of other good reasons to buy organics, and I do."[5]

One of the most common objections to organics is the cost. It is true that many organic foods are more expensive. I shop frequently at a local natural foods store and find that processed organic foods, and imported organic produce out of season, are expensive. So I don't buy those organic items, and nor would I if I were shopping for conventional produce. Organic meats are usually expensive, so I eat small portions and purchase less-expensive cuts, such as ground lamb instead of lamb chops. At holiday times, I buy free range turkey instead of organic. It's about half the price, and my feeling is that producers using free range practices are generally conscious about how they raise the animals.

According to Michael Pollan, one of the most common questions people ask him is which organic foods provide best value for the money when they are on a budget. This question often comes from parents, and his answer is simple: pay the organic premium on whatever your children eat and drink the most of.[6]

Other useful advice comes from the Environmental Working Group, which publishes a yearly shopper's guide to pesticides in produce. The 2012 list[7] identifies the "dirty dozen" fruits and vegetables that are grown with the heaviest use of pesticides—apples, bell peppers, blueberries, celery, cucumbers, grapes, lettuce, nectarines, peaches, potatoes, spinach, and strawberries. These would be the products to buy organic if you were on a limited food budget.

The "clean 15" are those with the lowest levels of pesticides—asparagus, avocado, cabbage, cantaloupe, corn, eggplant, grapefruit, kiwi, mangoes, mushrooms, onions, pineapples, sweet peas, sweet potatoes, and watermelon. If you need to buy some conventional produce, these would be the ones to choose. For a handy card to print and carry with you, go to the Environmental Working Group website at www.ewg.org/foodnews.

Think-abouts

Our greatest responsibility is to be good ancestors.
~Jonas Salk

It is common sense to take a method and try it. If it fails, admit it frankly and try another. But above all, try something.
~Franklin D. Roosevelt

There are two freedoms: The false, where man is free to do what he likes. The true, where man is free to do what he ought.
~Charles Kingsley

The greatest discovery of my generation is that a human being can alter his life by altering his attitudes.
~William James
philosopher

Living Consciously

Understanding the issues and their implications is vital to living consciously. So is maintaining your sense of perspective.

Maintain your sense of perspective...

It is my personal policy to eat organic foods as much as is reasonable, and I make an effort to maintain a balance between living that policy and not being obsessively devoted to it. This allows me to respond to life's realities and changing circumstances. Michael Pollan's last rule, number 83, reminds us to "Break the rules once in a while."

> Obsessing over food rules is bad for your happiness, and probably for your health too. Our experience over the past few decades suggests that dieting and worrying too much about nutrition have made us no healthier or slimmer; cultivating a relaxed attitude toward food is important. There will be special occasions when you will want to throw these rules out the window. All will not be lost (especially if you don't throw out number 79 [Treat treats as treats.]). What matters is not the special occasion but the everyday practice—the default habits that govern your eating on a typical day. "All things in moderation," it is often said, but we should never forget the wise addendum... "Including moderation."[1]

This viewpoint is worth remembering, and not only about food. Obsessing about anything puts us out of balance and causes a loss of perspective. It is what makes us into fanatics. *Merriam-Webster* defines a fanatic as being marked by excessive enthusiasm and often intense, uncritical devotion.

Uncritical devotion, even to our own personal policies, stops us from thinking; there is no need to consider something further when we already think we have the answer. Uncritical devotion either closes us off from new opportunities or makes us vulnerable to taking our direction from others with vested interests in our choices. For anyone living in a consumer culture, this leaves us at risk of making our decisions based on corporate interests rather than our own.

Develop discernment…

When we become fanatic supporters of a position—responding reflexively rather than consciously—we have lost our capacity to use discernment. *Discernment* is the quality of being able to grasp and comprehend what is obscure. It requires keen insight and good judgment, challenging us to go beyond superficial perception. As we practice our ability to be discerning, we develop a wisdom that enables us to understand difficult situations and to make good decisions in such circumstances. My encounter with food additives was the point at which I became aware of the importance of discernment. Since then, I have been continually challenged to be discerning, to determine what is constructive and what is not when faced with contradictory viewpoints about products available in the marketplace.

The ability to discern is fundamental to decision-making, and the quality of our decisions is affected by how discerning we are. The tricky part about discernment is that we are trying to understand what is obscure, to see beneath what is obvious on the surface. It is not a straightforward case of listing pros and cons to find the answer. Discernment involves more than information. It involves perceiving the true nature of something—being in touch with your gut feelings in addition to direct observations.

As a result, the usual sources of information are not enough. What you see, hear, and read is a start. However, discernment requires you to also engage your inner senses, your gut feelings, to experience beyond the limits of your five basic senses (hearing, seeing, tasting, touching, smelling). Multisensory perception is what gives you the strength to be an independent thinker and to make conscious choices. It gives you authentic power rather than external power.

When you are not discerning, you rely on external information only. This leaves you in a vulnerable state, one in which you can easily be exploited. Authentic power is grounded within and is achieved when you measure your choices against your inner core, where your *real* strength resides.

One way we shut down our thinking and turn over our personal power is by blindly following experts. Experts can be very convincing, and their advice usually carries a lot of weight because they have credentials in their field. Believing what they say and following their advice gives us a break from thinking. The psychological effect of expert advice on brain activity has been seen in brain scans. David Freedman is the author of *Wrong: Why Experts Keep Failing Us—and How to Know When Not to Trust Them*. In a 2010 interview with *Time* magazine, he explained:

> ...people have actually looked at this question of what happens to brain activity when people are given expert advice, and sure enough, you see that the brain activity dies out in a way that suggests the person is thinking for themselves less. The brain actually shuts down a bit in the face of expert advice. When we hear an expert, we surrender our own judgment.[2]

I'm not suggesting we disregard what experts tell us. But we do need to use discernment in considering their positions in the context of ourselves. We need to think in terms of what makes sense for us.

We also need to remember that experts are people with a special skill or knowledge derived from training or experience. This does not mean they are right in their judgments or that they have a corner on all the information in the field. What they know and how they frame it is largely dependent on two things: where they were trained and where they worked afterward. People take on the culture and ideology of their educational institution because they are at the developmental stage of their careers and are being trained by experts in the field. When they graduate and have jobs, they take on the culture and ideology of their workplaces; that's how they stay employed.

Expert opinion often depends on who employs the expert. We can see this in looking at scientific positions on the approval of aspartame. Some experts say it should not have been approved for widespread use until safety was proven, and others maintain that there are no safety issues. That's why consumers need to be aware of potential bias and conflict of interest when assessing expert advice. If someone is selling you investments, that person presumably has expertise in the field. However, his or her advice may be biased due to the commission earned from your purchases.

People with specialized training are not always right. Here are some facts from David Freedman's book, quoted in the previously mentioned *Time* article:

> As much as 90% of physicians' medical knowledge has been found to be substantially or completely wrong. In fact, there is a 1 in 12 chance that a doctor's diagnosis will be *so* wrong that it causes the patient significant harm. And it's not just medicine. Economists have found that all studies published in economics journals are likely to be wrong. Professionally prepared tax returns are more likely to contain significant errors than self-prepared returns. Half of all newspaper articles contain at least one factual error.[3]

That's the way it is. And that's why we need to filter expert advice through our own common sense, rather than allowing ourselves to be lulled into unconsciousness by a false sense of security. No one forces us to be unconscious; it's a choice we make.

Nurture common sense...

Keith Stanovich, professor at the University of Toronto and author of *What Intelligence Tests Miss: The Psychology of Rational Thought*, identifies three components of the thinking process: autonomous mind, algorithmic mind, and reflective mind. The first two are how we commonly engage with our minds, and the last one is where common sense resides.

Our *autonomous mind* is at work when we make automatic decisions without further thought. Sometimes this simplifies our lives, as in the example I gave earlier about my shopping strategies: I find brands I like and stick with them as long as they continue to work for me. That means I can buy many things on autopilot because the decision has been previously made and I have no need to change it. By going on autopilot, my mind is freed up to think about other things instead of being unnecessarily tied up in the clutter of potential choices in the store. However, autonomous mind does not help us deal with changing times and new experiences. It keeps us stuck in old patterns that may no longer work in the new circumstances.

The *algorithmic mind* is the information processor. This is the component cultivated in the education system and measured by IQ tests. It's the part of my brain I used when I initially decided which brands to buy, before I put the decision-making on autopilot. The trouble with using the algorithmic mind is that when we apply it, we tend to think we've done it all and know everything there is to know…that we can rest on our laurels, so to speak.

These two components of thinking—autonomous mind and algorithmic thinking—are the most commonly used. Yet decision-making is incomplete without the third—the *reflective mind*. The reflective mind gives depth and dimension to our thinking. It is what contributes to rational thought. The ability to think rationally—to use common sense—is an important skill that allows us to think on our feet as we sort out life's daily challenges. According to Stanovich, "To be rational means to adopt appropriate goals, take the appropriate action given one's goals and beliefs, and hold beliefs that are commensurate with available evidence."[4] He goes on to point out that when we don't do this, we are less satisfied with our lives.

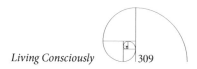

I've said before that it matters *what* we think. It also matter *how* we think. Why? I agree with Michael Bond, who said in an article in the *New Scientist*, "We need to be good at rational thinking to navigate our way around an increasingly complex world."[5] Because it helps us adapt sensibly to our environment, rational thinking is a crucial life skill.

Can it be taught? My theory is that common sense needs to be uncovered, not taught. I think most of us are born with the innate ability to look after ourselves, but the reflective commonsense mind has been discounted and disregarded in the culture. I have observed a high level of cultural admiration for academic algorithmic thinking to the exclusion of the reflective mind and common sense. This leads to a disproportionate trust in expert opinion and a loss of confidence in our own ability to make practical decisions.

I experienced this as a university student taking Economics 101. When we were presented with the concept that continual growth is essential for a healthy economy, it just didn't make sense to me. It seemed unnatural. I had a mental image of a balloon being blown bigger and bigger until it burst. I knew that when cells in a body grow without stopping, the overgrowth can destroy the system to which it belongs. We call that condition cancer, and the system is endangered by that continual growth. I couldn't see how it was any different for an economy.

I felt the same way when Canada undertook deficit budgeting a few years later. There were fancy theories about how this wasn't a problem, but it just didn't seem sensible. If a household can't sustain itself by continually spending more than it makes, how can it be any different for a country? At the time, there seemed to be no place for that point of view; I felt foolish and alone in my commonsense viewpoint. When this happens, a natural tendency is to "dumb down" our innate knowing, to disregard what our common sense tells us, and to follow the guidance of experts whose knowledge and advice have been cultivated in the education system. In other words, we defer to algorithmic thinking.

What might we do instead, to nurture common sense as a valued component of our thinking? Here are my suggestions:

- **Allow time to think**. This permits your reflective mind to work. When it does, the bigger picture of your life comes into focus and becomes part of your decision-making.

- **Uncover your common sense.** Clear away emotions and unproductive learnings that are masking your intrinsic common sense. Trust what you know.
- **Appreciate it when it shows up.** Use your common sense with confidence, knowing that practical intelligence is a legitimate part of your thinking toolkit.
- **Watch for it by being aware of incongruity.** If a decision or piece of information doesn't sit well with you, if there seems to be a mismatch with what you stand for, you may be hearing from your common sense.
- **Listen to it**. While it's not prudent to listen to every voice in your head, consider what comes up and see what fits with you.
- **Learn from experience.** We develop common sense by experiencing the consequences of our actions. Reflect on your experiences and what they have taught you.

The peril of not using common sense...

Experience is a great teacher. We also learn from stories, especially those that are enduring classics. One of my favourites is about the failure to apply common sense. "The Emperor's New Clothes" was written in 1837 by Danish author Hans Christian Andersen. Even though it describes an occurrence long ago and far away, it applies today. Here is the story as I have paraphrased it:

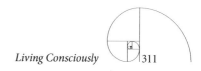

An emperor was approached by two weavers who negotiated a price to make him a splendid suit of clothes. What the emperor hadn't discerned was that they were scoundrels who were scamming him. They took the money to buy materials and turned up with beautiful, rich fabric supposedly in hand. Actually they had nothing, but did a great job of pantomiming the gestures as if they were showing sumptuous bolts of cloth to the emperor for his approval.

The emperor couldn't see anything, but their pitch had been clever: They had told him that only intelligent people would be able to see the cloth, and this would be a good way for him to identify the stupid people among his subjects. Naturally, the emperor did not say that he couldn't see the fabric because he certainly did not want to admit he was among the stupid.

The two men went away and came back in due course with a suit of clothes made from the "fabric" and fitted the garments on the king, all in an elaborate pantomime, of course. Once again, the king kept up the charade to avoid being thought stupid, even though his common sense told him there were not any clothes.

It didn't end there. When it was suggested that he parade through town so his subjects could see him in his finery, he had boxed himself into a corner. He couldn't back out, so the parade went ahead.

The townsfolk had heard that the clothes would be invisible to stupid people. They whispered about his nakedness among themselves as he paraded by, but were careful to make only the most complimentary statements aloud. They certainly did not want to risk seeming stupid. The pretense was broken when a little boy, who had not yet learned to deny his common sense and censor what he knew to be true, said: "But father, he has nothing on at all!"

Once the silence was broken, others began speaking the truth that they had also seen. As for the emperor, he saw no way out but to continue the farce to the end. The irony was that in trying to avoid looking like a fool, he put himself in the position of looking absolutely foolish. If only he had listened to his common sense instead of his fear.

The little boy did not see it as being complicated. He saw something different from what the others were talking about, and spoke the truth as he saw it. To him, it was simple: he saw the emperor walking through the streets without clothes, and he said so.

As long as we keep repeating what others are saying, instead of articulating what we think and know, we will go around in circles of comfortingly familiar thought. Myths will be perpetuated and common sense will be lost. One of my all-time favourite quotes is from Hungarian-born biochemist and Nobel Prize winner, Albert Szent-Györgyi: "Discovery consists of seeing what everybody has seen and thinking what nobody has thought."[6]

What if life really was meant to be simple?

We have made a complicated world to live in. But what if life *really* was meant to be simple? In *Small Is Beautiful*, E. F. Schumacher said, "Any intelligent fool can make things bigger, more complex, and more violent. It takes a touch of genius—and a lot of courage—to move in the opposite direction."[7]

Instead of mindless complication, we could strive for intentional simplicity. A simple life would not require us to drop out, do without, live in deprivation, or uncritically believe in the notion of scarcity. It would involve being more thoughtful about the way we live our lives and would allow us to engage with the consumer culture on our own terms, rather than reacting in knee-jerk fashion to the cultural meta-narrative, the overarching big-picture story that tells us how life ought to be. One semester, I asked my college students what life might be like, if it really were meant to be simple. Here are some excerpts from their collectively created vision:

- We would live as individuals, not as competitors in a mad rush to consume. Simplifying our lives would allow us to look around and enjoy life instead of seeing how fast we can get through it. Less time would be spent in paid employment, and more with friends and family. We would take responsibility for our actions, and the excuse "there isn't enough time" would have disappeared.
- We would not get caught up in the world's stereotypes and myths. We would make up our own minds about things. People who think differently would be valued because they don't see things in the "normal" way.

- There would be a spiritual quality to life. Not religion in the traditional sense, but recognition of the importance of life and our place in it. We would be in tune with ourselves, and value ourselves and the gifts we bring to the world.
- We would recognize that the world was never meant to be controlled by economics, money, commercialism, or time; that the world, and we in it, was created for a purpose. We would know that the world was created in perfect balance and symmetry to support life in a perfect way. We would no longer try to live life by the rules *we* make, but in harmony with the natural order of things.

I found a lot of wisdom in what they said. The full title of Schumacher's book is *Small Is Beautiful: Economics as if People Mattered.* The possibility that people could matter in an economic system has always appealed to me. It is expressed beautifully in the vision articulated by those students. Their ultimate world sounds like a place where people matter, and one where I'd like to live.

The world we live in and the lives we make for ourselves do not happen by accident. When you are conscious in your engagement with the consumer culture, you are more likely to end up living a life that is congruent with what you really want. Once we have recognized that what we think and how we act is important, it becomes a question of how could one do otherwise.

Think-abouts

Money is only a tool. It will take you wherever you wish, but it will not replace you as the driver.
~Ayn Rand

Our duty is to preserve what the past has had to say for itself, and to say for ourselves what shall be true for the future.
~John Ruskin

We need to teach the next generation of children from day one that they are responsible for their lives. Mankind's greatest gift, also its greatest curse, is that we have free choice. We can make our choices built from love or from fear.
~Elisabeth Kübler-Ross

There are people who have money and people who are rich. ~Coco Chanel

Strategies & Principles to Live By

Treat this like a trunk of old clothes. Take out a few and try them on. Put back the ones that don't work for you. And come back to it from time to time so you can see what suits you now that didn't the last time.

These are good habits to develop

- Keep an eye on your money (envelopes, jars, cheque register, subtraction record).
- Save in a savings account, not a chequing account.
- Control your expectations.
- Watch for the money leaks (small daily purchases, late fees, paying interest).

Important facts about money

- It is a basic principle of finance that the higher the interest rate, the more you pay in total interest over the life of the loan.
- It is also true that the higher your monthly payments, the shorter your loan. This reduces the total amount of interest you will pay.
- Conversely, the lower the monthly payments, the longer it takes to pay off the loan. This increases the amount paid out in interest. This is where many people get into financial difficulty—they go for the low payment now, rather than less interest in the long run.
- Credit cards have a period of a few weeks' grace before interest is charged. You can avoid paying interest simply by paying the bill in full before the due date.
- Debt consolidation propels a person into a never-ending cycle of debt unless it is used very skillfully.
- As for account overdraft and payday loans, they are best avoided completely.
- When it comes to money, it isn't just the math that counts, it's the psychology.
- Living consciously is where true power resides in your relationship with money.

Tricky things about credit cards

- The no-interest period of a credit card applies to purchases but not to cash advances or the cheques that credit card companies periodically send you in the mail.
- You don't pay interest on a credit card if you pay the balance in full by the due date. But it must be the full amount. Anything less and you will be charged interest back to the day when purchases were made.
- If you are working on clearing an unpaid balance off a card, the first thing to do is stop using the card.
- A credit card is a great convenience if you pay the balance off each month, but a huge burden when used as a source of borrowed money.

Exercise autonomy in making decisions

- Detach yourself from the cultural story.
- Think about how *you* would like to live.
- Re-engage with the consumer culture on your own terms.

Tips for navigating the consumer culture

- Understanding the cultural meta-narrative is crucial for successfully navigating through it.
- If we are unaware of it, we simply react in knee-jerk fashion to the stories that corporations would like us to believe about what makes life worth living.
- When we are aware of the narrative, we can decide for ourselves if that's how we want to live the story of our own lives.
- This requires willingness to question, to have an open mind, to look for other ways, and to develop a sense of what is important to us.
- If you learn how to identify enough, it will be much easier to navigate the consumer culture because more things will be non-issues.
- The challenge of uncertainty is that, since you don't know what will present itself, you can't rehearse your response.

Make decisions that will lead to a sustainable life

Common sense must be nurtured

- Allow time to think with your reflective mind.
- Uncover your common sense and trust what you know.
- Appreciate it when it shows up.
- Watch for it by being aware of incongruity.
- Listen to it and see what fits with you.
- Learn from experience.

Conflicting expert opinion is a fact of life

- Maintain healthy skepticism.
- Apply the precautionary principle.
- Take the simplest approach.
- Use natural alternatives.

Look after yourself in the marketplace

- Pay attention to your mindset.
- Adopt an attitude of healthy skepticism.
- Hold your boundaries.
- Learn how the systems work.
- Cultivate an assertive approach.

Steps to release unconscious motivators

- Increase your awareness about what isn't working.
- Ask yourself if the belief or feeling is serving you well.
- Let go of the outdated belief.
- Install a new belief.

Make a life that is deeply satisfying

- Write your own story.
- Use all your resources.
- Practice intentional simplicity.
- Consider "what if..."
- Know how much is enough.

Anticipate uncertain times

- Live lightly by avoiding a debt load.
- Retire existing debts rapidly.
- Build a stable and sustainable financial structure.
- Cultivate your innate common sense.
- Pay yourself first.

Establish a powerful relationship with money

- Uncover your unconscious motivators.
- Define value and worth for yourself.
- Experience the freedom of conscious choice.

Create financial security

- Do not incur destructive debt.
- Create an emergency fund.
- Consider your lifestyle.
- Be cautious and reasonable about constructive debt.

Reduce the mortgage interest you pay

- Shorten the amortization period.
- Prepay the principal.
- Pay weekly or biweekly.
- Increase your monthly payment.
- Shop for the best interest rate.
- Make the largest down payment possible.

Avoid credit card debt

- Anything you buy with your credit card will cost you a whole lot more than what's on the price tag—unless you pay off the entire balance before the grace period ends.
- Most of the minimum payment on a credit card goes to pay off the interest each month. That's why it takes a very long time to retire a loan if you only pay the minimum.
- Powerpay (snowball) your outstanding balance to short-circuit this if you have an ongoing credit card balance.

Protect your dependents with life insurance

- You need the most life insurance when your last child is born.
- Term insurance gives you the financial protection you need at a reasonable cost. Make sure it is renewable term.
- It makes no sense to use your insurance as an investment vehicle by purchasing a cash value policy. Invest the money yourself and you'll be farther ahead.

Mastering the art of living skillfully

- ✓ Think for yourself. Remember the principle of critical mass.
- ✓ Don't settle for ready-made answers. They are the anesthetic of the mind.
- ✓ Challenge the conventional wisdom; be skeptical of "experts."
- ✓ Look beyond the obvious. Think about possibilities. Ask questions that open doors in your imagination and allow creativity to occur. Two key questions:

  What are the possible ways I could ______________?

  What if ____________________________________?

- ✓ Steer away from fads. Instead, look for what endures. Fads are the creation of a market economy intent on getting you to keep parting with your money. Long-lasting items provide deeper satisfaction.
- ✓ Do not fall prey to insecurity and fear. Insecurity prevents us from thinking for ourselves. Fear causes us to be oblivious, paranoid, or somewhere in between. When you are not being controlled by insecurity and fear, you are better able to make conscious choices.
- ✓ Be prepared to see the truth, especially about yourself. Beware of self-deception and superficiality.
- ✓ Be mindful of who you really are and what makes life meaningful for you.

The Language of Financial Sustainability

This section is about learning the language. In any subject, there are words and concepts that articulate the field. When you have a sense of them, it's easier to grasp the significance of what the author says.

I've divided the subject of financial sustainability into its two major areas, self-management and money management, with a few sections under each. These sections deliver a snapshot view. As in the case of photography, the snapshots capture the subject from one perspective. This doesn't cover all the words you'll ever want to know on the subject. But for now, it is enough.

To start with, I suggest picking the topic that's of greatest interest and reading it through. The next time you return, read the one that is least familiar. Another time, choose the section you think will bore you the most.

The definitions and descriptions contain some italicized words. These are defined elsewhere in the section, and I've alerted you this way in case you want to look them up. Sections are laid out as follows:

Self-Management…

Thinking & Self-Responsibility

Active parenting: reducing children's vulnerability to pressures of modern life by teaching them how to think and be self-responsible. May include monitoring online activities, building their sense of self, increasing their understanding of ulterior motives in the marketplace, and helping them see through advertising claims and emotional appeals.

Aggressive approach: a rudely confrontational attitude during interpersonal communication. In consumer transactions, is not effective in achieving the desired results when there is a problem with a product or service.

Algorithmic mind: the aspect of thinking that involves information processing. This is the component cultivated in the education system and measured by IQ tests. The other two components are *autonomous mind* and *reflective mind.*

Aspirational gap: the difference between the cost of what we want and the amount we can actually afford.

Assertive approach: a communication strategy of stating what you want, firmly and without antagonism. Is usually the best way of achieving desired results, and very useful in consumer transactions.

Autonomous mind: the aspect of thinking that involves decisions made automatically, without further thought. The other two components are *algorithmic mind* and *reflective mind.*

Awareness: the state or condition of having realization, perception, or knowledge; consciousness.

Balance: a state of equilibrium that serves for the time being. Balance cannot be achieved and then ignored; it requires continual response to conditions and circumstances.

Boundaries, personal: the physical, mental, and emotional limits we establish to prevent being manipulated or taken advantage of. Boundaries communicate that we have self-respect and will not allow others to define us.

Common sense: sound and prudent judgment based on clear perception of the situation combined with what has been learned from past experience; a basic level of practical knowledge and judgment essential to helping us live in a reasonable and safe way. Related to *reflective mind.*

Conscious choice: the deliberate act of deciding between two or more possibilities; choosing with full awareness. The opposite is allowing chance to determine what happens.

Conscious spending: deliberate and mindful engagement with the consumer culture, rather than reacting in a knee-jerk fashion to external pressures. Requires us to think for ourselves and take responsibility for our actions. Based on the intention of meeting our needs without causing harm to other people and the environment.

Consume: use up, destroy, expend, or squander. *A consumer* is someone who consumes or buys things.

Consumer culture: a *culture* based on materialistic values. Instills a way of living that promotes buying, discarding, and using things up.

Consumer: a person or group of people that pays to own and use the goods and services produced in a society. The Western economic system is set up so that consumers are a key factor motivating production and keeping the economy moving.

Critical mass, theory of: a concept about group behaviour, often applied in marketing, that explains the phenomenon of dramatic increase in sales after a certain point which is known as the tipping point. The same phenomenon can occur with ideas as well as products.

Cultural meta-narrative: the big, overarching story of a *culture*. The meta-narrative is built by a group of people and transmitted from one generation to the next. Exists unseen and unidentified, yet exerts a surprisingly powerful effect on our lives. Also referred to as a *story field.*

Culture: a product of the arts, beliefs, customs, and institutions created by a society at a particular time. Expresses the values held by that society.

Discernment: the quality of being able to grasp and comprehend what is obscure. Requires keen insight and good judgment, challenging us to go beyond superficial perception. Enables the understanding of difficult situations and making good decisions in such circumstances.

Enough: occurring in such quantity, quality, or scope as to fully meet demands, needs, or expectations. From a broader viewpoint, "enough" is not a number, but rather what is deeply satisfying, without anything in *excess* to burden or complicate our lives.

Essential: of the essence—the inward nature, true substance, or constitution of anything, including ourselves.

Excess: surplus to requirement; surpassing usual, proper, or specified limits; undue or immoderate indulgence.

Expert failure: mistakes that occur in the work of people with a level of expertise that makes mistakes seem unthinkable. Malcolm Gladwell argues this is due to overconfidence on the part of the expert, who believes he or she has all the information needed in the situation. Is not the same as incompetence, and has potential to have far greater consequences. In view of this, we must use discernment in considering expert advice, and think in terms of what makes sense for us.

Fulfillment curve: a graph showing the effect of continual accumulation of goods and experiences. The apex of the curve is the point of *"enough"* and everything after that is *excess*. Developed by The New Road Map

Foundation and published in *Financial Integrity: Transforming Your Relationship with Money.*

Healthy skepticism: a state of not automatically believing a claim or statement without looking at the evidence to see if there are any other possible interpretations.

Holistic view: looking at the big picture instead of focusing on details. Associated with right brain functioning rather than the logical left brain. A necessary part of a comprehensive approach to decision-making. Sometimes written as "wholistic."

Intentional simplicity: a *paradigm* based on the premise that we can choose to see the world as a place of elegantly simple solutions, if we are willing to look for and apply them.

Living by default: letting society and those around you determine how you live. The opposite is *conscious choice.*

Mindfulness: attention of a particular kind—seeing both the deeper significance and the broader context. Gives an advantage over simple and superficial awareness when making decisions.

Mindset: a mental attitude or inclination; a fixed state of mind.

Multisensory perception: engagement of inner senses, sometimes described as "gut feelings," to experience beyond the limits of the five basic senses (hearing, sight, taste, touch, smell). Gives authentic power rather than external power, and the strength to be an independent thinker and to make *conscious choices.*

Navigating: to make one's way over or through.

Overconsumption: *consuming* to an excessive degree.

Paradigm: a philosophical or theoretical framework; a theory or group of ideas about how something should be done, made, or thought about.

Passive: a weak and withdrawn approach during consumer transactions. Ineffective in negotiations, and usually results in the other party having the upper hand.

Practical intelligence: mental ability to cope with the challenges and opportunities of life, making good judgments in real-life situations. Similar to *common sense* and "street smarts."

Rational thought: a type of thinking that allows us to think on our feet while sorting out life's daily challenges. Helps us adopt appropriate goals, take the suitable action in light of goals and beliefs, and hold beliefs that fit with available evidence—i.e., rational thought helps us be realistic.

Reflective mind: the aspect of thinking that contributes to *rational thought,* giving depth and dimension to thinking. Is the seat of *common sense.* The other two components of thinking are *autonomous mind* and *algorithmic mind.*

Resourcefulness: able to deal skillfully and competently with new or difficult situations, devising creative ways and means of solving problems. Also referred to as "self-reliance."

Responsible: able to be trusted to do what is right or to do the things that are expected or required; willing to answer for one's conduct and obligations; accountable. Capable of *rational thought* or action.

Self-awareness: an *awareness* of one's own personality or individuality.

Self-fulfilling prophecy: something that becomes real or true because it was predicted or expected. Occurs because the belief that something will happen causes a person to unconsciously act in ways that do make it happen.

Self-reliance: see *resourcefulness.*

Self-responsibility: the state of being *responsible* or accountable to oneself for actions undertaken.

Story field: see *cultural meta-narrative.*

Sufficiency: the quality or state of being adequate. Lynne Twist defines it as an experience, a context we generate, a knowing that there is enough. The opposite is "scarcity."

Sustainability: the capacity to endure; able to be maintained or kept going. Often thought of in relation to environmental issues, but also applicable to one's own life in that it makes sense to make decisions that will lead to a sustainable life.

Time poverty: the feeling that there is insufficient time to meet the demands on us.

Unconscious consumption: mindlessly *consuming* with little or no regard for what is deeply satisfying or socially and environmentally responsible. The opposite is *conscious spending.*

Uncritical devotion: a mindset of accepting what is presented without reflecting on the statements or claims to see if they make sense for you. Closes us off from new opportunities and makes us vulnerable to taking direction from others with vested interests in our choices.

Upscale emulation: the desire to imitate people who have more money than we do.

Values: deeply held beliefs; those things we deem fundamentally important. Truth, honour, courage, humility, order, and compassion are generally considered universal values.

Wholistic view: see *holistic view.*

Work-life balance: juggling competing factors related to work and family so they can exist in a harmonious whole.

Worldview: a person's view of how the world works; a comprehensive conception of the universe and of humanity's relation to it.

Ethics & Social Responsibility

Accountable: being obliged or willing to accept responsibility or to account for one's actions; answerable.

Boycott: a concerted refusal to have dealings with a business, usually to express disapproval of certain practices with the hope of causing a change in corporate behaviour.

Cash cropping: growing crops for export to meet obligations for international balance of trade payments. For this to happen, large corporate farms take over the land and it is no longer available to grow food for the local population. Usually a condition of developing countries.

Change: to make different; transform. May be viewed as a disconcerting loss or a challenging opportunity, depending on one's mindset.

Clone site: a bogus website set up by a scammer to mimic a legitimate one for the purpose of obtaining personal identity information for fraudulent use.

Code of conduct: see *code of ethics.*

Code of ethics: a public statement by a company or professional group that defines what is considered right and wrong in the practice of the business or profession. Intended to ensure fair treatment of consumers. Breaches of the code are punishable to varying degrees, depending on the severity.

Crowdfunding: a means of obtaining small amounts of capital from many people in the community who are interested in supporting the development of a project or business.

Earthships: Mike Reynolds's unique human dwellings that are entirely self-sustaining. Headquartered near Taos, New Mexico.

Ethical dilemma: a complex situation that often involves an apparent mental conflict between *moral imperatives*, in which following one would result in violating another.

Ethics: the principled choice between right and wrong, based on our values; what we do when no one is watching.

Fair trade: a philosophy meant to ensure that production is sustainable and workers in developing countries are paid fairly for their work and products. Includes commitment to a safe and healthy work environment, to not exploiting children as cheap labourers, to sustainability through improved environmental practices and responsible methods of production, and development of a producer's ability to remain independent.

Grameen Bank: a source of *microloans* that is tackling poverty by making business loans to the poorest of the poor. Started by economist Muhammed Yunus in Bangladesh in 1983. This model of lending has now spread to more than 100 countries. Professor Yunus and Grameen Bank were awarded the Nobel Peace Prize in 2006.

Identity theft: the stealing of pertinent personal information to use for fraudulent purposes. Has become an issue particularly in the digital age because it can be accomplished so easily.

Interface: Ray Anderson's flooring company that is waging a successful war on waste, as a result of his epiphany that he did not want to continue to be part of a huge problem, and that change was possible. Recognized worldwide as an inspiration to other businesses.

Justification: the act of rationalizing actions that are incongruent with our values by giving ourselves reasons why they are acceptable.

Living wage: the amount it takes to pay for basic food, shelter, and clothing. Usually used in connection with workers in Third World countries.

Microfinance: see *microloan.*

Microloan: small amounts of money lent to people living in poverty, with the intention of helping them start businesses and support themselves.

Mission statement: a statement of the purpose of a company or organization, developed to guide decision-making. Makes public its reason for existence, and its goals.

Moral imperative: a principle of right behaviour, held by a person to be unquestionably true and compelling him/her to act accordingly. May be described as the dictates of one's conscience.

Personal integrity account: a metaphor used by author Stephen Covey to describe how we build trust in ourselves and our ability to do the right thing. All our choices either contribute to our strength of character and personal integrity account, or they subtract from it.

Phishing: *(pronounced fishing) a* primary means of fraudulently obtaining identity information. Much phishing is done by e-mail, often urging an individual to click on a link that will unknowingly take them to a *clone site* where identity information can be gathered by the scam artist.

Public health care: see *universal health care.*

Rationalization: see *justification.*

Resource-based economy: a vision for an alternate way of organizing society, based on the scientific method and intelligent use of technology to create a better world for all with what we have. Developed by Jacque Fresco.

Responsible: able to be trusted to do what is right or to do the things that are expected or required; willing to answer for one's conduct and obligations; accountable.

RFID chip: a radio frequency identification chip in a credit card; allows payments to be made wirelessly. Fast and convenient, but leaves user wide open to card information being accessed and misused. A shielded wallet or wrapping the card in aluminum foil may prevent this.

Scams: schemes to take a person's money without providing value in return, even though something is promised in order to encourage participation. Enduring ones are known under names such as the bank inspector scheme, Nigerian money letter, and Ponzi scheme. Were previously conducted by telephone and mail; now e-mail provides cheap and easy access to potential targets. Some are highly sophisticated, others are not.

Shrink: retail losses due to theft by employees, customers, and organized crime. Global cost was $119 billion in the 12 months ending June 2011. In Canada, shrink averages about 3% of sales.

Smishing: a variation of *phishing*, used to reach a person via text. The individual is asked to click on a link in a message to deal with some "urgent" situation or to claim a prize. Takes person to a webpage where information is requested, or else downloads malware onto the cell phone, allowing the scammer to access banking information via the phone.

Social justice: a viewpoint based on making life better for others. Based on principles of equality, solidarity, human rights, and the dignity of every human being.

Social responsibility: to be *responsible* for, and take appropriate action to contribute to, the well-being of those beyond our own immediate family.

Subsistence farming: growing the plants and animals that families need to feed themselves, on small patches of land which are vulnerable to being seized for cash cropping. These families are forced to move to city slums, where they struggle to find work to earn money to buy food.

Sustainability: the capacity to endure; ability to be maintained or kept going.

Sweatshop: a production facility that employs workers at very low wages, for long hours, and in poor working conditions. Most frequently found in developing countries, where workers are not protected by legislation and have little choice or protection. Are an economic response to demand for cheap consumer goods in developed countries.

Universal health care: a system to provide health care to all citizens, regardless of income. Society supports the system through taxes, and costs are paid from the government budget. Also referred to as *public health care.*

Visionary: a person with foresight and imagination, able to express clear ideas about what should or could happen in the future. Often their ideas are controversial because thinking is far ahead of the general population. T. C. Douglas, known as the father of Medicare in Canada, is an example.

Health & Safety

Artificial sweetener: a synthetic *food additive* that duplicates the sweet taste of sugar with few or no calories. Used by diabetics. Also for weight control, although research is showing them ineffective for the latter purpose. Found in a wide variety of processed foods, often labeled as "sugar-free". Safety is controversial; some have been allowed, then later banned. See also *aspartame, cyclamates, saccharin.*

Aspartame: an *artificial sweetener* made from a combination of two proteins not usually found together in nature. Widely sold under brand names NutraSweet, Equal, and now AminoSweet. Most legislators are satisfied with safety, but reports of adverse effects including confusion, memory loss, night sweats, depression, and weight gain make their use controversial.

BHA (butylated hydroxyanisole): a chemical antioxidant added to food, cosmetics, and pharmaceuticals as a preservative. Found in fat-containing foods such as margarine, oil, processed meats, soups, baked goods, deep fried foods, and frozen entrees. Controversial. Avoidable by reading labels.

Closely related to *BHT (butylated hydroxytoluene).*

BHT (butylated hydroxytoluene): see *BHA (butylated hydroxyanisole).*

Bisphenol A (BPA): a plasticizer widely used in food containers, plastic bottles, and linings of food cans. Endocrine disrupter which interferes with natural production and function of the body's hormones. Babies and young children are especially sensitive to the effects of BPA, and its use in baby bottles and cans has been controversial.

Cold pressed (oil): process for extracting oil without heat in order to preserve maximum flavour and nutrients.

Cyclamates: an *artificial sweetener* introduced in the 1950s, very popular in diet soft drinks in the 1960s, banned in 1969 when a cancer connection was discovered.

DNA (deoxyribonucleic acid): a biological molecule, essential for life on Earth, that contains genetic instructions for the development and functioning of living organisms. The DNA segments carrying this genetic information are called "genes."

Food additive: any chemical substance added to food during preparation, packaging, or storage for the purpose of achieving a particular technical effect, which may include improved appearance, flavour, keeping qualities, or ease of manufacturing. Some are controversial.

Food irradiation: a process of exposing food to ionizing radiation with the intention of preventing food spoilage. Destroys microorganisms or insects present in the food, inhibits sprouting, and delays ripening. Also increases juice yield and improves rehydration. Foods do not become radioactive, but subtle chemical changes result when the energy of radiation breaks apart molecules to form free radicals. Is controversial for this and other reasons related to the safety of using and transporting nuclear energy.

Fungicide: see *pesticide.*

Genetic engineering (GE): see *genetic modification.*

Genetic modification (GM): manipulation of the fundamental material of living cells to create results that can't occur naturally, e.g., crossing of the species barrier. Also known as *genetic engineering.*

Genetically modified organism (GMO): a plant or animal that results from *genetic modification.*

Herbicide: see *pesticide.*

Hydrogenation: a chemical process in which liquid oil is treated with a metal catalyst and hydrogen under high temperature and pressure to turn it into a solid at room temperature. Saturated with hydrogen changes the molecular shape slightly, turning it into a *trans fat.* Found in fat-containing foods including margarine, cake mixes, baked goods, salad dressings, frozen pizzas, microwave popcorn, and some energy bars. Once widely accepted, now controversial.

Hydrolyzed vegetable protein (HVP): see *MSG (monosodium glutamate).*

Insecticide: see *pesticide.*

Interesterification: a chemical process that solidifies oils by heating with enzymes or chemicals and a small amount of *saturated fat* to move fatty acids around in the molecules without creating *trans fats.* However, like *hydrogenation*, it produces altered molecules that may not be assimilated well in the body. Found in similar fat-containing foods. Introduced as an alternative to *hydrogenation*; unclear if it is preferable.

Mercury: a toxic metal found in some fish (especially tuna), certain dental fillings (amalgams), and products such as batteries, thermometers, compact fluorescent lights, and fluorescent tubes. Affects the brain, liver, and kidneys, and can cause developmental disorders in children.

Monounsaturated fat: a fatty acid chain with one double bond between carbon atoms. Liquid at room temperature. Olive oil, nuts, and avocados are sources. Monounsaturated fat is now recommended by some instead of *polyunsaturated fat. See also saturated fat and unsaturated fat.*

MSG (monosodium glutamate): a chemical added to food to enhance flavour. Found in many processed foods as well as in Chinese restaurant food. Causes headaches and tightening of the chest in people who lack the enzyme to digest it. *Hydrolyzed vegetable protein (HVP)* may contain MSG.

Nitrate: a preservative used in processed meats, such as sausage and bacon, to prevent possible food poisoning from careless handling during processing and retailing. Known to form nitrosamine, a cancer-causing substance. Decision to permit use in food is based on a *risk-benefit analysis.*

Organic food: food produced without synthetic pesticides and fertilizers; and processed without using chemical solvents and *food additives,* or processes such as *food irradiation* and *genetic modification.*

Partially hydrogenated: see *hydrogenation.*

PBDEs (Polybrominated diphenyl ethers): chemicals used as flame retardants in synthetic materials. Typically found in electronics, and in foam used in furniture and carpet underlay. Linked to cancer, disruption of the developing brain, and immune and reproductive problems.

Pesticide: chemical preparation that destroys plant, fungal, or animal pests. Found on lawns and gardens treated with pesticide-containing products, as well as on food grown with pesticides. Causes a variety of health issues in the reproductive system, brain, and nervous system. More-specific terms are *herbicide* (for plants), *fungicide* (for fungi), and *insecticide* (for insects).

PFCs (Perfluorochemicals): chemicals applied to create a non-stick surface on some pots and pans, food packaging, clothing, upholstered furniture, windshield washer fluid, and lipstick. Cause brain and nervous system damage, birth and developmental effects, organ system toxicity, cancer, allergies, and fertility issues. Build up in the body over time.

Phthalates: chemicals used to give fragrance a lasting quality, and also to make vinyl products soft and flexible. In our bodies, may adversely affect reproduction and development. Found in body products, air fresheners, and soft plastics often used in shower curtains and toys. Identified on the label as "fragrance" or "parfum."

Polyunsaturated fat: a fatty acid chain with more than one double bond between carbon atoms. Liquid at room temperature. Common sources: nuts, seeds, and their oils (what we broadly refer to as vegetable oils). Thought to be the preferable form of fat for some time, but this has recently come into question. See also *saturated fat* and *unsaturated fat.*

Precautionary principle: a guideline for ensuring prudence in the adoption of new products in the face of *scientific uncertainty*. Instead of asking how much harm we are willing to permit, the precautionary principle asks how little harm is possible. It states: Where an activity raises threats of harm to the environment or human health, precautionary measures should be taken even if some cause-and-effect relationships are not fully established scientifically.

Recombinant DNA (rDNA): a modified *DNA* sequence that results when genetic material from various sources is combined in a lab to make DNA sequences that are not normally found in nature.

Risk-benefit analysis: a comparison of the risk of a situation to the benefits. Raises the fundamental question: How much harm is allowable? Has resulted in many new products being put into widespread use until unintended consequences begin to show up. *Trans fats* and *artificial sweeteners* are two examples.

Saccharin: an *artificial sweetener* introduced in the late 1800s and popular as a sugar alternative during the two World Wars. In the early 1970s, research showed it to be a cause of cancer in laboratory rats. Banned as an ingredient in packaged foods, although Canada continued to allow its sale as a table-top sweetener.

Saturated fat: a fatty acid chain with no double bonds between carbon atoms. Solid at room temperature. Animal products such as butter, cream, cheese, eggs and fatty meats are primary sources. For some time, saturated fats were thought to be bad for heart health, but that view is now being challenged. See also *monounsaturated fat* and *polyunsaturated fat.*

Scientific uncertainty: a fact of life. There are too many variables for science to give us definitive answers; what they report is limited to observations made in the study being reported upon. Waiting for definitive proof on big questions is not prudent. This is why the *precautionary principle* is important.

Sucralose: an *artificial sweetener* made from chlorinated sugar. 600 times sweeter; therefore, little is needed and it adds no calories to the food. Most widely known as Splenda. Can be produced in a form that allows substitution for sugar in most recipes, with appropriate adjustments in preparation methods and baking times. Has an advantage over *aspartame,* which breaks down when heated. Safety concerns are expressed by some.

Super-food: a product *genetically modified* to be hardier, more resistant to disease and insects, faster growing, and/or undamaged by pesticides. These measures are financially attractive to producers because of increased productivity and profitability of crops.

Superpest: see *super-food.*

Superweed: see *super-food.*

Synergistic effect: a state in which the total result is greater than the sum of the individual effects. Difficult for scientific study because combined effects are extremely complex and often unpredictable. Very limited research in this field, creating lack of clarity about the effect of combined human exposure to food additives and chemical toxins. At least one recent in vitro study of multiple additives confirmed a synergistic effect.

Trans fat: an altered molecular structure that results from *hydrogenation* of liquid fat to turn it into a solid at room temperature. Increases risk of heart disease because the body is unable to break it down normally. According to the Center for Science in the Public Interest, trans fat is the most harmful fat.

Triclosan: an antibacterial/antimicrobial chemical found in hand sanitizers, body products of many kinds, toothpaste, household cleaning supplies, some clothing (socks, sandals, and underwear), cutting boards, cleaning cloths, knives, and even aprons. Disrupts the endocrine system, which regulates growth and development. May contribute to development of antibiotic-resistant bacteria.

Unsaturated fat: a fatty acid chain with one or more double bonds between carbon atoms. Degree of saturation in a fat depends on the number of double bonds between the carbon atoms in the molecule. See *monounsaturated fat* and *polyunsaturated fat.*

Money Management...

Economics & Planning

Appreciation: an increase in value of something. The opposite is *depreciation.*

Assets: what you own. May include personal belongings, car, house, cash, and investments of all types. The opposite is *liabilities.*

Conflict of interest: a condition which exists when there are incompatible interests within the scope of an individual's authority and action, e.g., private interests and official responsibilities of a person in a position of trust. Could occur when a commission salesman (e.g., life insurance or investments) advises a client as to what product to buy.

Consignment store: a business that sells used clothing on behalf of the people who own it, and shares in the proceeds from the sale. Business structure is different from that of a *thrift store,* which sells donated goods and usually is attached to a charity.

Deficit budgeting: running a country, business, or household with expenses exceeding income. In simple language, spending more than you make. Raises the question: How can this be sustained?

Deficit: a shortfall. In finance, the amount by which expenditures exceed income.

Demand: in economics, the quantity of a product or service that customers are willing to buy at a given price.

Depreciation: a decrease in the value of something. The opposite is *appreciation.*

Depression: a *recession* that is severe or continues over a period of several years.

Emergency fund: a back-up sum of money for times when the unexpected happens. A prudent amount is six to eight months' living expenses in this account, to allow for major crises such as job loss.

Extraordinary income: lump sum payments (e.g., gift money, inheritance, loans, and scholarships) that are not received on a regular basis.

False economy: an action that seems to save money but in the long run costs more (e.g., driving across the city to save a few cents on a grocery item, and spending more on gas than was saved).

Financial advisor: a professional who assists clients with financial planning in areas such as estate planning, investments, and retirement savings. Frequently works for an investment company and sells its products.

Financial counsellor: a professional who assists clients with the daily practical issues of money—cash and debt management, budgeting to save for major purchases and retirement, and clarifying goals and values.

Free enterprise: an economic philosophy in which the marketplace is left to determine the price of goods through the action of supply and demand, without interference from authorities. Proposed by Adam Smith in *The Wealth of Nations* in 1776.

Frugality: economy in the use of resources.

Genuine Progress Indicator (GPI): an alternative measure of economic growth and progress. Includes *GDP*, but also incorporates a variety of social and environmental factors such as crime, education, oil spills, and natural disasters. These affect *quality of life* rather than just *standard of living;* therefore, it is believed this presents a more accurate picture of overall well-being.

Great Depression: a severe worldwide economic *depression* throughout the 1930s; the longest, most widespread, and deepest depression of the

20th century. Sometimes referred to as the "Dirty Thirties."

Gross Domestic Product (GDP): a measure of the amount of money that moves through an economy in a given year. GDP goes up when there is increased economic activity, which is said to indicate the economy is healthy.

Gross National Product (GNP): Similar to *GDP*, with some technical differences as to how it is calculated.

Guerilla marketing: undeclared advertising such as product placement, street promoting, and viral transmission of planted messages via digital social networks.

Invisible hand: Adam Smith's concept that individuals working in their own best interests would collectively do what was best for society. This was the basis for his belief that the market did not require regulation or interference.

Irregular expense: a budget item that occurs only occasionally during the year. Is predictable and therefore cannot be considered an emergency for financial planning purposes.

Latte Factor: the drain in money that occurs from small daily purchases which add up to enough to make a significant difference if invested for the long term. Popularized by financial writer and speaker David Bach.

Law of diminishing marginal utility: Stated plainly, this means that after a certain point, each item is of less use than the previous one.

Liabilities: what you owe. Includes all debts—outstanding balance on your credit cards, and other outstanding loans of all types (student, personal, car, home equity, mortgage, line of credit, consolidation, and loans from family members or friends). The opposite is *assets*.

Mass marketing: a selling strategy based on reaching the largest audience possible to maximize exposure to a product. Traditionally, mass marketing focused on radio, television and newspapers as the medium used to reach this broad audience. The digital age offers powerful new alternatives such as social media.

Mass production: manufacture of large numbers of standardized products by efficient means such as assembly lines in order to produce them as cheaply as possible. Emphasis is on low cost rather than quality.

Millionaire mentality: the mindset of the wealthy as described by Richard Paul Evans. Based on belief that freedom and power are better than momentary pleasure, and that wealth is built by reducing expenses and increasing income.

Net worth statement: a snapshot of financial worth at any given time. Calculated using the formula: assets – liabilities = net worth.

Opportunity cost: the cost of giving up something when you choose something else. In other words, when deciding on one option, you give up the benefits you would have gained from another.

Poverty line: see *standard of living.*

Quality of life: a measure of general well-being of individuals and societies. Goes beyond *standard of living* to include social and environmental conditions in addition to income. See *Genuine Progress Indicator (GPI).*

Real hourly wage: adjusted income divided by adjusted job hours. The adjustments take into account extra costs associated with having the job and extra demands on time because one is working.

Recession: half a year of decline in the *GDP* or *GNP.*

Regular income: predictable income received monthly, if not more often. Examples: biweekly paycheque, monthly allowance, planned amount withdrawn each month from savings set aside for future living expenses.

Amounts you can count on; form the basis of financial plans.

Standard of living: a measure of whether people have enough money to buy basic food, shelter, and clothing. Governments often identify a *poverty line,* which is the minimum amount required for an adequate standard of living, to determine which citizens have insufficient income for meeting basic needs.

Supply: in economics, the quantity of a product or service that sellers have available for customers to buy.

Thrift store: a retail establishment selling used clothing which has been donated, usually to raise funds for a charity. Different from a *consignment store,* which is a private business.

Thrift: see *frugality.*

Credit & Debt

Annual percentage rate (APR): a percentage number that represents the actual yearly cost of a loan including any fees or additional costs. Helps consumers compare loans from several sources by providing a standard means of expressing the cost.

Bad debt: see *consumer debt.*

Bankruptcy: a condition of financial failure caused by insufficient money to pay one's debts. A person who is bankrupt may go through a legal process of declaring bankruptcy, which is intended to give that individual a fresh start.

Collateral: something pledged as *security* that can be reclaimed if a borrower is unable to repay a loan. Savings bonds, term deposits, and property such as vehicles, furniture, or a house are typical examples.

Constructive debt: see *consumer debt.*

Consumer debt: borrowed money used by a household (as opposed to businesses and governments) to buy consumable goods. **Good or constructive debt** is used to buy something that can reasonably be expected to produce a return in the long run, such as a house or education. **Bad or destructive debt** is anything that loses value over time. Bad debt includes all *consumer goods,* both durable and nondurable.

Consumer goods: products purchased for use by consumers. They are not the same as investments. **Durable goods** are those with a life span of more than three years—cars, furniture, and appliances. **Nondurable goods** are those with a short lifespan—clothes, vacations, concert tickets, food, and gas for a car are examples.

Consumer Proposal: a plan to repay creditors on an adjusted schedule when a person is highly indebted but able to repay if monthly amounts are reduced and length of time is extended. A legal process which is undertaken through a bankruptcy trustee but is different from bankruptcy.

Cosigner: a joint signer on a loan, which may be required by a lender as security if there is uncertainty about the ability of the borrower to repay. A cosigner is responsible for payments if the borrower defaults, and the lender has a legal right to enforce that obligation.

Credit card: a card authorizing purchases or cash advances on credit. The card issuer creates a *revolving account* from which the user can borrow money for payment to a merchant or can receive a cash advance. Annual interest rate (*APR*) is typically around 20%. A grace period of about three weeks is usually allowed before payment for purchases is required. If full payment is made by then, no interest is charged. There is no grace period on cash advances, and the interest rate may be different from the rate charged on purchases.

Debt consolidation: a single large loan used to pay off several smaller loans, leaving the borrower with only one loan and one monthly payment. Can work to the borrower's advantage only if the interest rate on the consolidation loan is lower than that on the original small loans, and if the repayment time is the same or shorter. Otherwise, consolidation propels the individual into a never-ending cycle of debt.

Debt: see *consumer debt.*

Debt-to-income ratio: a means of expressing the rate of consumer indebtedness. A ratio of 150% or 150/100 means that $150 is owed for every $100 earned.

Destructive debt: see *consumer debt.*

Durable goods: see *consumer goods.*

Equity: the monetary value of a property in excess of claims or liens against it—i.e., the amount of the property that a person actually owns. Typically spoken of in relation to real estate, in terms of the market value minus the outstanding balance of the mortgage.

Good debt: see *consumer debt.*

Home equity line of credit (HELOC): a *line of credit* in which a homeowner is preapproved to borrow up to a certain percentage of the *equity* held in the house, in return for pledging it as *security.* The house will be repossessed if the borrower doesn't keep up the payments on the line of credit. Interest rate is lower than on a *personal line of credit* because the loan is secured by the property, reducing the lender's risk. However, the homeowner risks losing the house, so a HELOC should never ever be used to purchase consumer goods and services.

Line of credit: preapproval to borrow up to a specified amount of money without having to explain what it is being used for. Typically, interest rates are lower than for *personal loans.*

Nondurable goods: see *consumer goods.*

Overdraft protection: a means of borrowing from a bank by writing a cheque or using a debit card for more money than is in an account. The bank lends the amount that was overspent and charges interest to the account holder. As soon as money is deposited into the account, the bank reclaims the advanced amount plus interest owed for borrowing it. Attractive to the account holder because it prevents bounced cheques and rejected debit transactions. However, can lead to a cycle of perpetual debt.

Payday loan: a short-term loan used to fill an income gap until the next payday. Typically between $100 and $400, and used primarily to obtain emergency cash for necessities or unexpected expenses. Effective *annual percentage rate (APR)* could be up to 1000% or more. Can easily lead to a never-ending cycle of indebtedness. Sometimes called pay-advance loans.

Personal line of credit: a *line of credit*, usually for a minimum of $10,000. Borrower can spend any amount from within the limit provided regular payments are made as required depending on the outstanding balance. Like a bank account, it is *unsecured credit.*

Personal loan: a lump sum of money borrowed for a specific purpose, such as furniture or a car. The item becomes the *collateral*, and will be repossessed if the borrower doesn't make the payments.

Power paying: a method of reducing the repayment time on a loan or loans by paying an extra amount (beyond the minimum monthly payment) on one loan while maintaining the minimum payment on all others. When that one debt is repaid, all money paid toward it each month is applied to another debt. The monthly sum being paid is now substantial, allowing more rapid repayment of the second debt. When that's paid off, the third is repaid even more quickly. Sometimes referred to as "snowballing" your debt repayment.

Principal: an amount invested or borrowed.

Revolving account: a method of borrowing in which the full balance does not have to be paid back each month. Instead, a minimum monthly payment is charged, depending on the amount of the outstanding balance. As long as this minimum is paid each month, the account is considered to be in good standing. Typical of credit cards. Sometimes referred to as a "revolving charge account."

Security: something given, deposited, or pledged to ensure the fulfillment of an obligation. *Collateral* and a *cosigner* are two types of security.

Student loan: money borrowed for post-secondary education. Under government student loan programs, payments are typically deferred while the individual remains a student and for a six-month grace period after graduation. Beneficial because they may offer favourable interest rates and not require collateral or a credit check. However, it is easy for students to run up a lot of debt which is burdensome when they begin careers in entry-level jobs.

Unsecured credit: money borrowed without a form of *security* to back up the loan. Bank accounts and credit cards are typical examples.

Investing: General

Asset allocation: a strategy to balance risk and reward when investing. Takes into account a person's risk tolerance, financial goals, and age. Apportions investments appropriately between the three asset classes (debt, equity, and cash) to achieve balance.

Capital gain: the increase in value of an asset. Determined by the formula: selling price – purchase price = capital gain. If sold for less than it was bought for, then the formula results in a negative number and there is a **capital loss.**

Compound interest: interest paid or charged on both the principal and any interest from past years. Over time, interest increases exponentially when it is reinvested in this way, unlike *simple interest*, which increases linearly.

Debt investment: a type of investment in which money is lent to a person, company, or institution in return for interest. Examples: savings account, *term deposit, GIC*, Canada Savings Bond, and corporate bond.

Dividend: a distribution of a portion of a company's earnings to holders of particular types of shares. Mutual funds may also pay dividends to fund shareholders. Usually quoted in terms of "dividend per share."

Dollar cost averaging: an investing strategy to counter the problem of *market timing* through buying a fixed dollar amount of an investment on a regular schedule, regardless of the unit price. More units are purchased when prices are low, and fewer are bought when prices are high. Over time, it averages out. Can be purchased via an automatic bank withdrawal to ensure the regular schedule is maintained without effort.

Equity investment: a type of investment in which the investor becomes the owner of something that is expected to increase in value over time. *Return* is realized in the form of *capital gain* (loss) or *dividends*. Examples: house, stocks, precious metals such as gold, and collectibles such as fine art. Consumer goods are not considered equity investments because they depreciate in value.

Guaranteed investment certificate (GIC): a certificate of deposit in Canada wherein money is committed for a predetermined length of time, and the return is a stated percentage in interest. Interest may be forfeited if cashed before the specified time is up.

Inflation: a rise in the cost of living. Tracked monthly by Statistics Canada, using the Consumer Price Index—a basket of about 600 commonly used consumer goods and services.

Interest: the money paid by a borrower for the use of the money; also, money paid to an individual in return for investing it in certain places such as a bank account, GIC or Canada Savings Bond.

Invest: put money where it can reasonably be expected to produce a *return.*

Leveraging: an investment strategy in which borrowed money is used to buy an investment. The investor hopes value will increase enough to cover repayment of the loan plus interest, and still generate a profit. A risky practice if the investment is in the stock market, which is unpredictable and could result in the loss of the borrowed money (which will still have to be repaid).

Liquidity: the degree to which an investment can be cashed (or liquidated) without loss of *principal.* A bank account or *GIC* has high liquidity because the investor is assured of getting back the principal in addition to accumulated interest. Real estate is subject to market forces and therefore less liquid. If price drops below the amount that was paid and the property must be sold, there will be a loss of principal.

Market timing: the act of attempting to predict the future direction of the market in order to purchase investments at their highest prices. Requires continual attention and monitoring. Even then, difficult to accomplish because many forces affect stock prices. Is the reason many recommend *dollar cost averaging* and investing for the long run instead.

Money market fund: see *Treasury bill.*

Principal: an amount invested or borrowed.

Progressive tax system: a system by which a society generates money for public programs, based on the premise that people with low incomes should pay a lower percentage of income tax than high-income earners. In Canada, accomplished through the designation of four *tax brackets.*

Registered Retirement Savings Plan (RRSP): a tax sheltering account to hold savings and investments, established to encourage Canadians to save for retirement. May include savings accounts, *GICs*, bonds, *mutual funds*, and *stocks*, among others. Government regulates RRSPs in relation to tax benefits, but this does not guarantee their safety.

Return: money earned on an investment. May be in the form of interest, *capital gain* (loss), or *dividends*. Type of return becomes important when considering tax implications of the earnings on investments.

Risk: the degree of security of an investment. Risk implies the chance of losing part or all of the money in an investment. Sometimes a person can afford to take more risks than at other times, and this should be considered when making financial decisions.

Simple interest: interest paid or charged each year on the basis of the original principal only, thus ignoring potential increases due to *compound interest.* As a result, interest grows linearly rather than exponentially.

Tax avoidance: a legitimate means of reducing income tax paid. Examples: contributing to Registered Retirement Savings Plans and claiming approved deductions when filing income tax. Post-secondary students should be sure to know which deductions apply to them. Different from *tax evasion.*

Tax brackets: the divisions at which tax rates change in a *progressive tax system.*

Tax deferral: putting off paying income tax until a later time. Specifically pertains to RRSPs because income tax is paid when the money is taken out of a plan rather than when it is put in.

Tax evasion: non-payment of income tax that an individual is legally obliged to pay. Punishable under the Criminal Code, with penalties varying depending on the nature of the offence. Not claiming all of one's income, in particular income from doing work at home or from tips earned on the job, is considered by the tax department to be tax evasion. Not the same as *tax avoidance.*

Tax Free Savings Account (TFSA): a tax shelter which exempts Canadians from paying income tax on the *return* generated by this particular type of account. Can hold the same sorts of investments as an *RRSP.*

T-bill: see *Treasury bill.*

Term: the length of time money is locked into an investment.

Term deposit: similar to a *GIC*, but typically the term is less than a year.

Treasury bill: a short-term investment that pays a relatively high interest rate. Not particularly accessible to small investors because of the high minimum required. In a category called money market funds. Often called *T-bills.*

Investing: Buying a House

Amortization period: the length of time it takes to fully pay off a loan. Applies to any loan, including a mortgage.

Closed mortgage: restricts *prepayment* of the mortgage principal. This reduces the borrower's ability to pay off the mortgage quickly.

Condo: see *condominium.*

Condominium: a form of multi-unit housing involving individual ownership of the unit itself and joint ownership of common elements such as roof, outside walls, hallways, recreation areas, and the land on which it is built. Cost of maintaining common elements is covered by a monthly condominium fee. The complex is managed by a condominium board, usually made up of owners. Also known as a condo.

Detached house: a separate dwelling occupied by one household or family, as opposed to a multi-family complex. Depending on municipal zoning regulations, it may contain a separate living suite. Also called a *single-family dwelling.*

Equal blended payments: repayment structure of mortgages whereby the monthly payment is a fixed amount, but the portion of the payment going to interest and the portion going to repay the principal varies slightly each month. Initially most of the payment goes toward interest, resulting in slow repayment of the principal during the first years of a mortgage. That is why *prepayment* and other strategies are important if one wishes to reduce total interest paid.

Fixed rate mortgage: a loan on property in which the interest rate is established at the beginning of the mortgage *term.* That rate is fixed until the end of the term, then a new rate is agreed to for the next term, depending on market conditions. Monthly payments are the same throughout the term, but may be different in the next term if interest rates have gone up or down. Different from a *variable rate mortgage.*

Foreclosure: the process of repossessing real estate which has been pledged as security in the event that the borrower defaults on the monthly mortgage payments.

Homeowner's equity: the amount of the property that the borrower actually owns. It is the market value of the property minus the outstanding mortgage.

House poor: a condition arising from having committed to high mortgage payments relative to income, such that the monthly budget is stretched to the maximum and optional activities are severely curtailed. Leads to the risk of bad debt when homeowners use credit cards and lines of credit to make ends meet for daily purchases of consumer goods.

Mortgage: a loan for the purchase of real estate, with the property itself as the security. A mortgage is a means of leveraging investment in a house when an individual doesn't have cash to pay for it outright. Typical loan period is 25 years, but there are strategies to shorten the time and thus reduce total interest paid.

Open mortgage: allows *prepayment* of the principal without penalty at times other than the end of the term. Provides greater flexibility for paying off the mortgage quickly and reducing the amount of interest paid.

Prepayment (of a mortgage): payment of all or part of a debt obligation, in this case a mortgage loan, prior to its due date. Payment in excess of the scheduled debt repayment amount will pay off a loan faster because all of the excess goes directly toward reducing the principal. This means the borrower pays less total interest on the loan, and the loan will be completely retired in a shorter length of time than originally anticipated.

Single-family dwelling: see *detached house.*

Term (of a mortgage): the length of time within the total *amortization period* for which there is an agreement at a specific interest rate. Normally one to five years, although may be six months or even ten years. At the end of the term, a new term is negotiated.

Variable rate mortgage: a loan on property in which the interest rate varies as interest rates fluctuate in market. Monthly payment is typically fixed, but the amount of the payment going to interest varies depending on the current interest rate. When rates go up, more goes to interest and less is available to pay down the principal so it takes longer to pay off the mortgage. Some are now structured so payments change when the interest rate does, rather than remaining the same each month. A variable monthly payment has the disadvantage of creating uncertainty and making budgeting difficult. Different from a *fixed rate mortgage.*

Investing: Mutual Funds

Balanced fund: a mutual fund with investment in both debt investments and equity investments. Developed to combine the strengths of both—stability of debt investments and higher return of equity investments. As with any investment, profitability is not guaranteed. It depends on the particular fund and how it is managed.

Debt fund: a mutual fund with investment in debt investments only. Not subject to the ups and downs of the market, so generally recommended for older investors, whose age may preclude them from waiting for the market to go up before cashing in their investment.

Equity fund: a mutual fund with investment in equity investments only. Are usually more suitable for young people, who can weather ups and downs of the market because they have more time to keep the money in the investment. The long-term return of equity funds tends to be higher than debt funds, although this generalization does not apply in all cases.

Exchange-traded fund (ETF): similar to an *index fund.*

Index fund: a mutual fund invested in the same stocks that make up a particular market index, such as the TSX or the Dow Jones Industrial Average. The fund goes up and down in tandem with the particular market on which it is based. Reduces need for management decisions because composition of the fund is predetermined. This keeps *management expense ratio* low.

Load (mutual funds): a purchase fee for a mutual fund, tending to range from 5% to 9% A **no-load fund** has no purchase fee; this is typical of mutual funds bought at a bank. Funds can be either **front- or back-end loaded**. With a front-end load, fee is paid at time of purchase. A back-end load is paid when fund units are sold.

Management expense ratio (MER): the yearly fee charged to cover operating costs of managing a mutual fund. Taken out of fund earnings, so reduces the investor's profit.

Mutual fund: a professionally-managed investment vehicle that pools money from many investors to purchase securities. Widely available for purchase by the general public with relatively small sums of money. Attractive to small investors without enough money to adopt a strategy of diversification on their own.

Investing: Stock Market

Bear market: term used to describe the *stock market* when it is trending down. (Think of bear retreating to its cave to hibernate.)

Blue chip stocks: shares in solid, established companies that have a proven track record and can generally be counted on to yield good returns. Often pay *dividends.*

Bull market: term used to describe the *stock market* when it is trending up. (Think of a bull charging the matador in a bullfight.)

Buying on margin: a means of buying more shares than an investor can afford by borrowing money from the broker to purchase stock. Requires a margin account with the broker. Very risky because the lender can demand repayment of the loan if value of the stock falls too low, and the investor is obligated to come up with cash to cover that amount. Also called "margin trading."

Exit strategy: a plan for how an investor will deal with an investment if its value goes down. **Buy-and-hold** is based on the philosophy that the market goes up and down over the long term, and shares will eventually increase in value even if they go down for a period of time. **Cut-your-losses** is based on picking a point, such as drop of a certain percentage (e.g., 25% below its highest price) and automatically selling shares if they go below that.

Growth stocks: shares in young companies that are in the development stage, doing well, and putting profits back into the company rather than paying *dividends* to shareholders. Profitability to the investor comes through *capital gains* resulting from this growth.

Investor psychology: a frame of mind causing an investor to make counterproductive decisions. Instead of buying stocks at a low price and selling them for more, the person does the opposite and loses money.

Market: a medium that allows buyers and sellers of a specific good or service to interact in order to facilitate an exchange. Often used in reference to the general market where *securities* are traded. Market price is determined by several factors, including supply and demand.

Securities: a general term which includes both *stocks* and bonds.

Shares: see *stocks*.

Speculative stocks: shares in unproven companies where there is considerable risk that investors will lose their money. Gold mining is a classic example.

Stock broker: an individual or firm that is licensed to buy and sell shares on behalf of investors. May provide in-person or online services, and charge a fee or commission for executing the trade.

Stock exchange: a marketplace in which *stocks* are traded. Does not itself own the stocks, but exists to facilitate the process of fair, orderly, and efficient trading. May be a physical location where traders meet to conduct business or an electronic platform where this can occur.

Stock market index: a measuring tool that tracks the value of a representative group of shares on a particular *stock exchange*. Examples: Dow Jones Industrial Average (DJIA), NASDAQ-100, and Standard & Poors 100 (S&P 100) are the most commonly quoted U.S. indices. S&P/TSX

Composite Index is the general index for the Canadian stock market. Reported in "points," as in: The S&P/TSX has dropped 18 points today.

Stock market: a particular market where *stocks* are bought and sold.

Stock: a unit of ownership in a company. Value of these units fluctuates depending on a variety of factors, including consumer confidence, corporate management, and world events. Also referred to as *shares.*

Estate Planning

Estate planning: arranging affairs in advance to minimize difficulties for survivors when a person dies. Typically involves life insurance, a will, living will (personal directive), power of attorney, and sometimes income tax, depending on the size and complexity of the *estate.*

Estate: the property and money left behind when someone dies. Includes personal belongings (such as clothes, jewellery, furnishings, car) as well as house, bank accounts, and investments.

Life Insurance

Agent (insurance): a representative of one particular insurance company who sells that company's products exclusively.

Beneficiary (life insurance): someone who receives all or part of the *face value* of an insurance policy.

Broker: a person or company who represents several different insurance companies and searches the products of all those companies to find a policy that best suits the client.

Cash surrender value: the savings component of a *cash value insurance* policy. Cash value will be paid to the policyholder if policy is terminated before death, but not to *beneficiaries* after the policyholder has died (i.e., beneficiaries receive only the *face value*). Not usually a good investment because return is low considering the amount paid in premiums. Generally better to buy a *term* policy for the insurance you require, and look after your own investments.

Cash value insurance: a life insurance policy with both a *face value* and *cash surrender value.* Very expensive because of the *cash surrender value,* which requires you to pay high premiums so the company can invest your money for you. Generally not recommended. The other option is *term insurance.*

Direct seller (insurance): an insurance seller operating via telephone from a call centre rather than through a local *agent.*

Face value: the amount of money that a life insurance policy pays to *beneficiaries* when the insured person dies.

Group plan (insurance): provides life insurance to members of particular groups such as a workplace or university alumni. Only members of that group qualify to participate.

Life insurance: a protection against loss of income that would occur when a person dies. The *face value* of the policy is selected to replace income so the family has continued financial support, and the money is paid to the *beneficiary* who has been named in the policy.

Premium: the amount paid regularly, either yearly or monthly, to keep the policy in effect. Premiums of a *cash value policy* are much higher than for the same *face value* in a *term policy.*

Renewable term: a *term insurance policy* that will be automatically renewed at the end of each term (anywhere from 5 to 20 years) without requiring a medical exam. Protects policyholder from disqualification in the event of ill health.

Spreading the risk: an insurance principle whereby an insurance company collects money from a large number of people who wish to protect themselves from financial risk if a particular event occurs. From the pool of money collected each year, the company pays out to those participants who experience the insured event. The yearly *premiums* paid by participants are determined according to the probability of the insured event occurring.

Term insurance: a life insurance policy that has only a *face value* (i.e., no *cash value*). A straightforward policy that provides protection against the insured event (death of the policyholder). Should always be *renewable.* Generally recommended as a better option than *cash value insurance.*

Wills, Living Wills, Power of Attorney

Beneficiary (will): someone who inherits something from the *estate* of a deceased person.

Bequest: what the deceased leaves to his or her *beneficiaries* via the terms of the *will.*

Codicil: an amending document attached to a will. Must meet certain format requirements, including being signed and witnessed.

Executor: an individual appointed to administer the *estate* of a deceased person, ensuring that affairs are properly wrapped up and the estate is dispersed to the *beneficiaries.* Female form of the word, "executrix," is still used occasionally.

Godparent: an individual appointed under the authority of a church for the purpose of ensuring a child gets proper religious upbringing in that particular faith. Is not automatically assumed to be the *guardian* in the event there is no surviving parent of a minor child. If that is the wish of the *testator,* this should be stated in the will.

Guardian: an individual appointed by the court to act as a substitute parent until minor children have reached legal age and are able to live independently. Applies when a child is left with no surviving parents.

Holograph will: a will made completely by the *testator*, handwritten, dated and signed. Witnesses are not required. Legally valid in a limited number of places. This becomes important for a person who makes a holograph will and moves to another jurisdiction.

Intestate: dying without a valid will. In such case, legislation determines distribution of the deceased's assets and guardianship of children.

Living will: a legal document that comes into effect when an individual is alive but unable to make personal decisions. Also referred to as a personal directive. Does not apply to financial decisions (see *power of attorney).*

Power of attorney: a legal document granting an individual authority to deal with financial matters on someone's behalf. **Immediate Power of Attorney** is for a specific purpose or time period. **Enduring Power of Attorney** is set up in advance to take effect if a person become mentally incapable.

Personal directive: see *living will.*

Probate: the legal procedure for proving a will. Involves verifying that the person named in the will has died, that the will is valid, and that the executor is confirmed. Required before property may be sold or transferred, or funds released from the deceased's financial institution. Once the executor has completed necessary steps, an application for **grant of probate** is submitted to the government.

Testator: the person making a will.

Will: a legal document directing what happens to a person's assets upon his or her death. Also specifies guardianship of any minor children, which is around the age of 18 in most places.

Acronyms…

ADHD attention deficit hyperactivity disorder
APA Automobile Protection Association
APR annual percentage rate
ATM automated teller machine
BBB Better Business Bureau
BHA butylated hydroxyanisole
BHT butylated hydroxytoluene
BPA Bisphenol A
CAC Consumers' Association of Canada
CFCs chlorofluorocarbons
DJIA Dow Jones Industrial Average
DNA deoxyribonucleic acid
ETF exchange-traded fund
GDP Gross Domestic Product
GE genetic engineering
GIC guaranteed investment certificate
GM genetic modification
GMO genetically modified organism
GNP Gross National Product
GPI Genuine Progress Indicator
HELOC home equity line of credit
MER management expense ratio (mutual funds)
MSG monosodium glutamate
NASDAQ National Association of Securities Dealers Automated Quotation
NSF non-sufficient funds
NYSE New York Stock Exchange
PBDEs polybrominated diphenyl ethers
PFCs perfluorochemicals

PIN Personal Identification Number
PSRAST Physicians and Scientists for Responsible Application of Science and Technology
RFID radio frequency identification (chip)
RRSP Registered Retirement Savings Plan
S&P Standard & Poors
TFSA Tax Free Savings Account
TSE Toronto Stock Exchange (before 2002)
TSX Toronto Stock Exchange
FDA Food & Drug Administration (U.S.)
HVP hydrolyzed vegetable protein
rDNA recombinant DNA

Endnotes

For convenience, endnotes are published on www.TheUncommonGuides.com with hyperlinks to web references.

Welcome to the Voyage

1. Boldt, *Zen and the Art of Making a Living,* 541.
2. Chopra, *Life After Death,* 232–33.

Part 1

The Consumer Culture

1. "Onto the Global Stage: The 1960s and the End of Parochialism," (Royal Bank of Canada website), accessed August 22, 2012, http://www.rbc.com/history/quicktofrontier/chargex-visa.html
2. Ibid.
3. "Eaton's: The History and Legacy of a Canadian Institution," (Eaton's website), accessed August 22, 2012, http://www.eatons.com
4. "Our History: Timelines: Early Stores," (Hudson's Bay Company website), accessed August 22, 2012, http://www2.hbc.com/hbcheritage/history/timeline/early/

The Issues of Consumerism

1. Griffiths, *International Journal of Consumer Studies,* 230–36.
2. Stuart Stamp, "A Policy Framework for Addressing Over-Indebtedness," (Dublin, Combat Poverty Agency, 2009), 36, http://www.cpa.ie/publications/APolicyFrameworkForAddressingOverIndebtedness_2009.pdf
3. Kirby, *Macleans,* third paragraph.
4. Roger Sauvé, "The Current State of Canadian Family Finances, 2011-2012 Report," (Ottawa, The Vanier Institute of the Family, March 22, 2012), http://www.vanierinstitute.ca/include/get.php?nodeid=1779
5. Bank of Canada, "Highlights-Financial System Review, June 2010," http://www.bankofcanada.ca/wp-content/uploads/2010/09/highlights_0610.pdf
6. Moodie, *Roughing It in the Bush, 199.*
7. "The Urgent/Important Matrix," (Mind Tools website), accessed Aug 22, 2012, http://www.mindtools.com/pages/article/newHTE_91.htm
8. Ibid.

The Marketing of Culture

1. Noreene Janus, "Cloning the Consumer Culture," (Center for Media Literacy), accessed August 22, 2012, http://www.medialit.org/reading-room/cloning-consumer-culture
2. Klein, *No Logo, 75.*
3. Sutherland, *Kidfluence,* book jacket.
4. Course material for Bus106 at Seneca College, taught by Michael O'Neill, accessed August 26, 2012, http://www.mhoneill.com/106/articles/YTV_Kidfluence_2007.pdf
5. "Marketing in Schools," (Campaign for a Commercial-Free Childhood website), accessed August 27, 2012, http://commercialfreechildhood.org/factsheets/schools.pdf
6. "How Marketers Target Kids," (MediaSmarts website), accessed August 26, 2012, http://mediasmarts.ca/print/marketing-consumerism/how-marketers-target-kids
7. "Young Canadians in a Wired World, Phase III," (Media Smarts, 2012), 3, http://mediasmarts.ca/sites/default/files/pdfs/publication-report/summary/YCWWIII-youth-parents-summary.pdf
8. Robert D. Putnam, "Bowling Alone: The Collapse and Revival of American Community," accessed August 22, 2012, http://bowlingalone.com/
9. Sheri Candler, "What is Brand Integration?" (blog, December 4, 2009), http://www.shericandler.com/2009/12/04/what-is-brand-integration/
10. "Benefits of Product Placement," (MMI Product Placement Inc. website), accessed August 22, 2012, http://www.mmiproductplacement.com/
11. Klein, *No Logo,* 80.
12. Tom Atlee, "Story fields," (Co-Intelligence Institute, 1995, revised 2007), http://www.co-intelligence.org/StoryFields.html
13. Sut Jhally, "Film Transcript: Advertising and the End of the World," (Media Education Foundation, 1997), 6 & 18, http://www.mediaed.org/assets/products/101/transcript_101.pdf

The Economics Underlying Consumerism

1. Lebow, *Journal of Retailing*, 7.
2. "1992 World Scientists' Warning to Humanity: Introduction," (Union of Concerned Scientists website), accessed August 26, 2012, http://www.ucsusa.org/about/1992-world-scientists.html
3. Jhally, "Film Transcript," 17.
4. "Who We Are," (New Economy Working Group website), accessed August 22, 2012, http://neweconomyworkinggroup.org/about-us
5. David Korten, "Why This Crisis May Be Our Best Chance to Build a New Economy," *(Yes! Magazine,* posted June 19, 2009), http://www.yesmagazine.org/issues/the-new-economy/why-this-crisis-may-be-our-best-chance-to-build-a-new-economy
6. David Korten, "The Illusion of Money," (*Yes! Magazine*, posted January 18, 2011), http://www.yesmagazine.org/blogs/david-korten/the-illusion-of-money
7. Anielski, *The Economics of Happiness,* xviii.
8. Ibid., back cover.

9. "Ray's Legacy," (Interface website), accessed August 25, 2012, http://www.interfaceglobal.com/Company/Leadership-Team/Ray-Watch.aspx
10. "Ray Anderson Honoured at Ceremony," The Guardian Sustainable Business Awards: May 30, 2012, (*The Guardian website*), http://www.guardian.co.uk/sustainable-business/video/ray-anderson

Part 2

Some Thoughts about Ethics

1. Thomas Shanks, "Morality Requires Regular Reflection on the Day-to-Day Decisions That Confront Us." (Santa Clara University website), accessed October 28, 2012, http://www.scu.edu/ethics/publications/iie/v8n1/everydayethics.html
2. Reuters, "Global retail theft up 6.6 per cent in latest year," (Reuters website, October 18, 2011), accessed October 27, 2012, http://www.reuters.com/article/2011/10/18/us-retail-theft-idUSTRE79H0JR20111018
3. "Welcome," (Retail C.O.P. website), accessed August 25, 2012, http://retailcop.ca/
4. "Facts of the General Insurance Industry in Canada 2009," (Insurance Bureau of Canada), 8, http://www.ibc.ca/en/need_more_info/documents/facts%20book%20 2009_eng.pdf
5. Covey, Merrill, and Merrill, *First Things First*, 68–70 & 137–38.

Social Responsibility

1. "Values & Campaigns," (Body Shop Australian website), accessed July 22, 2011, http://www.thebodyshop.com.au/Content.aspx?Id=6
2. "Ben & Jerry's Mission Statement," (Ben & Jerry's website), accessed July 23, 2011, http://www.benjerry.com/activism/mission-statement/
3. "Our MEC Charter," (Mountain Equipment Co-op website), accessed August 25, 2012, http://www.mec.ca/Main/content_text.jsp?FOLDER%3C%3Efolder_id=2534374302887390
4. "Protecting Workers' Rights Worldwide," (Fair Labor Association website), accessed July 15, 2011, https://www.fairlabor.org/fla/_pub/SyncImg/flageneralbrochure.pdf
5. "Board and Advisors - Jessica Jackley: Co-Founder, Kiva" (Kiva website), accessed August 25, 2012, http://www.kiva.org/about/team/board
6. "About Us," (Kiva website), accessed August 25, 2012, http://www.kiva.org/about
7. "Our Approach," (Momentum website), accessed November 29, 2012, http://www.momentum.org/about-momentum/our-approach

Looking After Yourself in the Marketplace

1. Andy Greenberg, "Hacker's Demo Shows How Easily Credit Cards Can Be Read Through Clothes And Wallets," (Forbes magazine, January 30, 2012), http://www.forbes.com/sites/andygreenberg/2012/01/30/hackers-demo-shows-how-easily-credit-cards-can-be-read-through-clothes-and-wallets/print/

2. Susan Sproule and Norm Archer, "Measuring Identity Theft in Canada: 2008 Consumer Survey," (Ontario Research Network for Electronic Commerce), http://www.business.mcmaster.ca/IDTDefinition/WP23%20exec%20summ.htm
3. "Debit Card Fraud," (CTV website), accessed July 28, 2011, http://www.ctv.ca/CTVNews/WFive/20050108/wfive_debit_card_fraud_010801/
4. "Canadian Anti-Fraud Centre Annual Statistical Report 2011," 4, (Canadian Anti-Fraud Centre website), http://www.antifraudcentre-centreantifraude.ca/english/documents/Annual%202011%20CAFC.pdf
5. "Consumer Rights," (Consumers International website), accessed August 25, 2012, http://www.consumersinternational.org/who-we-are/consumer-rights
6. "Consumer Rights and Responsibilities," (Consumer Rights Commission of Pakistan website), accessed August 25, 2012, http://www.crcp.org.pk/cons_right_responsi.htm
7. *Definition of planned obsolescence:* A manufacturing decision by a company to make consumer products in such a way that they become out-of-date or useless within a known time period. The main goal of this type of production is to ensure that consumers will have to buy the product multiple times, rather than only once. This naturally stimulates demand for an industry's products because consumers have to keep coming back again and again. Products ranging from inexpensive light bulbs to high-priced goods such as cars and buildings are subject to planned obsolescence by manufacturers and producers. Also known as "built-in obsolescence." Accessed from *Investopedia,* August 26, 2012, http://www.investopedia.com/terms/p/planned_obsolescence.asp#axzz21HDhwGye

Part 3

Making a Life

1. Bernice Wood, "Don't Live in Default Mode," (Blog, March 7, 2011), accessed August 25, 2012, http://livingthebalancedlife.com/2011/dont-live-in-default-mode/
2. "What is Brain Gym?" (Brain Gym International website), accessed August 26, 2012, http://www.braingym.org/about
3. "Brain Gym: Educational Kinesiology," (The Skeptic's Dictionary website), accessed August 26, 2012, http://www.skepdic.com/braingym.html
4. Pink, *A Whole New Mind,* 2–3.
5. Boldt, *Zen and the Art of Making a Living,* 540.
6. "The Founder, Lynne Twist," (Soul of Money website), accessed August 26, 2012, http://www.soulofmoney.org/about/about-lynne-twist/
7. Twist with Barker, *The Soul of Money,* 74.
8. Ibid., 77.
9. Diagram reproduced with permission from *The Financial Integrity Program Guide (Canadian Version),* 21. This work is licensed under Creative Commons Attribution Share-Alike 3.0 U.S. License. It is based on the Financial Integrity materials developed

by the New Road Map Foundation, available for free at www.financialintegrity.org

10. *The Financial Integrity Program Guide (Canadian Version),* (The New Road Map Foundation, February , 2012), 20, http://www.financialintegrity.org/index.php?title=Downloadable_Guides
11. Ibid., 22.

Power and Money

1. "The Energy of Money," (Energy of Money website), accessed August 26, 2012, http://www.theenergyofmoney.net/aboutEOM.html
2. Opdyke, *Love & Money,* 85.
3. Rick Crawford, "Techno Prisoners," (article originally published in *Adbusters Quarterly,* no. 11), http://www.cs.unm.edu/~refromsn/tv/prisoners
4. *The Financial Integrity Program Guide (Canadian Version),* (The New Road Map Foundation, February, 2012), 22, http://www.financialintegrity.org/index.php?title=Downloadable_Guides
5. Ibid., 42.
6. Evans, *The Five Lessons,* 51.
7. *Ibid.,* 53.
8. *Ibid.,* 54.
9. Maich, "Hip Deep in Hock," paragraph eight.
10. "Canadians Get Poor Grades for Retirement Savings," (CBC News, posted Dec 30, 2011, last updated January 27, 2012), accessed August 26, 2012, http://www.cbc.ca/news/business/taxseason/story/2011/12/20/f-rrsp-savings-rate-graph.html
11. Evans, *The Five Lessons,* 55–60.

Dealing with Money

1. Rivers, *The Way of the Owl,* 101, 102, 104.
2. "CIBC Personal Car Loan," (CIBC website), accessed August 25, 2012, https://www.cibc.com/ca/loans/car-loan.html?WT.mc_id=AutoLending_campFY11-AutoLending_kwdcar||finance||loans_adgrpCar||Loan||Finance-E100
3. Cameron, "The Debt Bomb," 42.

Taking Your Situation in Hand

1. "Take The 'Start Over' Latte Factor® Challenge," (David Bach's Finish Rich website), accessed July 22, 2011, http://finishrich.com/lattefactor/
2. Chilton, *Wealthy Barber,* 33.
3. "Do You Want to Be Rich? Find Your Financial Freedom," (Lesley Scorgie's website), accessed August 26, 2012, http://lesleyscorgie.com/index.php
4. "Credit Counselling: The Orderly Payment of Debts Program," (Money Mentors website), accessed August 26, 2012, http://www.moneymentors.ca/our-services/credit-counselling.html

Impact of Your Generational Era

1. "Generation X: Overlooked and Hugely Important Finds New Study from the Center for Work-Life Policy," (PRWeb website), accessed August 26, 2012, http://www.prweb.com/releases/2011/9/prweb8803120.htm
2. Don Tapscott, "The Net Generation Takes the Lead," (*Businessweek*, December 22, 2008), http://www.businessweek.com/technology/content/dec2008/tc20081219_896789.htm
3. Brock, *Live Well on Less*, 9.
4. Ibid., 19.

Issues in Your Relationship with Money

1. Ryan T. Howell, "Active Money Management: A Road Map to a Sustainable Financial Future?" (*Psychology Today*, Mar 7, 2012), http://www.psychologytoday.com/print/89787
2. Gail Vaz-Oxlade, "Spending Journals Pay Off," (*MoneySense*, online only, April 19, 2012), http://www.moneysense.ca/2012/04/19/spending-journals-pay-off/
3. Schwartz, "The Tyranny of Choice," 71–5.
4. Barry Schwartz, "The Paradox of Choice," (TED talk, video format), accessed August 26, 2012, http://www.youtube.com/watch?v=VO6XEQIsCoM
5. Schwartz, "The Tyranny of Choice," 74.
6. A lien is a claim against property for satisfaction of a debt. If you buy a car with a lien against it, you may become responsible for that outstanding debt. That could make it a *very expensive* car!
7. Betty Moore-Hafter et al, *The EFT free Manual: Version 2.1*, 5, http://www.eftfree.net/get-the-eftfree-manual/

Growth of Money

1. David Chilton and Jordan E. Goodman, "Q and A: Some Advice from The Wealthy Barber: An Earful about Money from the Wealthy Barber," (*CNN Money*, March 1, 1994), http://money.cnn.com/magazines/moneymag/moneymag_archive/1994/03/01/88714/index.htm
2. An online compounding calculator I like: http://www.inspiredtosave.com/
3. "Students," (Canada Revenue Agency website), accessed August 26, 2012, http://www.cra-arc.gc.ca/tx/ndvdls/sgmnts/stdnts/menu-eng.html
4. Other countries will differ, so be sure to check what applies where you live. Also remember that if you are a Canadian living and working outside the country, you will need to check the tax implications particular to your situation.

The Costs of Money

1. "Loan Repayment Estimator," (CanLearn website), accessed August 26, 2012, http://tools.canlearn.ca/cslgs-scpse/cln-cln/50/crp-lrc/af.nlindex-eng.do
2. Gail Vaz-Oxlade, "So How Much Debt *Can* You Afford?" accessed August 26, 2012, http://www.gailvazoxlade.com/articles/students/how_much_debt_afford.html

3. Gail Vaz-Oxlade, "What's the Alternative to Debt?" accessed August 26, 2012, http://www.gailvazoxlade.com/articles/students/alternative_to_debt.html
4. Ibid.
5. Gail Vaz-Oxlade, "Managing Your Money for School," accessed August 26, 2012, http://www.gailvazoxlade.com/articles/students/managing_money_school.html
6. Gail Vaz-Oxlade, "Cutting Costs @ School," accessed August 26, 2012, http://www.gailvazoxlade.com/articles/students/cutting_costs_at_school.html
7. "Rates and Terms," (Dollars Direct website), accessed August 26, 2012, http://www.dollarsdirect.ca/fee-schedule-alberta.html
8. Payday loan APR calculator, accessed October 27, 2012, http://www.csgnetwork.com/apr4calc.html
9. Vaz-Oxlade, *Debt Free Forever,* 12–13.
10. "Credit Card Payment Calculator Tool," (Financial Consumer Agency of Canada website), accessed August 26, 2012, http://www.fcac-acfc.gc.ca/iTools-iOutils/CreditCardPaymentCalculator/CreditCardCalculator-eng.aspx
11. "Canadian Mortgage Payment Calculator," (CanEquity website), accessed August 26, 2012, http://www.canequity.com/mortgage-calculator/
12. Perry Goertzen, "How We Paid Off Our House in Three Years," (Moneyville, *The Toronto Star,* May 16, 2011), http://www.moneyville.ca/article/991896
13. Ibid.
14. A mortgage calculator I like, from CanEquity: http://www.canequity.com/mortgage-calculator/
15. Gail Vaz-Oxlade, "House Poor," accessed August 26, 2012, http://www.gailvazoxlade.com/articles/home_sweet_home/house_poor.html

Investing Your Money

1. Anthony, *Financially Fearless by 40,* 114.
2. Ibid., 114–16.
3. "S&P 100," (Standard & Poor's Financial Services website), accessed August 26, 2012, http://www.standardandpoors.com/indices/sp-100/en/us/?indexId=spusa-100-usduf--p-us-l--

Big-Picture Planning

1. Suze Orman on YouTube: "Suze Orman on Cash Value Life Insurance vs. Term Life Insurance.flv," http://www.youtube.com/watch?v=kkUkZFczj0A&feature=related AND "Suze Orman on Life Insurance: Term Life Insurance vs. Whole Life," http://www.youtube.com/watch?v=WzgtWfQngII&feature=related AND "Suze Orman on Life Insurance," http://www.youtube.com/watch?v=6vnN9liFWaE; AND "Suze Orman Weighs In Her Opinion On Life Insurance Term vs Whole Life Insurance.flv," http://www.youtube.com/watch?v=IPzems4fWE4; accessed August 26, 2012.
2. "Canada Life Insurance Quotes," *term insurance calculator,* http://www.life-insurance-quotes.ca/default.aspx?Section=Common&Page=Quote AND *cash value calculator,*

https://www.life-insurance-quotes.ca/default.aspx?Section=Common&Page=Quote&Whole=True, accessed August 26, 2012.
3. "What Happens to the Cash Value of a Life Insurance Policy When the Insured Dies?" (Insurance Providers website), accessed August 26, 2012, http://www.insuranceproviders.com/cash-value-life-insurance-policy-insured-dies
4. "How Much Life Insurance Do I Need?" (CalcXML website), accessed August 26, 2012, http://www.calcxml.com/calculators/how-much-life-insurance-need
5. See Note 2 for term and whole life insurance calculators.
6. *Making a Will in Alberta,* (Centre for Public and Legal Education Alberta, Edmonton, February, 2012), 15, http://pub.cplea.ca/sites/default/files/publications/MakingaWill-Feb16-2012.pdf
7. *Making a Will,* (Centre for Public and Legal Education Alberta, Edmonton, February, 2012). To download go to http://www.cplea.ca/ and click on "Publications."
8. *Making a Personal Directive,* (Centre for Public and Legal Education Alberta, Edmonton, January, 2012). To download go to http://www.cplea.ca/ and click on "Publications."

Part 4

Integrity of the Future

1. Hawken, *Blessed Unrest,* 172.
2. Erika Tucker, "Top 10 Memorable David Suzuki Quotes," (*Global News* website, April 13, 2012), http://www.globalnews.ca/david+suzuki+quotes/6442620434/story.html
3. Hawken, *Blessed Unrest,* 183–84.
4. Chopra, *The Spontaneous Fulfillment of Desire,* 284.
5. "Frequently Asked Questions From Over 25 Years – What is the Venus Project?" (The Venus Project website), accessed August 31, 2012, http://www.thevenusproject.com/en/the-venus-project/faq
6. "Technology," (The Venus Project website), accessed August 31, 2012, http://www.thevenusproject.com/en/technology
7. Turner, *The Geography of Hope,* 138.
8. Ibid., 68.
9. Ibid., 141.
10. Ibid., 260.
11. Ibid., 208.
12. Ibid., 288.
13. Ibid., 289.
14. Erika Tucker, "Top 10 Memorable David Suzuki Quotes," (*Global News* website, April 13, 2012), http://www.globalnews.ca/david+suzuki+quotes/6442620434/story.html

The Complexities of Health and Safety

1. Jacqueline Mroz, "One Sperm Donor, 150 Offspring," (*New York Times* website, September 5, 2011), http://www.nytimes.com/2011/09/06/health/06donor.html?pagewanted=all
2. Tom Blackwell, "Limit Pregnancies by Same Sperm Donor: Fertility Experts," (*National Post* website, Sept 7, 2011), http://news.nationalpost.com/2011/09/08/limit-pregnancies-by-same-sperm-donor-fertility-experts/
3. Carolyn Abraham, "Unnatural Selection: Is Evolving Reproductive Technology Ushering in a New Age of Eugenics?" (*Globe and Mail* website, January 7, 2012, last updated January 10, 2012), http://www.theglobeandmail.com/life/parenting/unnatural-selection-is-evolving-reproductive-technology-ushering-in-a-new-age-of-eugenics/article1357885/?page=all
4. Dan Bilefsky, "Black Market for Body Parts Spreads Among the Poor in Europe," (*New York Times* website, June 28, 2012), http://www.nytimes.com/2012/06/29/world/europe/black-market-for-body-parts-spreads-in-europe.html?pagewanted=all
5. David Kilgour and David Matas, *Bloody Harvest: Organ Harvesting of Falun Gong Practitioners in China,* (Seraphim Editions, Woodstock, Ontario, 2009).
6. James M. Griffin and Mauricio Cifuentes Soto, "U.S. Ethanol Policy: The Unintended Consequences," *(Energy Tribune* website, February 29, 2012), accessed August 31, 2012, http://www.energytribune.com/articles.cfm/9973/US-Ethanol-Policy-The-Unintended-Consequences
7. Ibid.
8. Ibid.
9. "Wingspread Statement on the Precautionary Principle," (The Global Development Research Center), accessed August 31, 2012, http://www.gdrc.org/u-gov/precaution-3.html
10. Nancy Myers and Carolyn Raffensperger, "A Precaution Primer: An Ounce of Prevention is Worth a Pound of Cure," (*Yes! Magazine* website, Sep 30, 2001), http://www.yesmagazine.org/issues/technology-who-chooses/461
11. "About Us," (Physicians and Scientists for Responsible Application of Science and Technology website), accessed August 31, 2012, http://www.psrast.org/aboutus.htm
12. Ibid.
13. Sharratt, "SmartStax Corn: Was Health Canada Wise to Rubber-stamp Its Approval?" 104.
14. Ibid.
15. "Scientists In Support Of Agricultural Biotechnology," (The AgBioWorld Foundation website), accessed August 31, 2012, http://www.agbioworld.org/declaration/petition/petition.php
16. "How to Avoid Genetically Engineered Food: A Greenpeace Shoppers Guide," (Greenpeace website), accessed August 31, 2012, http://gmoguide.greenpeace.ca/shoppers_guide.pdf
17. "Percy Schmeiser's Battle," (CBC News Online, May 21, 2004), http://www.cbc.ca/news/background/genetics_modification/percyschmeiser.html

18. "The American Academy of Environmental Medicine Calls for Immediate Moratorium on Genetically Modified Foods," (Press Advisory, American Academy of Environmental Medicine website, May 19, 2009), http://www.aaemonline.org/gmopressrelease.html
19. Greenpeace brochure, see #16.
20. Ibid.
21. Video of the toxic chemicals experiment, (Slow Death by Rubber Duck website), accessed August 31, 2012, http://slowdeathbyrubberduck.com/CAN/videos.html
22. Smith and Lourie, *Slow Death by Rubber Duck,* 3 & 4.
23. Ibid., 4.
24. "Phthalates Regulation," (Health Canada website, Fact Sheet, January, 2011), http://www.hc-sc.gc.ca/ahc-asc/media/nr-cp/_2011/2011_07fs-eng.php
25. "Perfluorochemicals (PFCs)," (Environmental Working Group website), accessed August 31, 2012, http://www.ewg.org/chemindex/term/496
26. Lisa Gue, "Is the Canadian Government Flaming Out on PBDEs?" (David Suzuki Foundation website, August 24, 2011), http://www.davidsuzuki.org/blogs/panther-lounge/2011/08/is-the-canadian-government-flaming-out-on-pbdes/
27. "PBDE Flame Retardants and Human Health," (Health Canada website, It's your Health fact sheet, August, 2009), http://www.hc-sc.gc.ca/hl-vs/alt_formats/pdf/iyh-vsv/environ/pbde-eng.pdf
28. "Summary of Research on Mercury Emissions from Municipal Landfills," (The Northeast Waste Management Officials' Association website, Fact sheet, last modified December 28, 2009), http://www.newmoa.org/prevention/mercury/landfillfactsheet.cfm
29. "Mercury and Human Health," (Health Canada website, It's your Health fact sheet, March, 2009), http://www.hc-sc.gc.ca/hl-vs/alt_formats/pacrb-dgapcr/pdf/iyh-vsv/environ/merc2008-eng.pdf
30. Ibid.
31. Smith and Lourie, *Slow Death by Rubber Duck,* 268.
32. Lyndsey Layton, "FDA Says Studies on Triclosan, Used in Sanitizers and Soaps, Raise Concerns," (The Washington Post website, April 8, 2010), http://www.washingtonpost.com/wp-dyn/content/article/2010/04/07/AR2010040704621.html
33. "Health Effects (pesticides)," (City of Toronto website, last updated April , 2009), http://www.toronto.ca/health/pesticides/health_effects.htm
34. Janet Raloff, "How to Disinfect Your Salad," (*Science News* website), accessed August 3, 2012, http://www.sciencenews.org/sn_arch/9-28-96/food.htm

Looking After Yourself

1. "Health Funding –Allocations for 2012-2013," (Alberta Health website), accessed August 8, 2012), http://www.health.alberta.ca/about/health-funding.html
2. *World Health Report 2000: Health Systems: Improving Performance,* (World Health Organization), 152, http://www.who.int/whr/2000/en/whr00_en.pdf

3. "Private Clinics and the Threat to Public Health Care," (The Council of Canadians website), accessed August 31, 2012, http://www.canadians.org/healthcare/issues/clinics.html
4. Devereaux, "Payments for Care," 1817–24.
5. "Healthcare and Public-Private Partnerships," (The Council of Canadians website), accessed August 31, 2012, http://www.canadians.org/healthcare/issues/P3.html
6. Kohler and Righton, "Overeaters, Smokers and Drinkers," 34-39.
7. Ibid., paragraph two.
8. "The Benefits of Quitting for Pregnant Women," (Health Canada website), accessed August 31, 2012, http://www.hc-sc.gc.ca/hc-ps/tobac-tabac/legislation/label-etiquette/message-eng.php
9. Morgan Spurlock, *Super Size Me,* (Alliance Films, DVD, 2004).
10. Kaplan et al, "Dietary Replacement in Preschool-Aged Hyperactive Boys," 17.
11. "A canary in a coal mine" is an early warning of a danger that may not yet be perceptible to most of us. The expression originated in British coal mining where a major danger is the presence of carbon monoxide and methane, odourless gases that are not readily detectable by humans but are lethal in an enclosed space. Canaries are much more sensitive to these gases. Until 1987, British miners brought a caged canary with them when exploring new areas of the mine. If the canary died, they knew that the air supply was not safe, so they evacuated the area immediately.
12. "The submission must contain detailed information about the additive, its proposed use, the results of safety tests, and information on the effectiveness of the food additive for its intended use. Scientists from Health Canada's Food Directorate, Health Products and Food Branch, conduct a detailed and rigorous pre-market evaluation of the submission that focuses on safety." From: "How Are Food Additives Regulated?" (Health Canada website), accessed August 3, 2012, http://www.hc-sc.gc.ca/fn-an/securit/addit/index-eng.php
13. Retraction Watch website, http://retractionwatch.wordpress.com/
14. Tavare, "Scientific Misconduct is Worryingly Prevalent in the UK, Shows BMJ Survey."
15. "Food Additives," (CBC News In Depth, last updated September 29, 2008), http://www.cbc.ca/news/background/foodsafety/additives.html
16. Lau et al, "Synergistic Interactions between Commonly Used Food Additives in a Developmental Neurotoxicity Test," 182.
17. Ibid., 183.
18. Laura J. Stevens et al, "Dietary Sensitivities and ADHD Symptoms: Thirty-five Years of Research," 279–93.
19. "Trans Fat," (Center for Science in the Public Interest), accessed August 30, 2012, http://www.cspinet.org/transfat/about.html
20. Sundram, Karupaiah and Hayes, "Stearic Acid-rich Interesterified Fat and Trans-rich Fat Raise the LDL/HDL Ratio and Plasma Glucose Relative to Palm Olein in Humans," page 10 of online document, http://www.nutritionandmetabolism.com/content/4/1/3

21. "Cyclamates' Sour Aftertaste," *Time,* 83.
22. Tasmin Carlisle, "FDA's Approval of Aspartame Under Scrutiny," (*Globe and Mail,* June 24, 1987), http://www.wnho.net/fdas_approval_of_aspartame_under_scrutiny.pdf
23. Janet Starr Hull, "Aspartame's FDA Approval Process Shows Significant Flaws," (posted April 28, 2006), http://www.sweetpoison.com/articles/0406/aspartames_fda_approval_p.html
24. (AminoSweet website), accessed August 28, 2012, http://www.aminosweet.info/index.asp
25. Humphries, Pretorius, and Naudé, "Direct and Indirect Cellular Effects of Aspartame on the Brain," 461.
26. Abou-Donia et al, "Splenda Alters Gut Microflora and Increases Intestinal P-Glycoprotein and Cytochrome P-450 in Male Rats," 1415.
27. Tordoff and Alleva, "Oral stimulation With Aspartame Increases Hunger." AND Rogers and Blundell, "Separating the Actions of Sweetness and Calories: Effects of Saccharin and Carbohydrates on Hunger and Food Intake in Human Subjects." AND Lavin, French, and Read, "The Effect of Sucrose- and Aspartame-sweetened Drinks on Energy Intake, Hunger and Food Choice of Female, Moderately Restrained Eaters."
28. Swithers and Davidson, "A Role for Sweet Taste: Calorie Predictive Relations in Energy Regulation by Rats," 161.
29. "Natural Sugar Substitutes: 10 Healthier Alternatives to Refined Sugar," (American Diabetes Services website), accessed August 10, 2012, http://www.americandiabetes.com/living-diabetes/diabetes-food-articles/natural-sugar-substitutes-10-healthier-alternatives-refined
30. Ibid.

Spending Consciously

1. Nestle, *What to Eat,* 17 & 20.
2. Schwartz, "The Tyranny of Choice," 71–75.
3. Pollan, *Food Rules,* 25.
4. "Doctors Sound Alarm Over Antibiotics in Livestock Feed," (The Vancouver Sun website, September 12, 2010), http://blogs.vancouversun.com/2010/09/12/doctors-sound-alarm-over-antibiotics-in-livestock-feed/
5. Nestle, *What to Eat,* 55.
6. "Michael Pollan Answers Readers' Questions," (*The New York Times Magazine,* October 6, 2011), http://michaelpollan.com/articles-archive/michael-pollan-answers-readers-questions/
7. "EWG's 2012 Shopper's Guide to Pesticides in Produce," (Environmental Working Group website), accessed August 13, 2012, http://www.ewg.org/foodnews/

Living Consciously

1. Pollan, *Food Rules,* Rule 83, unnumbered page.
2. Kayla Webley, "Experts and Studies: Not Always Trustworthy," (*Time,* Health, June 29, 2010), http://www.time.com/time/health/article/0,8599,1998644,00.html

3. Ibid.
4. Keith E. Stanovich, "Rationality versus Intelligence," (Project Syndicate website, Apr 6, 2009), http://www.project-syndicate.org/commentary/rationality-versus-intelligence
5. Bond, "It's how you use it that counts," paragraph five.
6. Quotation Details, (Quotation Page website), accessed August 10, 2012, http://www.quotationspage.com/quote/151.html
7. Find quotes, (Goodreads website), accessed August 10, 2012, http://www.goodreads.com/quotes/search?utf8=%E2%9C%93&q=e+f+schumacher&commit=Search

Bibliography

Abou-Donia, Mohamed B., Eman M. El-Masry, Ali A. Abdel-Rahman, Roger E. McLendon, and Susan S. Schiffman. "Splenda Alters Gut Microflora and Increases Intestinal P-Glycoprotein and Cytochrome P-450 in Male Rats." *Journal of Toxicology and Environmental Health, Part A: Current Issues*, 71, no. 21 (2008): 1415-29.

Anielski, Mark. *The Economics of Happiness: Building Genuine Wealth.* New Society Publishers, 2007.

Anthony, Jason. *Financially Fearless by 40: Simple Strategies for Upgrading Your Thirtysomething Lifestyle.* USA: Penguin, 2003.

Boldt, Laurence G. *Zen and the Art of Making a Living: A Practical Guide to Creative Career Design.* New York: Arkana: Penguin, 1993.

Bond, Michael. "It's How You Use It That Counts." *New Scientist*, 204, no. 2732 (2009): 36-39.

Brock, Fred. *Live Well on Less Than You Think: The New York Times Guide to Achieving Your Financial Freedom.* Henry Holt, 2005.

Cameron, Amy. "The Debt Bomb." *Macleans*, December 10, 2001: 38.

Chilton, David. *The Wealthy Barber: The Common Sense Guide to Successful Financial Planning.* Toronto: Stoddart, 1989.

Chopra, Deepak. *Life After Death: The Burden of Proof.* New York: Harmony Books, 2006.

—. *The Spontaneous Fulfillment of Desire: Harnessing the Infinite Power of Coincidence.* New York: Three Rivers Press, 2003.

Covey, Stephen R., Merrill, A. Roger, and Merrill, Rebecca R. *First Things First.* New York: Simon & Schuster, 1994.

Devereaux, P. J., Diane Heels-Ansdell, Christina Lacchetti, Ted Haines, Karen E.A. Burns, Deborah J. Cook, Nikila Ravindran, et al. "Payments for Care at Private For-profit and Private Not-for-profit Hospitals: A Systematic Review and Meta-analysis." *Canadian Medical Association Journal*, 170, no. 12 (2004): 1817-24.

Evans, Richard Paul. *The Five Lessons a Millionaire Taught Me.* Simon & Schuster, 2005.

Gardner, David, Tom Gardner, and Selena Maranjian. *The Motley Fool Investment Guide for Teens: 8 Steps to Having More Money Than Your Parents Ever Dreamed Of.* New York: Simon & Schuster, 2002.

Griffiths, Margaret. "Consumer Debt in Australia: Why Banks Will Not Turn Their Backs on Profit." *International Journal of Consumer Studies*, 31, no. 3 (2007): 230–36.

Hawken, Paul. *Blessed Unrest: How the Largest Social Movement in History Is Restoring Grace, Justice and Beauty to the World.* New York and Toronto: Penguin, 2008.

Humphries, P., E. Pretorius, and H. Naudé. "Direct and Indirect Cellular Effects of Aspartame on the Brain." *European Journal of Clinical Nutrition*, 62 (2008): 451–62.

Kaplan, Bonnie J., Jane McNicol, Richard A. Conte, and H.K. Moghadam. "Dietary Replacement in Preschool-Aged Hyperactive Boys." *Pediatrics*, 83, no. 1 (1989): 7-17.

Kasser, Tim. *The High Price of Materialism.* Cambridge: MIT Press, 2002.

Kirby, Jason. "Awash in a Sea of Debt." *Macleans*, February 8, 2010: 28–33.

Klein, Naomi. *No Logo: Taking Aim at the Brand Bullies.* New York: Picador, 2002.

Kohler, Nicholas and Barbara Righton. "Overeaters, Smokers and Drinkers: The Doctor Won't See You Now." *Macleans*, April 24, 2006: 34–39.

Korten, David C. *Agenda for a New Economy: From Phantom Wealth to Real Wealth.* San Francisco: Berrett-Koehler, 2009.

Lau, Karen, W. Graham McLean, Dominic P. Williams, and C. Vyvyan Howard. "Synergistic Interactions between Commonly Used Food Additives in a Developmental Neurotoxicity Test." *Toxicological Sciences*, 90, no.1 (2006): 178–87.

Lavin, J.H., S.J. French and N.W. Read. "The Effect of Sucrose- and Aspartame-Sweetened Drinks on Energy Intake, Hunger and Food Choice of Female, Moderately Restrained Eaters." *International Journal of Obesity*, 21, no. 1 (1997): 37–42.

Lebow, Victor. "Price Competition in 1955." *Journal of Retailing*, 31, no. 1 (1955): 5-10.

Lee, Ilchi. *Brain Wave Vibration: Getting Back Into the Rhythm of a Happy, Healthy Life.* Sedona: Best Life Media, 2008.

Maich, Steve. "Hip Deep in Hock." *Macleans*, December 6, 2004: 40.

Moodie, Susannah. *Roughing it in the Bush.* Toronto: McClelland & Stewart, 1970.

Nemeth, Maria. *The Energy of Money: A Spiritual Guide to Financial and Personal Fulfillment.* Ballantine, 1999.

Nestle, Marion. *What to Eat: An Aisle-by-Aisle Guide to Savvy Food Choices and Good Eating.* New York: North Point Press, 2006.

Opdyke, Jeff D. *Love & Money: A Life Guide for Financial Success.* John Wiley & Sons, 2003.

Pink, Daniel H. *A Whole New Mind: Why Right-Brainers Will Rule the Future.* New York: Riverhead Books, 2005.

Pollan, Michael. *Food Rules: An Eater's Manual.* New York: Penguin, 2011.

Putnam, Robert D. *Bowling Alone: The Collapse and Revival of American Community.* Simon & Schuster, 2000.

Rivers, Frank. *The Way of the Owl: Succeeding With Integrity in a Conflicted World.* San Francisco: Harper, 1996.

Rogers, P.J. and J. E. Blundell. "Separating the Actions of Sweetness and Calories: Effects of Saccharin and Carbohydrates on Hunger and Food Intake in Human Subjects." *Physiol Behav*, 45, no. 6 (1989): 1093-99.

Schor, Juliet. *The Overspent American: Why We Want What We Don't Need.* Toronto and New York: HarperPerennial, 1999.

Schwartz, Barry. "The Tyranny of Choice." *Scientific American*, April 2004: 71.

Sharratt, Lucy. "SmartStax Corn: Was Health Canada Wise to Rubber-Stamp Its Approval?" *Alive*, February 2010: 103.

Smith, Rick and Bruce Lourie. *Slow Death by Rubber Duck: How the Toxic Chemistry of Everyday Life Affects Our Health.* Toronto: Alfred A. Knopff Canada, 2009.

Stegman, Michael A. "Payday Lending." *Journal of Economic Perspectives*, 2, no. 1 (2007): 169-90.

Stevens, Laura J., Thomas Kuczek, John R. Burgess, Elizabeth Hurt, and L. Eugene Arnold. "Dietary Sensitivities and ADHD Symptoms: Thirty-five Years of Research." *Clinical Pediatrics*, 50, no. 4 (2011): 279–93.

Sundram, Kalyana, Tilakavati Karupaiah and K.C. Hayes. "Stearic Acid-Rich Interesterified Fat and Trans-Rich Fat Raise the LDL/HDL Ratio and Plasma Glucose Relative to Palm Olein in Humans." *Nutrition & Metabolism*, 4, no. 3 (2007).

Sutherland, Anne and Beth Thompson. *Kidfluence: Why Kids Today Mean Business.* Canada: McGraw-Hill Ryerson, 2001.

Swithers, Susan E. and Terry L. Davidson. "A Role for Sweet Taste: Calorie Predictive Relations in Energy Regulation by Rats." *Behavioural Neuroscience*, 122, no. 1 (2008): 161–73.

Tavare, Aniket. "Scientific Misconduct is Worryingly Prevalent in the UK, Shows BMJ Survey." *British Medical Journal*, 344, e377 (2012).

Time. "Cyclamates' Sour Aftertaste." October 31, 1969 : 83.

Tordoff, M. G. and A. M. Alleva. "Oral Stimulation with Aspartame Increases Hunger." *Physiol Behav*, 47, no. 3 (1990): 555–59.

Turner, Chris. *The Geography of Hope: A Tour of the World We Need.* Toronto : Vintage Canada, 2008.

Twist, Lynne with Teresa Barker. *The Soul of Money: Transforming Your Relationship with Money and Life.* New York and London: Norton, 2003.

Vaz-Oxlade, Gail. *Debt-Free Forever.* Toronto: Harper Collins, 2009.

Authors Whose Work Inspires Me

Many people have inspired and informed my work. Not all have been referenced directly in this book. The following list is compiled from books on my shelves combined with key authors mentioned in *Conscious Spending, Conscious Life.*

This concise form is an easy reference when you're in the frame of mind for more exploration. Pick a name, familiar or not, and do an Internet search to see what that person is about. Or check which of their books are in your public library. Or search an online bookstore and read customer reviews on that author's books. However you approach this list, it will enrich your experience of navigating the consumer culture in ways you might not anticipate.

Your Personal Index

Use this space to note topics and pages you'd like to return to.

Your Personal Index

Use this space to note topics and pages you'd like to return to.

Your Personal Index

Use this space to note topics and pages you'd like to return to.

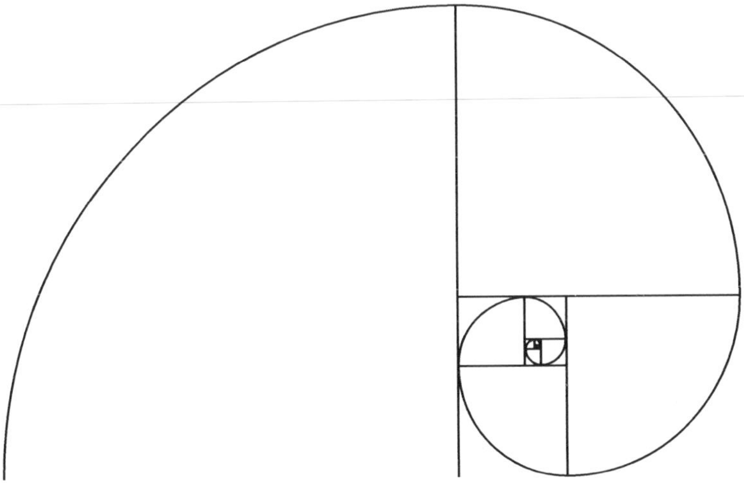

Why a spiral?

My long-standing fascination with ancient mysteries has drawn me to places that connect me with enduring wisdom. Spirals appear in many locations around the world.[i] As explained by Alex Whitaker, author of the ancient-wisdom website, "The synchronicity of the universe is determined by certain mathematical constants which express themselves in the form of 'patterns' and 'cycles' in nature. The outcome of this process can be seen throughout the natural world..."[ii] He shows photos of a passion flower, a spiral galaxy, the Giant's Causeway (a rock formation in Ireland), and a snail shell to illustrate this.

The spiral I have used is derived from the Fibonacci number sequence. This is a mathematical constant that was introduced into European mathematics in 1202 by Italian mathematician Leonardo of Pisa. The mathematical sequence is 1,1,2,3,5,8,13,21,34...ad infinitum. Each number is the sum of the previous two. The visual representation of this sequence is built from squares whose sides are the length of the numbers. The spiral is created by drawing curves to opposite corners through the squares.[iii]

If you take any two successive Fibonacci numbers, their ratio is very close to the golden ratio, also known as the golden section or the golden mean.[iv] Artists, mathematicians, architects, and scientists have long considered the golden mean to be a perfect proportion. It is featured in the architecture of ancient Greece and Egypt, and in da Vinci's work, including the Mona Lisa.[v] The golden mean was the inspiration behind photographer Steve Nelson's website. He describes it as "a mathematical concept which expresses the relationship of two parts of a whole with each other and with the whole.... it describes some of nature's most exquisite, complex, and orderly systems."[vi]

Galaxies, flowers, and nautilus shells are all exquisite, orderly, and complex systems based on the spiral. When we look around, we see that the spiral is imbedded in nature—elephant tusks, the unfurling shoots of plants, the inner ear of humans. Perhaps that's why ancient civilizations came to see the spiral as integral to strength and growth—in a word, life-supporting. The spiral became a symbol of unity connecting nature and human culture, and traditional cultures consider the spiral our connection to consciousness.

For my part, the spiral appeals to my right-brain intuitive self. I like the flow, the proportion, and the way it sustainably increases. The spiral is a link between my inner and outer worlds. It is a visual reminder that I must repeatedly spiral inward and then outward, if I am to engage with the consumer culture without losing myself in it. I imagine that each time I spiral back out, my ability to engage constructively has increased. That is the significance of the increasing spiral that appears on the four section pages of this book.

The spiral also reminds me that some things in life are mysteries. We can guess why the ancients carved spirals in so many places, but we don't really know. This keeps me humble and reminds me that I can't know everything.

---

i Photos, spirals in several locations, http://www.ancient-wisdom.co.uk/spirals.htm

ii http://www.ancient-wisdom.co.uk/sacredgeometry.htm

iii http://mathpaint.blogspot.ca/2008/10/fibonacci-spiral-in-nature.html

iv http://www.mathsisfun.com/numbers/golden-ratio.html

v Video, "A Synopsis of the Golden Ratio," http://www.youtube.com/watch?v=fmaVqkR0ZXg

vi http://www.thegoldenmean.com/why.html